Bill Mounce tackles a wide range of some of the most challenging questions about the origins and reliability of the Bible and boils them down to digestible size. Fully abreast of recent research, Mounce wears it lightly, even while giving important and practical answers to many thorny questions.

Craig L. Blomberg, distinguished professor
of New Testament, Denver Seminary

There remains much confusion about how the early church received the Bible, how manuscripts are utilized, and which translations are reliable. Assumptions need to be challenged to help people wade through false agendas and common misunderstandings. Dr. Mounce makes the confusing clear and brings understanding to both pastor and layperson alike. This book is a fascinating read that masterfully answers critical questions clearly and concisely. It is a must-read for every faithful follower of Jesus to understand why they can trust the Bible.

Rich Blum, Bethel Community Church

Why I Trust the Bible is a one-stop guide that is accessible and trustworthy for someone who has questions about the Bible or interacts with people who do. It's a most useful resource.

Darrell L. Bock, senior research professor of New
Testament studies, Dallas Theological Seminary

Bill Mounce has produced a remarkably clear, comprehensive, and level-headed resource that carefully and graciously explains each type of objection that has been lodged against the Bible, and then he answers each objection with convincing facts and arguments. I expect that all who read it will gain a deeper confidence in the trustworthiness of the Bible.

Wayne Grudem, distinguished research professor of
theology and biblical studies, Phoenix Seminary

Bill Mounce's book addresses many of the objections people raise against the Bible, answering them graciously. It's readable for a layperson, yet with insights even scholars may find helpful in their thinking and articulation.

Dr. Craig Keener, F. M. and Ada Thompson professor
of biblical studies, Asbury Theological Seminary

Christianity is under close scrutiny today—from the academy to the alley. Gen Z and millennials get their information from memes and YouTube videos that feed uninformed superstitions about the faith. As a pastor, I'm bombarded with questions about the Bible and the personhood and historicity of Jesus Christ on a regular basis. We now live in a time when truth is subject to a person's preferences, and what is called "truth" is really just a formulated montage of misinformation. We need accessible and accurate information for people in all walks of life. In *Why I Trust the Bible*, Bill Mounce invites Christ followers and doubters to consider the reasonable and sound answers he provides to today's tough questions.

Eric Mason, Epiphany Fellowship Church

Many wonder whether the Bible is true, whether we can truly trust the Scriptures. *Why I Trust the Bible* is a learned and accessible response to these questions. Bill Mounce examines the credibility of gospel accounts, so-called contradictions, the accuracy of narratives and speeches in the New Testament, apparent problems with the Old Testament, and more!

Thomas R. Schreiner, James Buchanan Harrison
professor of New Testament interpretation, The
Southern Baptist Theological Seminary

This excellent volume is a treasure trove of explanations of difficult texts and answers to skeptics' questions about the Bible. With each chapter I found my confidence in the integrity of the biblical text reaffirmed and strengthened. Bill Mounce is uniquely qualified to respond to the many arguments against the authority and trustworthiness of the Bible, and I highly commend this book to anyone who is struggling to believe that Scripture is genuinely God-breathed and inerrant. His response to Bart Ehrman is alone worth the price of the book, and although Mounce is primarily a New Testament scholar, his chapters on the Old Testament are superb.

Sam Storms, Bridgeway Church

In this practical volume, Dr. Bill Mounce responds to some of the toughest challenges commonly leveled against the Bible: Is the "Christ of faith" the real Jesus or a legend created by the early church? Are there contradictions in the Gospels? Was the biblical text hopelessly corrupted as it was hand-copied down through the ages? Mounce writes in an accurate yet accessible style that will strengthen believers and challenge skeptics.

Mark L. Strauss, university professor of
New Testament, Bethel Seminary

Anyone who reads the Bible will have honest questions about what they encounter in it. *Why I Trust the Bible* is accessible, up-to-date, and sympathetic to reader's questions. With Mounce's help, we are better prepared "to give an answer to everyone who asks you to give the reason for the hope that you have" (1 Peter 3:15).

Miles Van Pelt, academic dean and professor
of Old Testament and biblical languages,
Reformed Theological Seminary

WHY
I TRUST
THE BIBLE

ANSWERS TO REAL QUESTIONS AND DOUBTS PEOPLE HAVE ABOUT THE BIBLE

WILLIAM D. MOUNCE

ZONDERVAN
REFLECTIVE

ZONDERVAN REFLECTIVE

Why I Trust the Bible
Copyright © 2021 by William D. Mounce

Requests for information should be addressed to:
Zondervan, *3900 Sparks Dr. SE, Grand Rapids, Michigan 49546*

Zondervan titles may be purchased in bulk for educational, business, fundraising, or sales promotional use. For information, please email SpecialMarkets@Zondervan.com.

ISBN 978-0-310-10994-5 (softcover)

ISBN 978-0-310-13032-1 (audio)

ISBN 978-0-310-10995-2 (ebook)

Cover design: Brand Navigation
Cover images: Pexels; Brand Navigation
Interior design: Kait Lamphere

Printed in the United States of America

21 22 23 24 25 26 27 28 29 30 31 /LSC/ 15 14 13 12 11 10 9 8 7 6 5 4 3 2

CONTENTS

Abbreviations xi

Preface... xiii

The Historical Jesus

1. Jesus before the Gospels. 3
2. Jesus of the Gospels. 20

Contradictions

3. Contradictions in the Bible 45
4. Digging Deeper into Apparent Contradictions 67

The Canon

5. Why Do We Have the Twenty-Seven Books in the
   New Testament? 95
6. Digging Deeper into the Canon 113

Textual Criticism

7. Are the Greek Texts Hopelessly Corrupt? 129
8. Digging Deeper into Textual Criticism. 143
9. Digging Much Deeper into Textual Criticism 161

Translations

10. Translation Theory. 195
11. Digging Deeper into Translation 210

The Old Testament

12. The Character of God 229
13. The Historicity of the Old Testament 249

Conclusion: Why I Trust the Bible 267

General Bibliography 271

ABBREVIATIONS

General Abbreviations

ca.	*circa*, approximately
cf.	confer, compare
d.	date of the person's death
ed(s).	editor(s), edited by, edition
et al.	*et alia*, and others
MS(S)/ms(s)	manuscript(s)
MT	Masoretic Text
n.	note
NA[28]	Nestle-Aland, *Novum Testamentum Graece*, 28th revised edition, edited by Barbara and Kurt Aland et al. (2013)
NT	New Testament
OT	Old Testament
repr.	reprinted
rev.	revised
trans.	translated
UBS[5]	*UBS Greek New Testament*, 5th revised editon, edited by Barbara and Kurt Aland et al. (2014)
v(v).	verse(s)

Bible Versions

CSB	Christian Standard Bible (2017)
ESV	English Standard Version (2016)
KJV	King James Version (1611)
NASB	New American Standard Bible (1995)
NET	New English Translation (2019)
NIrV	New International Reader's Version (2014)

NIV   New International Version (2011)
NKJV   New King James Version (1982)
NLT   New Living Translation (2015)
NRSV   New Revised Standard Version (1989)

Biblical Books

Gen	Genesis	Mic	Micah
Exod	Exodus	Nah	Nahum
Lev	Leviticus	Hab	Habakkuk
Num	Numbers	Zeph	Zephaniah
Deut	Deuteronomy	Hag	Haggai
Josh	Joshua	Zech	Zechariah
Judg	Judges	Mal	Malachi
Ruth	Ruth	Matt	Matthew
1–2 Sam	1–2 Samuel	Mark	Mark
1–2 Kgs	1-2 Kings	Luke	Luke
1–2 Chr	1–2 Chronicles	John	John
Ezra	Ezra	Acts	Acts
Neh	Nehemiah	Rom	Romans
Esth	Esther	1–2 Cor	1–2 Corinthians
Job	Job	Gal	Galatians
Ps/Pss	Psalm/Psalms	Eph	Ephesians
Prov	Proverbs	Phil	Philippians
Eccl	Ecclesiastes	Col	Colossians
Song	Song of Songs	1–2 Thess	1–2 Thessalonians
Isa	Isaiah	1–2 Tim	1–2 Timothy
Jer	Jeremiah	Titus	Titus
Lam	Lamentations	Phlm	Philemon
Ezek	Ezekiel	Heb	Hebrews
Dan	Daniel	Jas	James
Hos	Hosea	1–2 Pet	1–2 Peter
Joel	Joel	1–3 John	1–3 John
Amos	Amos	Jude	Jude
Obad	Obadiah	Rev	Revelation
Jonah	Jonah		

PREFACE

The Bible makes some astonishing claims about itself. The apostle Paul tells his friend Timothy that every word of the Bible comes from the mouth of God (2 Tim 3:16). The Bible says God personally wrote the Ten Commandments with his own finger (Exod 31:18; Deut 9:10). Almost five hundred times, the prophets preface their prophecies with the claim "says the Lord." Jesus says, "I did not speak on my own, but the Father who sent me commanded me to say all that I have spoken" (John 12:49). Under normal circumstances, if someone says they speak for God, I doubt many of us would pay attention. But this is exactly what the Bible says about itself. Do you believe it?

We can no longer assume that people trust their Bible and believe what it says about itself. Western culture has shifted away from its Judeo-Christian heritage, and the popular media has launched such an attack on the believability of Scripture that many churchgoers have serious questions about the Bible. Genesis 1–11 reads more like a myth than history; people don't live 969 years (Gen 5:27). The God of the Old Testament is a moral monster who commands genocide, while the God of the New Testament is a loving God who would never send people to hell, if such a place were to exist. Did Jesus actually live? Did the biblical writers get it right, or did they slant, massage, or even create the Bible we have today? The Gospels were written long after Jesus lived; how can you trust them? How can you believe a Bible that's full of internal contradictions with itself and external contradictions with science and history? Why should we believe the right books are in the Bible? Many books were left out, like the Gospel of Thomas. Why trust the Bible when there are so many contradictory translations? If you are not aware of these questions, then watch Bill Maher's movie *Religulous*, or search YouTube for "Bart Ehrman."

Some people feel it's wrong to ask these fundamental questions; but if you never seriously ask them, you'll never be convinced that the Bible is true and trustworthy. So I invite you to ask the hard questions, read the controversies and solutions, and decide for yourself whether you trust your Bible. Does it contain the very words of God?

As I've been writing, I have kept university freshmen and their parents in mind. The first year at university is difficult enough, and it only gets more difficult with the barrage of attacks being leveled at the Bible and God. I trust this book will help.

It's been challenging to write a book that is based on academic research but also intends to convey its conclusions to a nontechnical audience. I have provided the necessary references to historical documents and modern writers in the chapter endnotes; there are no further discussions there, so they can be ignored for general reading.

Each of the six sections of this book has an opening chapter that introduces the topic, followed by a second or third chapter that delves more deeply into the content. While the content of these later chapters is typically more detailed than the first chapter, some readers will still have more questions, even after reading the in-depth chapters. To help those who want to dig even deeper, I have developed additional resources and made them available at www.BillMounce.com/trust. There you will find video introductions for each chapter, as well as additional content addressing several questions not specifically covered in this book.

I have picked a few primary books and referenced them heavily. These are the main books for further reading:

Blomberg, Craig. *The Historical Reliability of the New Testament: Countering the Challenges to Evangelical Christian Beliefs*. Nashville: B&H Academic, 2016.

Bock, Darrell L., and Daniel B. Wallace. *Dethroning Jesus: Exposing Popular Culture's Quest to Unseat the Biblical Christ*. Nashville: Nelson, 2007.

Komoszewski, J. Ed, M. James Sawyer, and Daniel B. Wallace. *Reinventing Jesus: How Contemporary Skeptics Miss the Real Jesus and Mislead Popular Culture*. Grand Rapids: Kregel, 2006, 121–66.

Kruger, Michael J. *The Question of Canon: Challenging the Status Quo in the New Testament Debate*. Downers Grove, IL: IVP Academic, 2013.

Jones, Timothy P. *Misquoting Truth: A Guide to the Fallacies of Bart Ehrman's* Misquoting Jesus. Downers Grove, IL: InterVarsity, 2007.

Special thanks go out to my friends who have read and critiqued the book. Having good friends is truly a gift from God: Darrell Bock, Craig Blomberg, Michael Kruger, Tom Schreiner, Mark Strauss, Miles Van Pelt, and Dan Wallace. I am also thankful for the excellent work of my Zondervan editors Ryan Pazdur and Dirk Buursma.

I have no compelling personal story. I was raised in a Christian family with a strong academic bent. I went to state schools and university (Western Kentucky University), except for my last year. I attended an evangelical seminary that exhibited the beginnings of a theological left-leaning tendency, and while it sowed seeds of distrust in the Bible, it did not convince me. I earned my PhD in Aberdeen, Scotland, which in typical British style was neither left nor right theologically but open to both. My professor, I. Howard Marshall, was a British evangelical who had a high view of Scripture but was not an inerrantist, and who probably would object to my discussion of harmonization in section 2. But my time there with Darrell Bock and Craig Blomberg (see chapter 3) continued to encourage me to believe that the Bible is wholly trustworthy, and Professor Marshall would never disagree with that. I taught in a Wesleyan university (Azusa Pacific University) and a Reformed seminary (Gordon-Conwell Theological Seminary). While I did try to question my faith so I would be an honest scholar, I never did have a crisis of faith. It would have made a good story, but I am thankful to the Lord that he granted me faith to persevere (1 Pet 1:5). My time in pastoral ministry further convinced me that a high view of Scripture is truly important for any Christian in order to face the challenges of life. After forty-nine years of consistent and serious study of the New Testament, I am more convinced than ever that the Bible contains the very words of God and is wholly trustworthy.

All authors think their books are important (why else write one?), and I am no exception. The attacks on the Bible and the subsequent lessening of God's glory are only increasing, and the material I cover is especially important today. I trust you'll find it helpful and affirming to your faith.

Bill Mounce, Ione, Washington, USA

THE HISTORICAL JESUS

Who Is Jesus?

Challenge

For decades, skeptics have challenged our understanding of who Jesus was. Some people claim there are no nonbiblical references to Jesus, and therefore conclude that Jesus never actually lived. Other people question whether the accounts of what Jesus did and taught were altered in the years between his life and when the Gospels were written. Other people question if the Gospel writers were even interested in writing accurate history. Didn't their beliefs slant their message? Did Paul change Jesus from being a human being into someone who thought he was God? Did Emperor Constantine create the idea of Jesus' divinity and invent the doctrine of the Trinity, as asserted in the fictional novel *The Da Vinci Code*?

A few months ago, I called a ride-sharing company to get a ride to the airport. I noticed that the driver was probably of Arab descent, and his prayer beads confirmed he was Muslim. I asked him a few questions about the beads, and he launched into a stereotypical discussion of why Jesus was only a human prophet, and that it was the church that claimed Jesus was the Son of God, a central anathema in Muslim theology.

It was actually a great conversation. I learned a lot about his point of view, but he wasn't really interested in hearing mine. He was surprised I knew what I believed as a Christian. But whenever I asked for facts or the reasons behind his assertions, he dodged the question and continued to make assertions. I could have had the same conversation with a well-informed skeptic.

I was just starting to write this book, and the incident encouraged me to continue focusing on the reader who might one day need a ride to the airport.

Chapter 1

JESUS BEFORE THE GOSPELS

 In this chapter, we will look at two issues: (1) the proof that Jesus actually lived, and (2) the time gap between Jesus' life and the writing of the Gospels, along with the nature of oral tradition.

Did Jesus Exist?

Would it not be strange if the single most influential person in the history of the world never existed? Yet there are people who affirm that Jesus never lived, that there is no evidence to the contrary, and that any historical reference to Jesus can't be trusted.

Earl Doherty defines "Jesus mythicism" as "the theory that no historical Jesus worthy of the name existed, that Christianity began with a belief in a spiritual, mythical figure, that the Gospels are essentially allegory and fiction, and that no single identifiable person lay at the root of the Galilean preaching tradition."[1] New Testament scholar I. Howard Marshall refers to a Russian encyclopedia written during the days of Communism that reserves one sentence for Jesus containing this phrase: "the mythological founder of Christianity."[2] All you have to do is google "Jesus never existed" or read the Wikipedia article on the "Christ Myth Theory" to see many more examples.[3]

It's amazing that this idea is repeated over and over again, despite clear, factual evidence to the contrary.

Josephus

One of the clearest nonbiblical references to Jesus is found in the writings of Josephus, a Jewish historian from the first century AD. He was not a Christian and therefore had no reason to embellish his mention of Jesus.

> Now, there was about this time Jesus, a wise man, *if it be lawful to call him a man*; for he was a doer of wonderful works, a teacher of such men as receive the truth with pleasure. He drew over to him both many of the Jews, and many of the Gentiles. *He was [the] Christ*; and when Pilate, at the suggestion of the principal men amongst us, had condemned him to the cross, those that loved him at the first did not forsake him, *for he appeared to them alive again the third day, as the divine prophets had foretold these and ten thousand other wonderful things concerning him*; and the tribe of Christians, so named from him, are not extinct at this day.[4]

I italicized a few of the phrases because they certainly are additions made by a Christian; they are statements no Jewish non-Christian would ever say. However, most scholars agree that the rest of the citation comes directly from Josephus. Most importantly for our discussion, Josephus clearly affirms the existence of Jesus.

Elsewhere we read what Josephus writes about James, the brother of Jesus: "Festus was now dead, and Albinus was but upon the road; so he assembled the sanhedrin of judges, and brought before them the brother of Jesus, who was called Christ, whose name was James."[5] Here Josephus refers to Jesus (Christ) without first identifying him, which suggests that Josephus had earlier identified Jesus, lending support to the idea that the first quote cited was written by Josephus and is an authentic witness to Jesus' existence.[6]

Nonbiblical Sources

Four Roman (and, more importantly, non-Christian) writers mention Jesus and some of the events of his life.[7] These references are from the first and early second century.

Pliny the Younger was a Roman governor of Bithynia-Pontus (modern-day Turkey). He wrote to the emperor Trajan ca. AD 112 because he was not sure how to deal with Christians, since they wouldn't worship the emperor's image. Pliny (*Letters* 10.96.7) added that the Christians met together on a regular basis and sang hymns "to Christ as if to a god."[8]

Suetonius was a Roman historian and wrote about a riot in Rome for which Emperor Claudius expelled the Jews in AD 49 (possibly referenced in Acts 18:2). He said the riot was caused "at the instigation of Chrestus" (*Claudius* 25.4).[9] Almost all scholars today agree that Suetonius confused "Chrestus" with "Christus," and that this is a reference to Jesus Christ.

Tacitus was perhaps the greatest of Roman historians. He said the name "Christian" comes from "Christ," a person who had been executed as a criminal by the procurator Pontius Pilate in the reign of Tiberius (*Annals* 15.44).[10] This reference not only confirms Jesus' existence but also gives a time frame for his death between AD 26 and 36. Tacitus also confirms that Jesus' followers increased in number after his death, moving from Jerusalem all the way to Rome. The writings of Tacitus are so well-attested as historically reliable by scholars that we could argue for Jesus' existence based on this witness alone.[11]

Thallus was a first-century historian who wrote about the darkness that occurred during the time of the crucifixion.[12]

In addition to Roman writers and historians, two Greek writers also told us about Jesus. Lucian of Samosata (writing in the early second century) ridiculed Christians because they worshiped a man, and he called Jesus a "sage" whom the Jews executed (*Death of Peregrine*, 11–13).[13] Mara ben Serapion (writing in the second century) described Jesus as a "wise King" whom the Jews killed. He also talked about the "wise King's" teachings and the exile of his followers.[14]

Craig Blomberg quotes Origen's reference to the pagan apologist

Celsus (*Against Celsus* 1.28), who "attacks Christian beliefs on numerous fronts. But he never denies that Jesus was a historical figure. Instead, Celsus disparages Jesus' lineage and socio-economic status, calls his mother Mary an adulteress, attributes his miraculous powers to sorcery that he learned in Egypt, and charges that he used these powers erroneously to claim his own divinity."[15]

As you might expect, Jewish sources from this time tended to expunge Jesus from their history, and yet there are still some references to Jesus and his followers.[16] Jewish writings that date to the early centuries of Christianity tell us that Jesus was a sorcerer from Egypt (*Shabbat* 104b) who led Israel astray (*Sanhedrin* 107b), that Jesus was born out of wedlock (the son of "Pandera"),[17] and that he was hanged on Passover Eve (*b. Sanhedrin* 43a):

> It was taught: On the day before the Passover they hanged Jesus. A herald went before him for forty days [proclaiming], "He will be stoned, because he practised magic and enticed Israel to go astray. Let anyone who knows anything in his favour come forward and plead for him." But nothing was found in his favour, and they hanged him the day before Passover.[18]

This passage from the Talmud, a Jewish religious text, certainly had no motivation to support the Christian movement, but this acknowledgment points to Jesus' existence as a real, historical figure.

In addition, Paul Barnett cites a Jewish prayer (*Benediction Twelve*), formulated in the decade after the fall of Jerusalem (AD 70), in which "Nazarenes" and "minim" refer to Christians:

> For the renegades let there be no hope, and may the arrogant kingdom soon be rooted out in our days, and the Nazarenes and the minim perish as in a moment and be blotted out from the book of life and with the righteous may they not be inscribed. Blessed art though, O Lord who humblest the arrogant.[19]

So let's summarize what we can know about Jesus from these non-biblical sources.

1. Jesus lived.
2. He was Jewish.
3. He lived in the first third of the first century.
4. People believed he had been born out of wedlock.
5. Jesus' ministry overlapped with John's.
6. Jesus worked wondrous feats.
7. He gathered disciples.
8. Jesus lived in conflict with the Jewish authorities.
9. Jesus was described as a sorcerer who led Israel astray.
10. Some believed him to be the Messiah.
11. Jesus was crucified under Pontius Pilate (AD 26–36).
12. One Talmudic tradition says he was "hung" (*b. Sanhedrin* 43a), but some early writings use "hung" for suspension on a pole.
13. Jesus was believed to have been seen raised from the dead by his followers, who now worship him as a god.
14. His brother James was martyred in AD 62 by the high priest Ananus.

Given the abundance of nonbiblical information on Jesus, it almost seems to be willful ignorance to deny his actual existence.

Why Not More References?

Given the importance of Jesus, especially in the years after his death and the rise of Christianity, we may question why there aren't more historical references. Shouldn't the pages of history be replete with references to the founder of what would become the world's largest religion?

The answer is simple. While he was alive, Jesus was relatively unimportant. He was a Galilean from the unimportant town of Nazareth in the relatively unimportant country of Israel. He had no political power.

In the decades following his life, the movement he started was viewed as a Jewish sect and not a religious movement in its own right. Ancient biographies and histories were not written about people like Jesus.

Biblical Witnesses

Although some historians discount biblical writings as historically unreliable, the early church did not. There is no hint in the New Testament that the Christian religion was based on ethical or spiritual principles. Instead, it was based on the person and work of a real human being. Ideas are not crucified, but people are.

> Peter preaches, "Therefore let all Israel be assured of this: God has made this Jesus, whom you crucified, both Lord and Messiah" (Acts 2:36).

> Paul writes, "For I resolved to know nothing while I was with you except Jesus Christ and him crucified" (1 Cor 2:2). "If Christ has not been raised, our preaching is useless and so is your faith" (15:14).

If Paul had lived decades after Jesus, his witness to Jesus' existence might be less meaningful. But we can date Paul's trip to Corinth (Acts 18:1) to AD 50 because we know from other sources that the Jews were expelled from Rome in AD 49. We also know that Gallio (Acts 18:12) was proconsul starting in July AD 51. Working backward from these dates and the time frame given in Galatians, we can conclude that Paul was converted about one or two years after Jesus' death (AD 30). Paul obviously believed Jesus existed, and it seems doubtful Paul could have been deceived about the existence of a person who had died a mere two years before his own conversion.

In light of all this, Craig Blomberg calls it a "silly and nonsensical notion" that Christian writers cannot relate accurate history and that we should only accept evidence coming from non-Christian sources.[20] Think of how irrational this is if applied to other forms of knowledge.

Should we deny the evidence of the Holocaust that comes from modern Jewish writers? Certainly not. We don't discount history about World War II that was written by the Allies and accept only what was written by people who did not experience the war. Yes, when someone has a faith commitment to a historical event, we don't automatically accept everything they say. We all have biases and a subjective interpretation of events we have experienced. Rather than reject experiential knowledge, we weigh what is written and evaluate it. People sometimes lie, and we all make mistakes. But not necessarily.

Another key factor in proving the existence of Jesus has to do with attributing a cause to the Christian movement. Large world-changing movements do not arise out of thin air. The earliest disciples clearly believed Jesus lived and died and rose again. It's hard to imagine the Christian movement starting and growing if there were no historical Jesus. There is sufficient secular historical data to corroborate the biblical testimony of the New Testament book of Acts that the Christian movement spread quickly and in large numbers throughout the Roman Empire. For example, the ever-reliable Tacitus refers to an "immense multitude" of Christian believers in Rome.[21] This is highly unlikely to have happened if the originator of the movement never existed.

There is only one obvious conclusion to draw from the available evidence: Jesus did exist, and therefore the reliability of the Bible is not up for debate on this point.

Oral Tradition

Most scholars accept that there was a twenty-five- to sixty-year time gap between the events of Jesus' life and the writing of the Gospels. If Jesus died around AD 30, Mark was probably written in the mid-50s to early 60s AD, and John in the 90s. During this time, the stories of Jesus' actions and teaching were passed on primarily through word of mouth (i.e., "oral tradition"). One common challenge made by skeptics of the Bible is that memory is faulty. It "leaks" and cannot be trusted over a long period of time. This means the Bible likely has errors and embellishments that were introduced during this time gap.

Reference is often made to the telephone game. A group of people line up; the first person whispers something to the second person and so forth until the message gets to the final person. The joke is that what the last person hears is rarely what the first person said. If a group of similar people in the same context can't remember and accurately pass on a saying, how can we trust decades of faulty memory? This is an understandable question, especially when asked by someone from a non-oral culture.

An oral culture is a culture in which stories are learned and passed on primarily by word of mouth. People tend not to rely on written accounts. Because the United States and Western Europe are not oral cultures, many people in these cultures struggle to understand how facts can be reliably communicated orally. But there is ample evidence that people who do live in oral cultures are capable of seemingly near-impossible feats of memory and accuracy.

So let's put this analogy to rest right now. Oral tradition has very little in common with the telephone game. In the game, the message is heard and passed along *one person at a time*. There are *no controls* over the message, and there is *no cost* attached to reliable or unreliable transmission. All of this makes it fundamentally different from the oral transmission of the Gospels.

The biblical stories were relayed in communities (not one-to-one), and when the stories were shared in community, many people knew the stories and would correct mistakes relayed in the retelling. The people retelling the stories had a strong personal interest in the truthfulness of what they were saying, especially when persecution of the church increased. The joke of the telephone game is irrelevant to this discussion.

Human Ability

Human beings are capable of great mental feats. I have a friend who has memorized, word for word, both the English Bible (755,976 words) and the Greek New Testament (138,213 words). We may be tempted to write this off as a rare exception, and yet we know that many ancient Greek children memorized the entire *Iliad* and *Odyssey*, ancient Greek works totaling around 200,000 words. We also know that many Jewish rabbis memorized the entire Hebrew Bible,[22] which in our current Hebrew text is around 309,000 words; I am told the same is true for clerics (and, to some extent, children) memorizing the Qur'an. Far from the exception, this was the common expectation of a good education in an oral society.

Teacher repetition and student memorization were the primary tools of instruction. When I was teaching in the university, I recall asking the students to stop taking notes, to put their pens down (or, today, to close their computers), and to intentionally listen to what I was saying, processing the meaning and significance of what I was teaching them. I did this because students would quite often let the lecture go from their ears to their fingers, bypassing the brain (so to speak). They would not really "hear" or remember what I taught. Today, teachers have the additional distractions of texts, social media platforms, and emails—and when students are at home, the temptation to binge-watch TV shows.

None of this was a problem in Jewish oral culture. Jewish boys learned to read by reading the Hebrew Bible. Each student had to memorize a passage perfectly before he could discuss it in class. Jewish children heard the words of Scripture repeated in many contexts—school, synagogue, dinner discussions, festivals. They were expected to learn and remember what they were hearing. Since most of us reading this book belong to a non-oral culture, we need to realize that the human brain is capable of far more than what our non-oral society expects from it. If these Jewish students played the telephone game today, the last person would undoubtedly accurately repeat what the first person said.

It's difficult for those from non-oral cultures to understand and accept how different that culture is. But for those versed in the study of orality, the ability of the human brain to remember accurately is an accepted fact.[23]

Guarded Tradition

It's helpful to analyze the nature of orality. In other words, this isn't just a matter of arguing that people in oral cultures memorize better than we do. There are three different kinds of oral cultures:

1. **Formal controlled tradition** means that stories and teachings can only be retold by people in formal positions of authority. This principle applied to Rabbinic Judaism. In ancient Jewish culture, the rabbis were the formal authority who guaranteed the accuracy of the teachings.
2. **Informal uncontrolled tradition** is the opposite of formal controlled tradition. In this situation, any person can retell the traditions, and no one is responsible to make sure the retelling is accurate.
3. **Informal controlled tradition** means that anyone can retell the stories, but people in authority are able to say whether or not the retelling is accurate.

Much of our understanding of the role of orality in biblical studies began with the work of Kenneth Bailey, a missionary to the Bedouin tribes in the Middle East.[24] The culture of the Bedouin was an oral culture, and Bailey would go to one area of the Middle East and hear a tribe tell a story. He would then travel hundreds of miles away to another tribe—one that had no apparent connection with the first tribe, where he would hear the same story, making the same main points with only minor variations. How can we account for the consistency and yet the variety? It happens because different people could tell the stories, but the Bedouin elders guarded and maintained their accuracy. The Bedouin took the telling of their stories seriously, and they made sure they were retold accurately from one generation to the next.

As we compare this to stories told in the Synoptic Gospels (Matthew, Mark, Luke), we see that formal controlled tradition doesn't explain the variations we find in the different accounts. Each gospel writer doesn't tell the story in *exactly* the same way. Moreover, informal *uncontrolled* tradition doesn't explain the similarities among the different accounts. But informal *controlled* tradition best explains how gospel stories can be consistent in their core elements and yet vary in the incidentals. For this reason, many scholars accept informal controlled tradition as an accurate picture of how the church retold the stories of Jesus.

The "informal" part allowed for some flexibility. As we will learn in later chapters, the Gospels are summaries, paraphrases, and abridgments, with the biblical writers selecting and arranging their materials in accordance with their individual goals. This accounts for the differences among the various gospel stories. But there were always key parts to each story that formed the basic structure of the event, and those parts were included in the different gospel accounts, which explains the consistency. For example, despite the slight differences in the retelling of the story of the paralyzed man who was lowered down through the roof, the core elements are present in all three gospels (Matt 9:1–8; Mark 2:1–12; Luke 5:17–26). The man was brought to Jesus by others; Jesus saw their faith and forgave the paralyzed man; the teachers of the law objected. Jesus knew what they were thinking. He used the visible healing as proof of the key statement, that the Son of Man has authority on earth to forgive sins. Flexibility and consistency.

The "controlled" part of this definition would refer to the eyewitnesses and church leaders who served as the guardians of the tradition—the apostles, the group of disciples who followed Jesus (120 in Acts 1:15), the 500 to whom Jesus appeared after his resurrection— "most of whom are still living" (1 Cor 15:6)—and the leadership of the church, such as Jesus' brother James (Acts 15:13). They collectively knew what Jesus had done and taught, and there is every reason to believe they provided a level of protection over the material that they so fervently believed. You can see the value placed on eyewitnesses when the apostles replaced Judas, and the criterion was to select a man who had "been with us the whole time the Lord Jesus was living among us, beginning from John's baptism to the time when Jesus was taken up from us" (Acts 1:21–22).

Craig Blomberg helpfully looks at the characteristics of oral traditions in nonbiblical contexts. When we compare two accounts of the same event, there is generally around a 10 percent variation in the details, but rarely more than 40 percent. It is interesting to find these same percentages when we compare the Synoptics Gospels. This confirms that the Bible, and in particular the gospel accounts of the life of Jesus, reflects a cultural understanding of the freedom and controls of oral tradition.[25] We can safely conclude that oral tradition faithfully guards the basics of the stories of Jesus, even if there are slight differences in the details.

Social Memory

Another factor to consider is the phenomenon of "social memory," which recognizes that when groups of people remember and reflect on the same events or teachings, memory can be more accurate. The more that stories are retold by more and more people in community, the better the chance that the members will accurately remember the key points of the story.[26]

One of our family favorite movies is *What about Bob?* I know that some people find this movie annoying (like Robin, my wife), but I don't know how many times I've said, "Guess what? Ahoy, I sail, I'm a sailor, I sail!" and the person I'm with knows exactly what I'm referring to. Like Bob, I say this when I'm doing something new or difficult and am enjoying myself. Or if I'm having a bad day, I'll say, "I feel good, I feel great, I feel wonderful!" My two nephews have heard me do this often enough that they fill in the blanks and know I'm having "a Bob day." Why do we remember lines like these so well? Because we have repeatedly heard the story together, and we've repeated the central lines over and over together until we remember them. "Baby steps!"

Personally Important

If an event is personally important, you are more likely to remember it accurately. The best examples are the historical discussions of the Holocaust by surviving Jewish authors. It was critical that these accounts be fastidiously accurate. If errors were found in their historical recollections, the writers would run the risk of having their entire accounts discounted. At the same time, because the people lived and survived the horrors of these camps, what they experienced has become part of who they are. The experiences were intensely personal, which helped with memory accuracy. To be honest, this fact can also act in reverse; because the Holocaust is such a personal memory, the facts could become clouded. That's why this argument is merely one among many.

Another way to state this is to ask if the person remembering has something at stake. If you were to ask me a question about something I read in the news or something a friend told me in passing, and it was a topic I wasn't interested in or involved in, my memory might be faulty. I could forget the details. Truth be told, I have trouble remembering a person's name a few minutes after meeting them if I don't actually engage in dialogue with them. But ask me about something that matters to me, something I have a personal stake in, and my memory is much better. I was a pastor for many years. Ask me about the building of the new worship center in the church I helped found, and I remember the details. Since I'm an Apple fan, ask me about the development of the Macintosh computer (not Windows). Since I'm a student of the Greek New Testament, ask me about a lecture I heard on Greek linguistics (not Hebrew). When we have a stake in something, we remember better. When something is important to us, we tend to remember better.

The apostles and the early church had a personal stake in remembering the life and teachings of Jesus—so they were extra careful to get the details right.

Note-taking

Because Jesus' world was an oral culture, many skeptics assume that notes were not taken by Jesus' followers or by those who witnessed the events recorded. But why not? Why should we assume the disciples or some of Jesus' followers outside the inner group were not taking notes as they traveled? The tax collector Matthew was certainly literate, and others may well have been able to write. We know that some rabbis at that time did encourage note-taking, even though memory was the primary learning tool,[27] although note-taking was banned by some rabbis (Babylonian Talmud, *Temurah* 14b).

Others argue that because the early church believed Jesus was going to return relatively soon, the disciples may have seen no reason to take notes. I will discuss this topic in more detail later, but the simple point I want to make now is that even if the followers of Jesus believed Jesus was returning relatively soon, wouldn't they still want to preserve his teaching, even if it were only for a matter of a few years? They must have assumed there would be some time before he came back. Why else would Jesus have talked so much about ethics and right living if he didn't expect some period of time to pass before he returned?

Paul

We know at least two things stand in the time gap between the events of Jesus' life and the writing down of those events: the nature of oral tradition and eyewitnesses. But there is a third, and it's a man named Paul.

Paul was converted sometime in the early to mid-30s on his trip to Damascus (Acts 9; Gal 1:13–2:10). Our best estimate as to the death of Jesus puts this event at either AD 30 or 33. This means the time gap between Jesus' ministry and death and the personal testimony of Paul is only a matter of a few years. Of added significance is the fact that Paul inherited an entire body of oral tradition. The largest section we know about is found in Jesus' instructions about the practice of Communion (1 Cor 11:23–26). Paul also quotes Jesus directly, saying that Christian workers should be paid (1 Cor 9:14) and that a married couple should not divorce (1 Cor 7:10). Yet these statements are not found in the written Gospels. Paul stands in the gap between the events of Jesus and the writing of the Gospels. He knows at least some of the traditions of Jesus and records them for us in his writings (cf. Rom 13:7; 14:13–14).[28]

The Holy Spirit

There is one final point that will have no influence on those who are skeptical of the Bible, but it is significant for a Christian who follows Jesus. Jesus makes a promise to the apostles in his Upper Room Discourse: "The Advocate, the Holy Spirit, whom the Father will send in my name, will teach you all things and will remind you of everything I have said to you" (John 14:26).

This is a promise to the eleven disciples (Judas had left at this point) that God's Spirit would supernaturally help them accurately remember what Jesus had taught. I find it personally comforting to know that when I read the Gospels, I'm reading words aided (and inspired) by the Holy Spirit, which leads me to trust that the words are accurate.

Conclusion

The evidence that Jesus existed is convincing. Considering the fact that he lived in relative obscurity, it's surprising how much we do know about him from nonbiblical sources.

There was a short time gap between Jesus' life and the writing of the Gospels, but it's safe to say that the gospel of Mark was written, at the latest, by the middle of the 60s—only three decades after Jesus— and the other gospels were written within a generation.

In the meantime, we know that the oral culture of the Bible followed an informal controlled tradition pattern in which anyone could retell the stories, but there were authorities who would guard the tradition. What's more, when your life and death are dependent on certain historical realities, you remember better.

Notes

1. Earl Doherty, *Jesus: Neither God nor Man—The Case for a Mythical Jesus* (Ottawa, ON: Age of Reason, 2009), vii–viii; for more examples, see Bart D. Ehrman, *Did Jesus Exist? The Historical Argument for Jesus of Nazareth* (San Francisco: HarperOne, 2012), 11–34.
2. I. Howard Marshall, *I Believe in the Historical Jesus* (Vancouver, BC: Regent College Publishing, 2004), 15.
3. See "Christ Myth Theory," Wikipedia, https://en.wikipedia.org/wiki /Christ_myth_theory. See also the talk by Craig A. Evans, "True or False: Is the New Testament Historically Reliable?" where he addresses mythicism (https://gk2.me/evans-mythicism, 11:08). He points out that some mythicists even denied the existence of Pilate and Nazareth until archaeological evidence proved them wrong.
4. Josephus, *Antiquities of the Jews* 18.3.3, www.pbs.org/wgbh/pages /frontline/shows/religion/maps/primary/josephusjesus.html.
5. Josephus, *Antiquities of the Jews* 20.9.1. Josephus goes on to say that James was stoned by the Sanhedrin in the 60s. He also mentions John the Baptist (*Antiquities of the Jews* 18.5.2).
6. See F. F. Bruce, *The New Testament Documents: Are They Reliable?* 6th ed. (Grand Rapids: Eerdmans, 1981), 105–15.
7. See the discussion in Craig L. Blomberg, *The Historical Reliability of the Gospels*, 2nd ed. (Downers Grove, IL: IVP Academic, 2007), 249–51.
8. Quoted in Blomberg, *Historical Reliability of the Gospels*, 249.
9. Quoted in Blomberg, *Historical Reliability of the Gospels*, 250.
10. Cited in Blomberg, *Historical Reliability of the Gospels*, 250.
11. For a fuller discussion of these writers, see Paul Barnett, *Is the New Testament Reliable?* 2nd ed. (Downers Grove, IL: IVP Academic, 2003), 22–24; Peter J. Williams, *Can We Trust the Gospels?* (Wheaton, IL: Crossway, 2018), 17–27.
12. Thallus was cited by the third-century historian Julius Africanus (Felix Jacoby, *Die Fragmente der griechischen Historiker* [Berlin: Weidmann Buchhandlung, 1923], 1156–58), https://infidels.org/library/modern /richard_carrier/jacoby.html.
13. Cited in Blomberg, *Historical Reliability of the Gospels*, 250.

14. Cited in Blomberg, *Historical Reliability of the Gospels*, 250.
15. Quoted in Blomberg, *Historical Reliability of the Gospels*, 251.
16. For more details, see Blomberg, *Historical Reliability of the Gospels*, 251–54; Barnett, *Is the New Testament Reliable?*, 30–31.
17. Origen (*Against Celsus* 1.32) tells us that the Jews taught that Jesus' father was a Roman soldier named "Pandera" (or "Panthera"). It's not a normal Roman name but could be an alteration of the Greek word for "virgin" (*parthenos*).
18. Quoted in Barnett, *Is the New Testament Reliable?*, 30.
19. Quoted in Barnett, *Is the New Testament Reliable?*, 30.
20. Craig Blomberg, "Lecture 10: More Reasons to Believe the Bible Is Credible History: Non-Christian Testimony to Jesus," in "Why We Trust Our Bible," Biblical Training Institute, https://gk2.me/we-trust.
21. Barnett, *Is the New Testament Reliable?*, 27.
22. Christians tend to call the first part of the Bible the "Old Testament" in distinction from the "New Testament." Since Judaism did not accept Jesus as the Messiah, they see nothing "old" with their Scriptures, so I tend to refer to the "Old Testament" as the "Hebrew Bible."
23. For an academic discussion of this topic, see Craig S. Keener, *Christobiography: Memory, History, and the Reliability of the Gospels* (Grand Rapids: Eerdmans, 2019), especially chaps. 14–16; Birger Gerhardsson,
24. All three of these categories were defined by Kenneth Bailey in *Jesus through Middle Eastern Eyes: Cultural Studies in the Gospels* (Downers Grove, IL: InterVarsity, 2008); see Kenneth E. Bailey, "Informal Controlled Oral Tradition and the Synoptic Gospels," *Themelios* 20, no. 2 (January 1995): 4–11, www.thegospelcoalition.org/themelios/article/informal-controlled-oral-tradition-and-the-synoptic-gospels.
25. See Craig Blomberg, "Reliability of the Oral Tradition (Part 2)," Biblical Training Institute, https://gk2.me/reliability-oral-tradition.
26. See Richard Bauckham, *Jesus and the Eyewitnesses: The Gospels as Eyewitness Testimony* (Grand Rapids: Eerdmans, 2006), 310–18.
27. See Allan Millard, *Reading and Writing in the Time of Jesus* (Sheffield, UK: Sheffield Academic Press, 2001), 202.
28. For a summary of what Paul knows about Jesus, see Craig L. Blomberg, *The Historical Reliability of the New Testament: Countering the Challenges to Evangelical Christian Beliefs* (Nashville: B&H Academic, 2016), 415–35.

Chapter 2

JESUS OF THE GOSPELS

In this chapter, we will look at the authorship of the Gospels, and whether the writers were in a place to tell us about Jesus accurately, or whether they changed our understanding of who he is.

Challenge

Skeptics frequently state that we don't know who wrote the Gospels.[1] Some will say that the gospel writers never met Jesus. They believe that someone wrote the stories and then attached the Gospels to a well-known person in the church to give their stories credibility. In addition, some skeptics say the gospel writers were not even concerned about history and had no desire to be historically accurate. They use the phrase "Jesus of history" to describe who they think Jesus *really* was, and they use the phrase "Christ of faith" to describe who the church presumably turned him into. For example, some would say the Jesus of history was merely a man; the Christ of faith was portrayed as God.

Who Wrote the Gospels?

Issues of authorship and dating are difficult when looking at ancient literature. The authors of the Gospels don't identify themselves, and we often have to rely on historical references from the second, third, and fourth centuries. The situation is different for the epistles, since they all state who wrote them (except for Hebrews). We'll look at the authorship of the epistles in chapter 5. In this chapter, we'll focus on who wrote the Gospels. The important question is whether or not the writers were in a position to retell the story of Jesus accurately.

External evidence for ancient historical documents is often scant. For almost all ancient documents, our understanding of who wrote them and when they were written is based on very little information. It's not like there were publishing houses that guaranteed authorship, and ancient books didn't have copyright notices with the year attached. So historians have to proceed based on the information they have, even if it is limited.

Titles

It has long been said that the Gospels are anonymous. At one level, that's true. The names of the authors are not embedded in the text of the Gospels. But it is false to suggest that their names are not attached in other, less direct ways.

Martin Hengel makes the argument that titles like "According to Mark" were used much earlier than previously suspected.[2] These titles were added sometime before the end of the first century, prompted most likely by the presence of two or more gospels that needed to be distinguished. Part of Hengel's argument is that the authorship of the four gospels was unanimously attributed to Matthew, Mark, Luke, and John by the middle of the second century, and the only way for this to have happened was for the church to have known for quite some time who wrote the Gospels. If the authors' names were truly not attached to their writings, multiple names would have been attached (as is the case with Hebrews).[3] To state it simply: if nobody knew for six decades who wrote the Gospels, the second-century witness wouldn't have been unanimous. Rather, it would have been highly contested, and we'd have records of that. Instead, we find the traditional names as the *only* names.

This is especially significant when we realize that the Gospels spread throughout the Roman Empire as Christianity exploded onto the scene, and yet everywhere we look, the same four names are attached to the same four gospels. The ancient world was obviously not as well-connected as we are today. If people in one area arbitrarily attached the name "Matthew" to the first gospel, it would be an astoundingly rare coincidence for people in another country to do the same. And yet in different countries throughout the ancient world, "Matthew" was always attached to the first gospel.

Craig Evans adds an even stronger argument. He states, "In every single text that we have where the beginning or the ending of the work survives, we find the traditional authorship."[4] In $\mathfrak{P}^{75}$ (the $\mathfrak{P}$ means it's written on a papyrus), a papyrus from the middle of the third century, we read "on leaf 47 (recto), where Luke ends (at Luke 24:53), the words εὐαγγέλιον κατὰ Λουκᾶν ["Gospel according to Luke"]. Below these words is a blank space, the equivalent of two to three lines. Below this space follow the words εὐαγγέλιον κατὰ Ἰωάνην [Gospel according to John] [sic][5] and then the opening verses of the Gospel of John."[6] Evans summarizes, "There are no anonymous copies of the Gospels, and there are no copies of the canonical Gospels under different names. Unless evidence to the contrary should surface, we should stop talking about anonymous Gospels and late, unhistorical superscriptions and subscriptions."[7]

The Church Fathers

Below is a summary of the evidence of gospel authorship we have from the early church fathers, most of whom wrote in the second, third, and fourth centuries.[8]

Mark

The church father Papias was the bishop of Hierapolis in Asia Minor until about AD 130. He was a disciple of the apostle John, and therefore his information is only one step removed from the eyewitnesses. Unfortunately, his writings have been lost. Fortunately, we know much of what he said because he was quoted by later writers, most importantly by the church historian Eusebius, who wrote at the beginning of the fourth century. According to Eusebius, Papias said:

> And the presbyter used to say this, "Mark became Peter's inter-preter [or, translator][9] and wrote accurately all that he remembered, not indeed, in order, of the things said or done by the Lord. For he had not heard the Lord, nor had he followed him, but later on, as I said, followed Peter, who used to give teaching as necessity demanded but not making, as it were, an arrangement of the Lord's oracles, so that Mark did nothing wrong in writing down single points as he remem-bered them. For to one thing he gave attention, to leave out nothing of what he had heard and to make no false statements in them."[10]

If the "presbyter" is in fact the apostle John, Papias's teacher, then we have a direct reference to Markan authorship from a first-generation Christian.[11] Clement of Alexandria in the late second century said that Mark wrote to the Christians in Rome at their request.[12] Justin Martyr (*Dialogue with Trypho* 106) in the mid-second century says that Mark's gospel was based on Peter's "remembrances" (possibly "memoirs"). Other church fathers who assert Markan authorship include Irenaeus, Tertullian, and Origen.[13]

In addition, the only person named (John) Mark in the first cen-tury who could be so named without further explanation is the Mark we read about in the Gospels, Acts, and the Pauline epistles. Most importantly, Peter writes from Rome and says Mark is his "son" (1 Pet 5:13). This suggests a close relationship and fits what we know of the Mark mentioned in Scripture.

There is good evidence that both Peter and Paul were martyred under Nero in the mid- to late sixties. We also know that Peter and Mark were in Rome by the early 60s. Because Matthew and Luke incor-porate most of the material in Mark's gospel, we believe Mark's gospel was probably written first. Clement of Alexandria writes:

> When Peter had publicly preached the word at Rome, and by the Spirit had proclaimed the Gospel, that those present, who were many, exhorted Mark, as one who had followed him for a long time and remembered what had been spoken, to make a record of what was said; and that he did this, and distributed the Gospel among those that asked him. And that when the matter came to Peter's knowledge he neither strongly forbade it nor urged it forward.[14]

This account could push the date of Mark's writing back into the late 50s, but certainly no later than the 60s.

Matthew

Papias says (alternate translations are in brackets), "Matthew composed [compiled] his λόγια in the Hebrew [Aramaic] language [dialect, style], and everyone translated [interpreted] it as they were able."[15]

Logia could refer to certain sayings of Jesus, but more likely it refers to both the sayings and the actions of Jesus. The church fathers believed that Matthew was the first to write a gospel (not Mark) and that he did so in Hebrew or Aramaic, but it's also possible that Matthew initially wrote a collection of Jesus' sayings and later turned them into a full-blown gospel. Eusebius quotes Irenaeus (*Against Heresies* 3.1.1, late second century), telling us that Matthew wrote "while Peter and Paul were preaching at Rome, and laying the foundations of the Church."[16]

All the church fathers without fail believed that Matthew wrote the gospel that now bears his name. Many scholars date the writing of Matthew in the 70s or 80s, but it certainly was written sometime after the writing of Mark.

Luke

The early church was in unanimous agreement in believing that the third gospel and Acts were written by the physician Luke, Paul's traveling companion. Luke is specifically named by the second-century Marcion, the Muratorian Canon (about AD 180), and Irenaeus (*Against Heresies*

3.1.1; 3.14.1). The oldest Greek manuscript we have of Luke (late second century), the Bodmer Papyrus XIV ($\mathfrak{P}^{75}$), identifies Luke as the author.

Like Matthew, Luke uses Mark as a source, so it must be dated after the writing of Mark. Luke states that his gospel is the "former book" (Acts 1:1), so the third gospel would have been written before Acts, and Mark and Acts are the chronological bookends to Luke's gospel. The final events in Acts 28 are dated in AD 62. Assuming one of Luke's purposes in writing Acts was to have documentation for Paul's trial, then Acts must have been finished soon after AD 62. Thus the most likely chronological sequence of books would be Mark, Luke, and then Acts. Most scholars date Luke in the 70s. Because it was written before Acts, I suspect it was written in the 60s, but that's a minority position.

John

As I said earlier, Papias was a disciple of John, and Papias tells us that he tried to find out any information he could about the apostles.[17] Along with John the Beloved, he also speaks of "John the Elder." We are not sure which of these two men Papias is speaking about when he says "John" wrote the fourth gospel, but the church fathers unanimously attributed the gospel to John the beloved disciple, the apostle of Jesus. In fact, there are good arguments that John the Elder and John the Apostle were the same person. John appears to have written at the end of the first century to churches in the area of Ephesus.

More conservative scholars date Mark in the 60s, Matthew and Luke in the 70s to the 80s, and John in the 90s. While the average life expectancy of a male in the first-century Eastern Mediterranean world was the late forties, we do know that some people lived to the age of one hundred.[18] If John was a young man when he began to follow Jesus, perhaps a teenager, this would mean John was in his seventies when writing his gospel, a believable scenario.

Some scholars place Mark in the 70s, Matthew and Luke in the 80s, and John in the 90s. But wherever you land on this discussion, we can affirm that the four gospels are first-century documents written by eyewitnesses or secondhand witnesses, relaying traditions that could be checked and corrected by the community. Simply stated, the writers of the Gospels were in a good position to write faithfully about Jesus' life and teachings.

Why These Writers?

The challenge at the beginning of this chapter pointed out that some skeptics believe an anonymous person wrote a gospel story and then attached it to a well-known person in the church in order to give it credibility. It is true that we know many of the apocryphal gospels were anonymous and were attributed to well-known people like Mary, Nicodemus, or an apostle such as Thomas or even Judas. However, if someone says this is what happened with the canonical gospels, the first question we should ask is why Matthew, Mark, and Luke were chosen as the supposed authors. If you were going to attach a false gospel to a famous person, would you have picked one of these three?

Let's first consider Mark (also named John Mark). He abandoned Paul and Barnabas on the first missionary journey (Acts 13:13) and later split the friendship between the two (Acts 15:39). It's also possible that he is the person who ran naked from Gethsemane when Jesus was arrested (Mark 14:52). Why would you attach your story to this person? Why not to Peter? Or another disciple?

Earlier we heard from Eusebius, who told us that Papias believed the second gospel was actually from Peter, and that Mark simply wrote down the words. Yet if this is true, why not call it the "Gospel of Peter"? That would give the writing considerably more credibility than attributing it to Mark. Here is the point to consider: even though the church knew the gospel ultimately came from Peter, they refused to use Peter's name. They were serious about attributing the correct authorship to the Gospels.

What about Matthew? The case here is not much better. It's hard for us today to fully understand the hatred the Jews felt toward another Jew who capitulated to the foreign invaders from Rome. Matthew was a tax collector, someone who took money from his fellow Jews to support the occupation by Rome. If you're going to write your own gospel, why choose Matthew as the author?

Or consider Luke. Luke admits right up front that he never saw Jesus (Luke 1:2). He was probably a Gentile, and in fact we know very little about him. Yet his writing comprises 27 percent of the New Testament. Wouldn't a smart forger have chosen someone other than a little-known Gentile who wasn't even an eyewitness?

We can't know for sure, but it stretches the truth to think that the supposed authors of these three gospels would have chosen these three names—out of all the names they could have picked—to give their gospels credibility. It's far more likely that Matthew, Mark, and Luke were the actual authors.

Why Later?

Why were the Gospels written so much later than the events they record? There are two good explanations for this. First, Papias told us he would rather hear the "living and abiding voice" of someone than read about it.[19] In other words, he preferred stories as they were told through oral tradition. But when those "living and abiding" voices, the eyewitnesses, were dying, there was a need for their testimony to be written down. We see this need demonstrated in the accounts of the Holocaust that were written as survivors began to die.

Second, we need to acknowledge that in the context of ancient literature, the time gap between the life of Jesus and the writing of the Gospels is incredibly short. In most ancient documents, hundreds of years passed between the events and the author's writing down of those events. For example, Alexander the Great died in 323 BC, but it wasn't until the late first century and early second century AD that

Plutarch wrote about Alexander's exploits—more than four hundred years after Alexander's life.[20] That would be roughly similar to me writing a book today about the events that led up to the American Revolutionary War in 1775. Despite the time gap that spans the lives of Alexander and Plutarch, historians are still confident they can piece together Alexander's life. The few decades between Jesus' life and the writing of the Gospels are just a blink of the eye in the realm of history, and this gives us unusual confidence that what we read is reliable.

Was Authorship Important?

Some skeptics contend that the actual author of a document was not significant, but is there any factual evidence that this was the case? Did the church think apostolic authorship of the accounts of Jesus was important? All evidence says yes.

The Muratorian Canon states about a pseudepigraphical letter, "There is current also [an epistle] to the Laodiceans, [and] another to the Alexandrians, [both] forged in Paul's name to [further] the heresy of Marcion, and several others which cannot be received into the catholic church—for it not fitting that gall be mixed with honey."[21]

Eusebius mentions that Serapion of Antioch (ca. 190) found the apocryphal gospel of Peter being used in Cilicia and wrote the following to the church at Rhossus in Cilicia: "We receive both Peter and the other apostles as Christ, but the writings which falsely bear their names we reject, as men of experience, knowing that such were not handed down to us."[22]

There also was a letter called 3 Corinthians, which was actually accepted by some as canonical. It was written by a second-century bishop in Asia out of "love for the apostle." When the author confessed that his work was a forgery, his actions were condemned. He was removed from office, and his forgery was rejected. Tertullian (*On Baptism* 17) writes:

But if the writings which wrongly go under Paul's name claim Thecla's example as a license for women's teaching and baptizing, let them know that, in Asia, the presbyter who composed that writing, as if he were augmenting Paul's fame from his own store, after being convicted, and confessing that he had done it from love of Paul, was removed from his office.[23]

In rejecting forgeries and disciplining those who wrote them, the early church showed its concern for truth in authorship. The church carefully examined the issue and rejected those writings that were questionable.

Jesus of History or Christ of Faith?

One of the discussions in academic circles today is whether or not our understanding of Jesus is historically accurate. Did the gospel writers describe Jesus accurately, or did they say he did things and taught things that he never did? For example, did Jesus say he was God, or did the church make it up?

Skeptics use the phrase "Jesus of history" to refer to who they think Jesus "really" was. They use "Christ of faith" to refer to who the church, especially Paul, supposedly changed Jesus into. This is essentially the same debate I mentioned in the introduction when I talked with my Muslim driver about Jesus on the way to the airport.

The history of the debate has produced versions of Jesus that are quite different. According to some, Jesus was a political or social revolutionary, a cynic-like philosopher, a charismatic holy man, a Jewish sage, an eschatological prophet,[24] or a simple Galilean man teaching the "brotherhood of man" and the "fatherhood of God." What they all agree on is that the Christ we read about in our gospels is not an accurate portrayal of who the real Jesus is, and hence the Bible cannot be trusted.

The influential German scholar Rudolph Bultmann said, "I do indeed think that we can know almost nothing concerning the life and personality of Jesus."[25] The Jesus Seminar was a collection of New Testament scholars who met to decide which sayings of Jesus in the Gospels were, in their opinion, authentic. Their conclusion was this:

> The Jesus of the gospels is an imaginative theological construct, into which has been woven traces of that enigmatic sage from Nazareth— traces that cry out for recognition and liberation from the firm grip of those whose faith overpowered their memories. The search for the authentic words of Jesus is a search for the forgotten Jesus.[26]

In other words, there is almost no correlation between who Jesus was and what we read about him in the Gospels.

Many full-length, scholarly books have been written on this topic,[27] but some things are worth saying in summary.

Assumptions

We must be careful whenever we assign motives, but in some cases, skeptics of the Bible will admit they come to the text with a priori assumptions and anti-supernatural ideologies, and then proceed as if these assumptions and ideologies were facts. For example, a skeptic might say:

- We know there are no such things as miracles, so all miracles must have been added to the historical account.
- No one is born of a virgin, so the story was added to parallel the supposed virgin births of other significant people.
- We know God can't become human, and so Jesus never would have said he was God.
- Jesus never intended to start a church, so any references to the church are later additions.
- God is a God of love, not wrath, so final judgment (if there is such a thing) must result in universal salvation, and all discussion of hell must be rejected.

Consider the early twentieth-century scholar Albert Schweitzer. He wrote that Jesus thought he could force God's hand in sending his kingdom to earth, eventually by being crucified. When Jesus was hanging on the cross and realized he had been unsuccessful, he cried out in despair, "My God, my God, why have you forsaken me?" (Mark 15:34). Schweitzer believed that the historical Jesus was a deluded, apocalyptic prophet. Or consider Rudolph Bultmann, who argued that modern people are rationalistic and do not accept the prescientific worldview of the biblical writers who believed in miracles and a three-level universe of earth, heaven, and hell.

But these assumptions about God and reality run contrary to what the Bible teaches and what Christians have always believed. We believe God is all-powerful, and he can do whatever he wants to do, including becoming human. As God, he can be born of a virgin, perform miracles, and die as a substitute for human sin. God (the Father) can raise God (the Son) from the grave.

These are, to be accurate, faith-based assumptions by Christians, but skeptics also base their conclusions on their faith-based, unprovable assumptions. If you believe there is no such thing as a miracle, then you will expunge the gospel of any mention of the miraculous. But if you hold these beliefs, there is no reason to remove the miraculous from the gospel accounts. To put it simply, to a large extent, your assumptions and beliefs about Jesus will determine your understanding of who the historical Jesus was.

Darrell Bock pursues a different course of argumentation. He starts with the accepted rules of the historical Jesus debate and uses them to show that many parts of the Gospels can be "proven" to be true.[28] These discussions can be quite technical at times, but in the end, they give positive arguments for the believability of the historical Jesus—all the while playing by the rules of skeptical biblical scholarship.

Theology and History

Skeptics will sometimes charge that theology has a bias toward history. In other words, because the gospel writers believed things about Jesus, their accounting of the historical realities is skewed and untrustworthy.

It is certainly true that if you believe something deeply, you *may* not see reality clearly. Those who follow cult leaders provide ample evidence that human beings can be blinded by faith commitments and are therefore unable to see and evaluate facts and truth. But while this is possible, it is not necessary. It doesn't follow that my beliefs *must* distort my understanding of history. I have already mentioned the faithfulness of Jewish historians in their description of the Holocaust. I've argued that the gospel writers felt a need for historical accuracy in remembering the person of Jesus. While sometimes true, the charge of bias is not always true, and this means the skeptic cannot just broadly dismiss an argument because it comes from a person of faith. Each situation needs to be tested individually.

Mark Strauss examines the charge of bias by acknowledging that everyone has a bias, both believer and skeptic. However, this doesn't mean our recounting of historical events must necessarily be skewed.

> Were the gospel writers biased historians? If we mean by biased "holding certain convictions," then the answer is yes, because there is no such thing as an unbiased historian. Everyone has a worldview and a belief system through which he or she processes reality, whether that worldview is theistic, atheistic, pantheistic, animistic, or agnostic. The gospel writers passionately believed in the message they proclaimed and desired for others to believe it ... [However], those passionately interested in the events are often the most meticulous in recording them.[29]

Were the Gospel Writers Interested in History?

Skeptics also question whether the gospel writers thought that accurate history was even important. After all, weren't they writing theological documents meant to convert nonbelievers? Aren't their writings nothing more than theological propaganda?[30] As we will see, there are several good reasons to believe the gospel writers were intentionally seeking to get their facts right.

First, the Christian faith requires Jesus to have been a real person. While many religions and philosophies don't require a real, historical person at their core, Christianity docs. The church was claiming that the person of Jesus Christ was unique in history. He was God made flesh. He lived without sin, preached, did miracles, fulfilled prophecy, was executed, and was raised from the dead. Christianity claims that these acts in history actually accomplished our salvation. Jesus did not just describe reality or tell people how to be saved. He had to be a real person; otherwise, the entire Christian belief structure falls apart. As Paul said, if there was no resurrection (of a real person), then the Christian faith is futile (1 Cor 15:15–20). This is why there was an emphasis on the historicity of Jesus in the early creeds. For example, the Apostles' Creed (ca. fourth century) reads, "I believe in Jesus Christ, his only Son, our Lord; who was conceived by the Holy Spirit and born of the virgin Mary. He suffered under Pontius Pilate, was crucified, died, and was buried." It is central and essential that Jesus existed, lived a certain kind of life, died a certain kind of death, and was raised from the dead to prove that he had won the victory over sin and death so that we too could be raised with him. The historical veracity of the church's belief about Jesus is crucial; Christianity is not just a good moral system.

Second, adding false information would have made an already difficult task even harder. Jesus' followers already faced an uphill battle, teaching as they did that Jesus is the fulfillment of the Jewish hope, a sinless human being, a resurrected man who was God. There would have been no reason to add false information into the Gospels that would have made their task even more difficult.

Third, the argument has been made that the early church believed Jesus would return soon, and therefore there was no need for accurate history. There are two answers to this argument: (1) While they believed in Jesus' return, they also believed in the importance of living out his teachings and commands. How could they know what to believe or how to live if their historical documents were unreliable? They had to learn how to relate to one another and to the government. They had to watch for the signs of Jerusalem's collapse and live in preparedness for Jesus' return. History was critical, even if it ended up lasting only a few years. (2) While the early Christians thought Jesus *could* return soon, that didn't mean they thought he *had* to return soon. Just as the Jewish people had lived for centuries with the expectation of the coming day of the Lord (Psalm 90:4), so Christians lived with an expectation of Jesus' second coming. But in the meantime, however long that time would be (2 Pet 3:8), they needed to know what Jesus did and said, and those historical records had to be accurate.

Yes, the gospel writers were interested in accurate history. Without it, there is no gospel.

Difficult Verses

We may also ask whether anything in the Gospels themselves suggests that the writers were faithful in their portrait of Jesus. Is there evidence they were trying to be accurate, or do we see signs that they were willing to change Jesus into something else—the "Christ of faith"? There are three arguments that point to the faithfulness of the writers.

One, the Gospels contain some "embarrassing" verses. It's frequently pointed out that if the writers were willing to play fast and loose with the historical facts, they would not have included stories and sayings that are embarrassing to the church. Why not remove them? The fact that they were not removed suggests the writers desired accuracy.

Peter became the head of the (Jewish) church, and yet Jesus says to him, "Get behind me, Satan! . . . You do not have in mind the concerns of God, but merely human concerns" (Mark 8:33). Jesus could not perform many miracles in his hometown (Mark 6:5). But these embarrassing sayings and others were left in the Gospels, signifying that the authors were trying to be faithful to the historical record rather than protecting the good reputation of the church leaders and even Jesus.

Two, the Gospels have many "hard" sayings. These are statements that trouble people. For example, Jesus tells the disciples that "you will not finish going through the towns of Israel before the Son of Man comes" (Matt 10:23), and yet Jesus did not return by the end of the disciples' ministry. Jesus seems to speak against the fifth commandment when he says, "If anyone comes to me and does not hate father and mother, wife and children, brothers and sisters—yes, even their own life—such a person cannot be my disciple" (Luke 14:26). The Gospels claim that Jesus was the Son of God, and yet he doesn't know when the end of the world will come: "But about that day or hour no one knows, not even the angels in heaven, nor the Son, but only the Father" (Mark 13:32). In speaking of the end of time, Jesus says, "This generation will certainly not pass away until all these things have happened" (Matt 24:34); two thousand years later, we're still here. Jesus even calls his own followers "evil" (Matt 7:11). Of course, there are good interpretations for these verses that make them easier to understand (e.g., Matt 24:34 is speaking of the destruction of the temple and not the end of time), but they tend to be difficult for many people to grasp when first read. Why include these verses when they could have been removed? The fact that these hard sayings were left in the Gospels once again suggests that the authors were intentionally being faithful to the historical record.

Three, the Gospels have several "missing" sayings. There were issues in the early church that could have been quickly solved if a gospel writer simply would have made up a new saying of Jesus. For example, the first theological battle of the church was over the relationship between Judaism and Christianity—specifically, about whether a Gentile converting to Christianity had to be circumcised in order to be saved. Why not make up a saying supposedly from Jesus that would solve the debate? Or what about a verse that defines the Trinity or clearly explains how Jesus can be both fully God and fully human (the incarnation)? New sayings from Jesus would have solved these theological conflicts, but instead they were not added to the Gospels.

The simplest explanation is that the gospel writers were intent on being honest and weren't willing to change or omit a verse just because it was embarrassing or difficult, nor were they willing to make one up to solve a current church dilemma.

Did Paul Change Jesus' Message?

In the supposed process of changing the Jesus of history into the Christ of faith, Paul is often cited as one of the main culprits. I've already addressed some of the more technical arguments, but let me share a more practical example.

A good friend was struggling with her faith. She had been raised in a conservative church, but her faith was based more on experience than on the teachings of the Bible. As a result, her theological footing was rather slippery. She told me, "Jesus I believe; I don't have to believe Paul." Her point was that Jesus and Paul did not preach the same gospel.

I responded with a basic set of questions:

Me: How do you know about Jesus?
My friend: I read about him in the Bible.
Me: Who wrote the gospels about Jesus?
My friend: Apostles.
Me: Who was Paul?
My friend: An apostle.
Me: Who was Mark?
My friend: I'm not sure, but he wasn't an apostle.
Me: How about Luke?
My friend: Same answer.

My point in asking these questions was to help her see that what we know about Jesus and Paul both come through the apostles (or in Luke's case, the friend of an apostle). If she agreed that an apostle's writing should be accepted, as she did with Matthew, Mark (Peter), Luke, and John, then the writing of all apostles should be accepted. The church as a whole certainly believed that Paul spoke with apostolic authority (1 Cor 7:17; 2 Thess 3:10–12, 14) equal to any other apostle (Acts 15:1–29; Gal 1:6–2:14).

The real issue my friend had was that Jesus and Paul sounded different to her. In her reading of the Bible, she thought Jesus was a kind, gentle, loving person, and Paul was severe, judgmental, and demanding. So I showed her that Jesus could be just as harsh (Matt 23), judgmental (Matt 5:20; 7:21–23), and demanding (Luke 14:26) as Paul. And Paul, with all his talk of grace, can sometimes sound just as loving as Jesus. It's difficult to find any personal characteristic in Jesus you can't find in Paul, and vice versa (other than Jesus' divinity).

But her struggle gets at a deeper issue. Are Jesus and Paul theologically compatible? Do they teach the same truths, or do they disagree with each other? While their teachings may seem to be in conflict at times, we need to realize that they are communicating in two different contexts. Jesus was the Messiah who came to bring the kingdom of God into the world through his life, death, and resurrection. Jesus taught how to enter and how to live in this kingdom. This is the message of the Gospels. In contrast, Paul had to deal specifically with the Jewish misunderstanding of salvation by faith versus obedience to the law, and much of his letters deal with answers to specific questions from the churches. The contexts are different and the vocabulary they use is different, but their teachings are compatible.

Craig Blomberg argues that some of the perceived differences between Jesus and Paul are not contradictory, citing justification and the kingdom of God, the role of the law, the Gentile mission and the church, women's roles, Christology, and discipleship.[31] For example, the concept of "church" is explained by Paul but only mentioned three times by Jesus (Matt 16:18; 18:17). And yet Jesus certainly envisioned a community of followers that would exist long after he was gone; otherwise, why all the ethical instructions? Both saw a future time of persecution followed by Jesus' second coming and life forever with God, even if they spoke about it in different terms.

Many have wondered why Paul doesn't quote Jesus more often, but once again, Jesus and Paul are in two different contexts. The Gospels were written to tell people about Jesus. Paul was writing to specific churches to give specific answers to specific questions, and many of the questions were not discussed (as far as we know) by Jesus. Paul also was writing with the absolute authority of an apostle. This meant he did not have to quote anyone else for support, not even Jesus. And yet from time to time we do find examples of Paul directly referencing Jesus, as well as alluding to what Jesus taught.[32]

Conclusion

There are many more things I could discuss. Craig Blomberg, Paul Barnett, Peter Williams, and F. F. Bruce have done a great service in showing how so many details of the New Testament fit neatly into first-century culture.[33] Williams includes a fascinating discussion of names, drawing from the work of Richard Bauckham, and the way names tend to be specific to certain locales, as well as the difficulty of faking a gospel and getting the names right. For those who want to dig in further, these books are well worth reading.

On the question of who wrote the Gospels, we don't have a surplus of evidence, as is typical of most ancient literature. But what we have is sufficient to accept the uniform church tradition as to the traditional authorship of the four gospels. We therefore have eyewitnesses or secondhand witnesses who were in a place to know and accurately report the actions and teachings of Jesus.

We have also seen that, due to the nature of Christianity, it was essential that the church's memory of Jesus be real. Christianity is about the person and work of Jesus of Nazareth. As long as we don't have preconceptions about the impossibility of the miraculous, there is no reason to see a distinction between the Jesus of history and the Christ of faith.

For Further Reading

Blomberg, Craig L. *The Historical Reliability of the Gospels.* 2nd ed. Downers Grove, IL: IVP Academic, 2007).

———. *The Historical Reliability of the New Testament: Countering the Challenges to Evangelical Christian Beliefs.* Nashville: B&H Academic, 2016.

Bock, Darrell L., and Daniel B. Wallace. *Dethroning Jesus: Exposing Popular Culture's Quest to Unseat the Biblical Christ.* Nashville: Nelson, 2007.

Bruce, F. F. *Jesus and Christian Origins outside the New Testament.* Grand Rapids: Eerdmans, 1974.

———. *The New Testament Documents: Are They Reliable?* 6th ed. Grand Rapids: Eerdmans, 1981.

Evans, Craig. *Fabricating Jesus: How Modern Scholars Distort the Gospels.* Downers Grove, IL: InterVarsity, 2006.

Komoszewski, J. Ed, M. James Sawyer, and Daniel B. Wallace, eds. *Reinventing Jesus: How Contemporary Skeptics Miss the Real Jesus and Mislead Popular Culture.* Grand Rapids: Kregel, 2006.

Pitre, Brant. *The Case for Jesus: The Biblical and Historical Evidence for Christ.* New York: Image, 2016.

Roberts, Mark D. *Can We Trust the Gospels? Investigating the Reliability of Matthew, Mark, Luke, and John.* Wheaton, IL: Crossway, 2007.

Strauss, Mark. *Four Portraits, One Jesus: A Survey of Jesus and the Gospels.* 2nd ed. Grand Rapids: Zondervan, 2020.

Strobel, Lee. *The Case for the Real Jesus: A Journalist Investigates Current Attacks on the Identity of Christ.* Grand Rapids: Zondervan, 2007, 23–63.

Williams, Peter J. *Can We Trust the Gospels?* Wheaton, IL: Crossway, 2018.

Advanced

Beilby, James K., and Paul Rhodes Eddy, eds. *The Historical Jesus: Five Views.* Downers Grove, IL: IVP Academic, 2009, especially the chapter by Darrell Bock, 249–81.

Bird, Michael F., ed. *How God Became Jesus: A Response to Bart D. Ehrman.* Grand Rapids: Zondervan, 2014.

Bock, Darrell. *Who Is Jesus? Linking the Historical Jesus with the Christ of Faith.* New York: Howard, 2012.

Carson, D. A., and Douglas J. Moo. *An Introduction to the New Testament.* 2nd ed. Grand Rapids: Zondervan, 2005.

Notes

1. For example, see Bart D. Ehrman, *Forged: Writing in the Name of God—Why the Bible's Authors Are Not Who We Think They Are* (San Francisco: HarperOne, 2011).

2. Martin Hengel, *Studies in the Gospel of Mark* (Minneapolis: Fortress, 1985), 64–84; see D. A. Carson and Douglas J. Moo, *An Introduction to the New Testament*, 2nd ed. (Grand Rapids: Zondervan, 2005), 140–41; Simon J. Gathercole, "The Titles of the Gospels in the Earliest New Testament Manuscripts," *Zeitschrift für die Neutestamentliche Wissenschaft* 104, no. 1 (January 2013): 203. Written in English, it is available online (www.academia.edu/7968624/The_Titles_of_the _Gospels_in_the_Earliest_New_Testament_Manuscripts); Craig A. Evans, *Jesus and the Manuscripts: What We Can Learn from the Oldest Texts* (Peabody, MA: Hendrickson, 2020), 130–203.

3. Tertullian argued that the author of Hebrews was Barnabas (*On Modesty* 20). Origen said that some believed the author was Clement of Rome or Luke (Eusebius, *Ecclesiastical History* 6.25.11–14). Eusebius thought it was Paul (*Ecclesiastical History* 6.14.2–4). Origen concluded, "In truth God knows."

4. Evans, *Jesus and the Manuscripts*, 53.

5. Evans presumably adds "[*sic*]" because John's name is being spelled with one *nu*.

6. Evans, *Jesus and the Manuscripts*, 53.

7. Evans, *Jesus and the Manuscripts*, 53; see Simon Gathercole, "The Alleged Anonymity of the Canonical Gospels," *Journal of Theological Studies* 69, no. 2 (October 2018): 447–76.

8. For a more detailed discussion of the issues of authorship and dates for the Synoptics, see Carson and Moo, *Introduction to the New Testament*, 140–56, 172–82, 203–10, 229–54; Timothy P. Jones, *Misquoting Truth: A Guide to the Fallacies of Bart Ehrman's* Misquoting Jesus (Downers Grove, IL: InterVarsity, 2007), 95–120; Evans, *Jesus and the Manuscripts*, 2–26.

9. *Hermēneutēs* could mean that Mark translated Peter's Aramaic into Greek, or that Mark shared Peter's teaching.

10. Quoted in Eusebius, *Ecclesiastical History* 3.39.15.

11. Simon Gathercole comments, "Attribution of the second Gospel to Mark goes back to John the elder in the first century. This cannot be more than about 20 years after the composition of the Gospel. In the light of this,

it seems extremely unlikely that there was a time when Mark was not associated with the Gospel" ("The Alleged Anonymity of the Canonical Gospels," *Journal of Theological Studies* 69, no. 2 [October 2018]: 475).

12. Cited in Eusebius, *Ecclesiastical History* 6.14.6–7.

13. Irenaeus (*Against Heresies* 3.1.2); Tertullian (*Against Marcion* 4:5); Origen, *Commentary on Matthew* (cited in Eusebius, *Ecclesiastical History* 6.25.5).

14. Quoted in Eusebius, *Ecclesiastical History* 6.14.5–6.

15. Quoted in Eusebius, *Ecclesiastical History* 3.39.16, translation with alternate translations from Craig L. Blomberg, *The Historical Reliability of the New Testament: Countering the Challenges to Evangelical Christian Beliefs*, 2nd ed. (Nashville: B&H Academic, 2016), 6.

16. Quoted in Eusebius, *Ecclesiastical History* 5.8.2–4.

17. Cited in Eusebius, *Ecclesiastical History* 3.39.4.

18. A tractate of the Jewish Mishnah, *Pirke Aboth* 5:24, discusses characteristics of people based on age and goes all the way to one hundred.

19. Fragment 3.3, cited in Eusebius, *Ecclesiastical History* 3.39 (see *The Apostolic Fathers*, 3rd ed., trans. Michael Holmes [Grand Rapids: Baker, 2007], 735).

20. Diodorus wrote in the first century BC and Quintus Curtius in the first century AD, but the works by Plutarch and Arrian (early second century) are the ones we typically go to to learn about Alexander (see Blomberg, *Historical Reliability of the New Testament*, 18–19).

21. Edmon L. Gallagher and John D. Meade, eds., *The Biblical Canon Lists from Early Christianity: Texts and Analysis* (Oxford: Oxford University Press, 2017), 180–81 (lines 63–67).

22. Eusebius, *Ecclesiastical History* 6.12.2–3.

23. Quoted in Tertullian, *Latin Christianity: Its Founder, Tertullian*, vol. 3 of *Ante-Nicene Fathers*, ed. Allan D. Menzies (Grand Rapids: Eerdmans, 1957), 677, www.ccel.org/ccel/schaff/anf03.vi.iii.xvii.html. I wrote extensively about the value of authorship in my commentary, *Pastoral Epistles*, in the Word Biblical Commentary series (2000; repr., Grand Rapids: Zondervan, 2016), cxxiii–cxxvii.

24. For a description of each of these positions, see the summaries in Mark Strauss, *Four Portraits, One Jesus: A Survey of Jesus and the Gospels*, 2nd ed. (2007; repr., Grand Rapids: Zondervan, 2020), 439–56.

25. Rudolph Bultmann, *Jesus and the Word*, trans L. P. Smith and E. H. Lantero (New York: Scribner, 1958), 8.

26. Robert W. Funk, Roy W. Hoover, and the Jesus Seminar, *The Five Gospels: The Search for the Authentic Words of Jesus* (San Francisco: HarperSanFrancisco, 1993), 4.

27. For a summary and short critique of this position, see Darrell L. Bock and Daniel B. Wallace, *Dethroning Jesus: Exposing Popular Culture's Quest to Unseat the Biblical Christ* (Nashville: Nelson, 2007), 183–91. For an academic debate see Michael F. Bird, ed., *How God Became Jesus: A Response to Bart D. Ehrman* (Grand Rapids: Zondervan, 2014). Also James K. Beilby and Paul R. Eddy, eds., *The Historical Jesus: Five Views* (Downers Grove, IL: IVP Academic, 2009); Darrell Bock is the evangelical contributor; see pp. 249–300.

28. Darrell L. Bock, *Who Is Jesus? Linking the Historical Jesus with the Christ of Faith* (New York: Howard, 2012); Bock, "The Historical Jesus. An Evangelical View," in *The Historical Jesus: Five Views*, 254–81. Bock was the cochair of the Institute for Biblical Research Jesus Group, a regular gathering of biblical scholars, where many of these issues are discussed and debated.

29. Strauss, *Four Portraits*, 465.

30. See James K. Hoffmeier and Dennis R. Magary, eds., *Do Historical Matters Matter to Faith? A Critical Appraisal of Modern and Postmodern Approaches to Scripture* (Wheaton, IL: Crossway, 2012).

31. Blomberg, *Historical Reliability of the New Testament*, 439–57.

32. 1 Cor 7:10; 9:14; 11:23–26. For more on Paul's influence see Bock and Wallace, *Dethroning Jesus*, 173–92.

33. Blomberg, *Historical Reliability of the New Testament*; Paul Barnett, *Is the New Testament Reliable?* 2nd ed. (Downers Grove, IL: IVP Academic, 2007), 54–66, 77–88, 145–58; Peter J. Williams, *Can We Trust the Gospels?* (Wheaton, IL: Crossway, 2018), who covers the topics of geography (bodies of water, roads and travel, gardens), people's names, the Jewishness of the Gospels, botanical terms, finance, and customs; F. F. Bruce, *The New Testament Documents: Are They Reliable?* 6th ed. (Grand Rapids: Eerdmans, 1981).

CONTRADICTIONS

Are There Contradictions in the Gospels?

Challenge

How can any thinking person believe the Bible? It's so full of contradictions that its teachings can't be trusted. It's full of teachings that we know are false because they contradict science, history, and common sense. It talks about miracles, such as Jesus' healing of diseases, walking on water, and being raised from the dead—things we know just don't happen. It's a book of fables and spiritual nonsense.

Chapter 3

CONTRADICTIONS IN THE BIBLE

 In this chapter, we will look at how apparent contradictions in the Gospels can be solved through correct interpretation and an understanding of how the Gospels were compiled.

The best educational experience of my life was the Thursday afternoons I spent in Aberdeen, Scotland, while working on my PhD. I had developed friendships with two fellow students—Craig Blomberg and Darrell Bock. Craig's office was one level below mine, and Darrell lived in a little town outside of Aberdeen called Torphins. Each week, I would meet them on Thursday afternoon. We'd eat lunch and then spend the afternoon in wonderful debates. We discussed everything related to the Bible and theology—from inerrancy to women's roles in ministry to dispensationalism and beyond.

If you're involved in biblical scholarship, you may recognize these two names. Both men went on to have long careers in teaching and academic research and writing. Craig spent most of his career at Denver Seminary, and his books on the historical reliability of the Bible, especially the Gospels, are my primary resource for the next two chapters. Darrell spent his career at Dallas Theological Seminary and has written extensively on the issue of the historical Jesus.

But those Thursday afternoon lunches had a profound impact on my life, reorienting my perspective on the Bible. I had gone to an evangelical seminary, but it was quite comfortable believing that the Bible has errors. What the Bible says about history and science, my professors would argue, is outside the scope of inspiration and is not necessarily correct. But Darrell and Craig disagreed. Darrell had attended Dallas Theological Seminary and Craig had gone to Trinity Evangelical Divinity School, both of which taught their students to believe in and fight for the inerrancy and reliability of Scripture. Both believed the Bible was true in *everything* it taught.

Week after week, no matter what problem I brought up at lunch, they had a believable solution. As the months passed, they slowly convinced me that the Bible is true in all that it affirms—as long as it is understood properly and within its cultural context. After my PhD studies, I spent my teaching career at Azusa Pacific University and Gordon-Conwell Theological Seminary, encouraging students to do what Craig and Darrell had taught me to do—to think through the issues and believe in the whole Bible, in every word. While there are admittedly a few issues I have yet to resolve, I decided to accept the reliability of Scripture and seek to give it the benefit of the doubt. My goal in these two chapters is to encourage you to do the same.

University students are often hesitant to answer the question I like to ask them: "Do you really believe that the Bible is true, that it contains the words of God breathed out of God's mouth, as 2 Timothy 3:16 says?" Today, there is a general sense in the evangelical church that certain questions should not be asked, that it is irreverent to do so. But nothing could be further from the truth. If you don't ask the question for yourself and think through the issues for yourself, you'll never be truly convinced the Bible is true. And more importantly, you won't rely on it when you need it the most.

My wife and I have had two children die. Rose died in a miscarriage, and Rachel died of a rare genetic disease as I held her in my arms four hours after her birth. If I had waited until those moments to decide if I thought the Bible was true, I don't know if I would have held on to my belief that God is all-knowing, all-powerful, and all-loving. The pain of loss was simply too great. But because I had worked through the issues and had become convinced that the Bible is wholly true, my faith in God was there when I needed it the most.

These next two chapters are critically important. Ask the hard questions, and don't be satisfied with pat, shallow answers. Someday your life may depend on it.

The Real Issue

One of the most frequent objections to the Bible has to do with the apparent contradictions and errors found in the Bible itself. Many of these questions are easily answered, but others are more complicated. I can't address all the issues in this book, but I will focus on a few of the more prominent questions. For this, I'm especially indebted to Craig Blomberg, not only for our times together in Scotland but for his many excellent books.[1]

Our starting point is very simple and something you need to remember whenever the Bible is challenged. If someone tells you they don't trust the Bible because it has so many errors and contradictions, there's one, and only one, question you should ask: "Can you show me one?"

Ask it nicely. You can say, "If I'm going to work with you on this issue, I need an example of what concerns you." How the person answers your clarifying question will reveal the real issue they are raising.

If they can't identify a potential error, you'll know this isn't the real problem for them. It's probably a smoke screen, meaning they have other issues, and you need not waste your time answering questions they aren't really asking. They're using the Bible to hide their *real* issues. That said, if they can identify specific issues with the biblical text, then you need to read the biblical text with them and pursue a solution. That's where this chapter may be of some help.

Incorrect Interpretation

Many of the issues that people have with apparent contradictions or errors in the Bible are due to an incorrect interpretation of a biblical passage. These are the easy ones to answer.

"There is a contradiction between what Paul and James teach on justification by faith." In Romans 4:3, Paul quotes Genesis 15:6 and the example of Abraham to show that justification is by *faith*: "Abraham believed God, and it was credited to him as righteousness." "Justification" is the doctrine that we are declared not guilty of our sins and therefore ushered into a relationship with God. It's one of Paul's central teachings that we are made right before God not by what we do but by what we believe about who Jesus is and what he did.

James likewise cites Genesis 15:6 and the example of Abraham (Jas 2:23), but he uses it to show that justification is by *works*, that we are justified by what we do. This apparent contradiction is so pronounced that ever since the early centuries, the church questioned whether the book of James should even be in the Bible, and Martin Luther was famous for his dislike of the book.

The solution is simple. To be declared "righteous" and to be "justified"—both English words translate the same Greek word—can describe *both* the process of becoming righteous and the living of a righteous life. Paul is emphasizing how one *becomes* righteous by faith, and James is emphasizing how one *lives* a righteous life, a life that in turn demonstrates that the person has true faith.

Paul's Jewish audience believed a person was made right with God by doing certain things, like being circumcised, following Sabbath laws (what one could or couldn't do on Saturday), and giving money to the temple. Paul's response is to say that being made right with God is a matter of faith. In contrast, James is addressing a different situation in which his audience is claiming they can have faith, but their faith is not changing their lives. His response is to argue that faith that is not accompanied by "deeds," by the actions of a changed life, is a dead and useless faith (Jas 2:26).

The NIV's and NLT's translation of James 2:24 is brilliant. Most other translations read, "a person is *justified* by works" (ESV, CSB, NRSV, NET, NASB), making the contradiction seem more obvious. The NIV reads, "a person is *considered righteous* by what they do," and the NLT reads, "we are *shown to be right* with God by what we do." These two translations make it clear that James is not contradicting Paul.

"Jesus contradicts himself in saying we are both for him and against him." In Matthew, Jesus is accused of exorcizing demons by the power of Beelzebul. He responds, "Whoever is not with me is against me" (12:30; parallel at Luke 11:23). In other words, if you're not actively for Jesus, you are in fact against him; if you are sitting on the fence, you are in fact actively opposing him. However, elsewhere we read that the disciple John said, "Teacher, we saw someone driving out demons in your name, and we tried to stop him because he wasn't following us." Jesus responded with these words: "Don't stop him . . . because there is no one who will perform a miracle in my name who can soon afterward speak evil of me. For whoever is not against us is for us" (Mark 9:38–40 CSB). In other words, apparently if you're not actively against Jesus, you are in fact for him.

These sayings sound contradictory, but context shows that Jesus is speaking about two different things. The first passage deals with conflict with people who are *not* his disciples; if they don't decide "for" Jesus, they will in fact be "against" him. In the second passage, the person who was driving out demons was surely a follower of Jesus ("in your name") but not part of the inner circle of the Twelve. John was objecting that someone other than the Twelve was performing a miracle, and Jesus says that if a follower of his is performing a miracle in his name, even if he is not part of the Twelve, if he is not "against" Jesus, then he is "for" Jesus. Though the sayings are formulated similarly, these are two totally different contexts and there is no contradiction between them.

"Jesus did not return in the time he said he would return." In Mark 13, Jesus has been prophesying about the destruction of the

temple and his second coming. He says, "Truly I tell you, this generation will certainly not pass away until all these things have happened"
(Mark 13:30; cf. Matt 24:34; Luke 21:32). The problem is that Jesus
did not return forty years later (the length of a generation), and the
prophecy is often used as an example of an error, essentially concluding
that Jesus is a false prophet.

The solution is to read the passage in context. "These things"
(ταῦτα) is a pronoun, and pronouns have antecedents—the word or
words they refer back to. "These things" connects back to the same
word ταῦτα in the previous verse: "Even so, when you see *these things*
happening, you know that it is near, right at the door" (Mark 13:29,
italics added). In this verse, "these things" refers to the signs of the coming destruction of the temple, which took place in AD 70, a generation
later. The "things" don't refer to Jesus' second coming; thus this is not a
false prophecy.

"The gospels give different timelines for the death of Jesus." In
the Synoptics, this is the sequence of events starting on Friday morning:

- Jesus' visit to Pilate occurred "early in the morning" (πρωΐα,
  "early," Matt 27:1; πρωΐ, "early," Mark 15:1; ὡς ἐγένετο ἡμέρα,
  "daybreak," Luke 22:66).
- After taunting Jesus, the soldiers began to crucify him at 9:00
  a.m. (ὥρα τρίτη, "third hour," Mark 15:25 ESV).
- Darkness came "about noon" (ὡσεὶ ὥρα ἕκτη, "about the sixth
  hour," Luke 23:44 NIV and ESV; Matt 27:45 and Mark 15:33
  don't have "about").
- Jesus died at about 3:00 p.m. (περὶ . . . τὴν ἐνάτην ὥραν, "about
  the ninth hour," Matt 27:46 ESV; ὥρας ἐνάτης, "ninth hour,"
  Luke 23:44 ESV, which carries the force of the approximate
  ὡσεί, "about," from the first time designation earlier in the
  verse; Mark 15:34 doesn't have "about"). It appears that Luke is
  being more precise by including "about," following the lead of
  Matthew 27:46.

However, the two time designations in John are:

- when the Jews took Jesus to Pilate in the "early morning" (πρωΐ, "early," 18:28), and
- when Pilate turned Jesus over to the soldiers "about noon" (ὥρα ἦν ὡς ἕκτη, "about the sixth hour," 19:14 NIV and ESV).

So was it the third or the sixth hour (9:00 a.m. or noon) when Jesus was crucified? Two points to consider:

First, for the most part, the Synoptics and John give approximate time designations, usually explicitly approximate. Given the fact that the ancient world did not have a way to give exact time designations, both the "third hour" and the "sixth hour" could mean the same as our expression "midmorning." If Jesus was crucified at approximately midmorning, both time designations would be approximately accurate. Second, Craig Blomberg points out that the only time designations in the Synoptics, except for one (Matt 20:9), are the "third," "sixth," and "ninth" hours.[2] Because time designations were not precise, it's possible these divisions refer not to a specific hour but to one of the four divisions of the day. (The night also was divided into four watches.) So the "third hour" refers to 9:00 a.m. to 12:00 p.m., and the "sixth" hour refers to 12:00 p.m. to 3:00 p.m. If an event occurred at the end of the time period designated by "third hour" or at the beginning of the time period designated by the "sixth" hour, we can see that there is little difference between Mark and John.

"The Bible contradicts science." It is often said that the Bible contradicts science, and therefore the Bible is wrong and untrustworthy, assuming, of course, that science is always right. The biblical account of creation is often cited as a primary example. Science says the earth could not have been created in six literal days, and hence Genesis 1 is in error. But it is possible that Genesis 1 is primarily a theological statement and not a scientific treatise. Since it would not be claiming a time frame of six twenty-four-hour days, there is no necessary conflict.

Science says the earth is millions of years old, and some older Bibles have a heading on the page or in the marginal notes of Genesis 1 claiming that creation occurred in 4004 BC. As far as I can tell, the first Bible to include the 4004 BC date was published by Oxford University Press in 1679.[3]

People will say this is an error because science assures us that the world is much older than six thousand years. Without getting into a debate over creation, it's easy to point out that this date is not part of the Bible; Genesis itself never gives a date for creation. In the seventeenth century, James Ussher, the archbishop of Armagh and the primate of all Ireland, concluded that the earth had been created in 4004 BC, basing his conclusions primarily on the Old Testament genealogies. This belief made its way into some Bible printings, but it was never part of the Bible itself, and hence there is no contradiction.

"The Bible has inaccurate historical and geographical references." When there seems to be a contradiction between the Bible and history or geography, the issue can be our inaccurate understanding of the latter. For example, Matthew writes, "When Jesus had finished saying these things, he left Galilee and went into the region of *Judea to the other side of the Jordan*" (19:1, italics added). The supposed conflict is that Judea is to the *west* of the Jordan, and Matthew is saying that Judea (or part of Judea) is to the east. However, Pliny the Elder Pliny (*Natural History* 5.15.70) makes it clear that an area *east* of the Jordan could be called "Judea," perhaps using Roman terminology: "Beyond Idumaea and Samaria, Judaea extends long and wide. The part of it [i.e., of Judaea] adjacent to Syria is called Galilee, but the part next to Arabia and Egypt is called Peraea, which is covered with rough mountains, and separated from the other Judaeans by the river Jordan."[4] This clearly shows that in Pliny's time (AD 50s–70s), Peraea on the other side of the Jordan could be considered part of Judea.

Archaeology can, in fact, be marshaled to support the accuracy of the Bible's historical and geographical statements. A famous example is that of William Ramsay, an archaeologist from Oxford University who tried to disprove the historicity of Acts. His research convinced him that Luke was extremely accurate in his descriptions, and eventually this led Ramsay to become a Christian.[5] Craig Evans talks about modern Jewish (non-Christian) archaeologists (some of whom he works with) who use the Gospels and Acts to help in their research.[6]

Many technical books convincingly argue that the Bible is accurate in its historical and cultural descriptions. For example, see the magisterial work by K. A. Kitchen, *On the Reliability of the Old Testament*,[7] Jeffery Sheler on archaeology and the Old Testament,[8] Walter Kaiser on the history of the Old Testament as well as archaeology,[9] and Craig Blomberg and Paul Barnett on archaeology and the New Testament.[10]

Many apparent contradictions can be solved through correct interpretation of the Bible, science, and history.

How the Gospels Were Written

A correct, biblical understanding of how the Gospels were written enables us to handle other supposed contradictions. The most important statement in this regard can be found in the introduction to the gospel of Luke:

> Many have undertaken to draw up an account of the things that have been fulfilled among us, just as they were handed down to us by those who from the first were eyewitnesses and servants of the word. With this in mind, since I myself have carefully investigated everything from the beginning, I too decided to write an orderly account for you, most excellent Theophilus, so that you may know the certainty of the things you have been taught.
>
> *Luke 1:1–4*

What does Luke say about his book? Here are five points to consider:

1. There were many written stories about Jesus before Luke wrote. They may have been entire books, like the gospel of Mark, or they may have been individual stories or collections of stories.

2. Luke was not an eyewitness, but eyewitnesses who were with Jesus from the very beginning "handed down" the accounts to Luke about what Jesus did and said. They were also people who were actively involved in Jesus' ministry ("servants of the word"); they were not casual bystanders.

3. Luke shows he was concerned with history. He carefully investigated everything from the beginning of the story of Jesus. It appears from some of the literary characteristics that Luke's research would have included not just gathering written documents but also speaking with eyewitnesses. How would Luke know about the angels' visits and the rest of the personal and private information he includes in his first two chapters? He probably talked with Mary, possibly during Paul's two-year imprisonment in Caesarea (Acts 24:27). While Luke 3–24 is written in proper Greek, Luke 1–2 and its very personal stories carry a decided Aramaic flavor. Aramaic was the language of Zechariah, Elizabeth, Mary, and Joseph, and the style of writing reflects the authenticity of his historical research.

4. Luke was not writing the story in chronological order; he was writing an "orderly" account. Sometimes he arranged his material chronologically, and other times thematically, pulling stories from different historical settings and presenting them together.

5. Luke had a specific purpose in mind—namely, to assure Theophilus that what he had been taught was historically accurate. His gospel certainly had an apologetic thrust. Luke covered other themes too, such as Jesus' involvement with the social outcasts and downtrodden, but the historicity of Jesus' life and teaching was paramount.

The gospel of John also contains an explicit purpose statement: "Jesus performed many other signs in the presence of his disciples, which are not recorded in this book. But these are written that you may believe that Jesus is the Messiah, the Son of God, and that by believing you may have life in his name" (20:30–31). Later, John writes, "Jesus did many other things as well. If every one of them were written down, I suppose that even the whole world would not have room for the books that would be written" (21:25). What we read in John's gospel is not everything he knew, but only some of what he thought would help people see that Jesus is the Messiah, that the Messiah is the Son of God, and that a belief in who Jesus is leads to eternal life.

Mark has a purpose statement as well, but it's not as obvious. The title to his book (or at least to the first part of his book) is, "The beginning of the good news about Jesus the Messiah, the Son of God" (Mark 1:1). Mark is telling the story of Jesus so that people will see who he is—the Messiah, the Son of God.

This is a far cry from modern biographies, which are intent on telling more details and background information. It's also (thankfully) a far cry from someone telling their life story on social media in which they think we want to know what they had for lunch and see yet another picture of their children, as cute as they may be.

It's difficult to nail down the specific genre the Gospels fit into, although Greco-Roman biography is the closest and most likely. The Gospels are stories about Jesus that the authors found relevant for their specific purposes. Stories of Jesus' boyhood, as curious as we may be about them, are not relevant to the writers' purposes, except for Luke's recounting of Jesus' visit to Jerusalem when he was twelve years old. Like ancient biographies, the gospel writers centered on major events and teachings and sometimes passed by the minutiae.

The point is that the gospel writers knew much more than what they wrote about, and their specific purposes in writing controlled both their selection and the arrangement of the accounts that eventually became their gospels. Armed with this information, you'll find that many of the apparent contradictions are solved. Here are a few examples.

"The Bible is not clear about what happened with the thieves on the cross." All four gospels say that Jesus was crucified between two insurrectionists (Matt 27:38; Mark 15:27; Luke 23:32; John 19:18). However, only Luke tells the story of the repentant rebel:

> One of the criminals who hung there hurled insults at him: "Aren't you the Messiah? Save yourself and us!"
>
> But the other criminal rebuked him. "Don't you fear God," he said, "since you are under the same sentence? We are punished justly, for we are getting what our deeds deserve. But this man has done nothing wrong."
>
> Then he said, "Jesus, remember me when you come into your kingdom."
>
> Jesus answered him, "Truly I tell you, today you will be with me in paradise."
>
> *Luke 23:39–43*

Is it a contradiction for Luke to say that one of the thieves repented? No. The gospels don't claim to tell us everything; they're being selective. All four gospels say there were two insurrectionists, and Luke adds that one of them repented.

Why did Luke include this story? We rarely know the answer to this kind of question, but it may have been because Luke had a heart for the socially disenfranchised, and here is a story of Jesus promising salvation to a dying political rebel. It fits one of Luke's purposes for writing. Perhaps both thieves "hurled insults at him" at first. What do you think Jesus did on the cross? Is it reasonable to think he said nothing? Or perhaps he talked with the thieves, and one came to change his mind about Jesus.

This brings up the important point of the burden of proof. Do I have to prove that the harmonization actually happened, or does the skeptic have to prove that the harmonization could not have happened? To be fair, neither option is possible. I am unable to prove that Jesus had an extended discussion with one of the rebels that was recorded by Luke, and the skeptic is unable to prove that this did not happen. Because I believe the Bible is basically reliable, I'm going to be more comfortable with giving it the benefit of the doubt and accepting possible harmonizations. Because skeptics do not believe the Bible is basically reliable, they will argue that the burden of proof is on me to prove my harmonization, which, as I have said, is impossible. For me, if a harmonization is plausible, if it does not create additional issues, and if it's consistent with what we know from other passages in the Bible, then I am content believing a harmonization and would argue that the skeptic must prove that the harmonization could not have happened.

Besides, how do you prove that an event is true? If multiple believable people personally witnessed something and wrote it down immediately—and if those manuscripts were available to us today—perhaps you could claim proof. But if that's what a historian requires, then to be honest, we know almost nothing about history. The vast majority of our historical documents were not written at the same time as the events they describe, and we have none of the original documents.

Tacitus (AD 56–120) was perhaps the greatest Roman historian, but we have only three manuscripts of parts of his work, with the oldest dating to the ninth century, and yet modern historians tend to believe what he wrote.[11] The oldest manuscript of Julius Caesar's account of the Gallic Wars (58–50 BC), *Bellum Gallicum*, is MS Amsterdam 73, dated in the later ninth century AD, almost a thousand years after the actual military campaigns. How can you prove that anything either writer said is true? You can't. The point is that the time gap between an event and the writing, and between the writing and our earliest manuscript of the writing, is usually a significant amount of time. Any unbiased historian understands the nature of historical writings and is willing to accept the historicity of many events without eyewitnesses and original manuscripts. The same methodology should be applied to the Gospels, which can make the claim of harmonization plausible without concrete proof.

"The Bible contradicts itself in telling how many angels were at the tomb." All four gospels tell us that an angel met the women at the tomb to tell them that Jesus had risen (Matt 28:1–2; Mark 16:5). However, Luke and John say there were two angels (Luke 24:4; John 20:11–12). Is this a contradiction?

If I tell you I went on a vacation with my son Hayden and only later mention that my wife, Robin, was there as well, is that a contradiction? Is it a contradiction to talk about one person without mentioning all the people present? Of course not. If I had said that *only* Hayden went on a vacation with me, then yes, that would be a contradiction, but that is not the case here.

It's interesting that John writes this about the angels: "They asked [plural] her, 'Woman, why are you crying?'" (20:13). In Luke, "the men [i.e., the angels] said [plural] to them, 'Why do you look for the living among the dead?'" (24:5). The Greek verbs in both verses are explicitly plural, but in reality I wonder if both angels in fact asked the question. Why would two angels speak in unison? Probably only one angel actually said the words. Can I prove that? Of course not. But is it a believable scenario? Yes. Can the skeptic prove that only one angel could not have said the words, that both angels must have spoken the same words at the same time? No.

In addition, consider that Matthew tells us that Mary Magdalene and Mary were at the tomb (28:1). Mark tells us that Salome was one of the women (16:1). Luke says it was Mary Magdalene, Joanna, Mary (the mother of James), and others (24:10). John mentions only Mary Magdalene (20:1). Is this a contradiction? No. The gospel writers were selective in what they wrote.

"The order of Jesus' temptations is different in Matthew and Luke." A common example of an apparent contradiction in the Bible is the order of the temptations. Matthew 4 recounts the order as turn stones to bread, jump off the temple, and then worship Satan. However,

Luke 4 reverses the order of the last two: turn stones to bread, worship Satan, and then jump off the temple.

The answer has to do with a difference between English and Greek and how we hear a series. In English, when we hear a series, by default we picture a sequence. If I said, "I went to the store, saw Ed, and had some coffee," we generally would think that I went to the store and *then* I saw Ed and *then* I had coffee. Certainly this isn't always the case, but by default I believe that's how we hear a series. So when we read about Jesus' temptation, we tend to hear turn stones to bread and *then* jump off the temple and *then* worship Satan.

In Greek, a series is not heard in the same way. Greeks don't hear the "then" that is implicit to our ears. This is one reason the Greek language prefers to start every sentence with a conjunction as a way of explicitly indicating the relationship between the two sentences. For example, Greeks would tend to say, "*and* Jesus said," "*then* Jesus said," or "*therefore* Jesus said" to make the connection between sentences explicit and clear.

The Greek that lies behind the English is interesting. In Matthew we read, "Tell these stones to become bread," and "then [τότε, *tote*] ... 'throw yourself down [from the temple],' and "again [πάλιν, *palin*] ... 'bow down and worship me [Satan]'" (4:3, 5–6, 8–9). Both conjunctions explicitly indicate sequence. However, Luke doesn't use sequential conjunctions. He writes, "Tell this stone to become bread," "[and, καί, *kai*] worship me [Satan]," "[and, δέ, *de*] throw yourself down from here [the temple]" (Luke 4:3, 7, 9). In fact, καί and δέ are so minor that the NIV simply translates them with punctuation marks and not with words. They don't necessarily indicate sequence, and hence there is no contradiction. Luke is simply saying there were three temptations.

Why did Luke change the order? Again, we can only speculate, but from a literary standpoint, Jerusalem is an important city for Luke. In Luke 9:51, while still early in his ministry, Jesus "resolutely set out for Jerusalem" because no prophet dies outside of Jerusalem (Luke 13:33).

For Luke's literary purposes, jumping off the temple holds a deeper significance because it's in Jerusalem, and so he creates a literary crescendo by changing the order of the last two temptations, but without claiming chronological sequence.

This is why the translation of καθεξῆς (*kathexēs*) in Luke 1:3 is so important. The 1995 edition of the NASB translated Luke as saying that he was writing his gospel "in consecutive order," presumably following the KJV translation "in order," thus creating an insurmountable problem. Many of the stories in the Gospels are told in a different chronological order. All the other major translations properly translate καθεξῆς as "orderly" (NIV, ESV, CSB, NRSV, NET) or "accurate" (NLT). "I too decided to write an *orderly* account for you, most excellent Theophilus, so that you may know the certainty of the things you have been taught" (Luke 1:3–4, italics added). Luke was not writing in strict chronological order. He was selecting and grouping his information according to different standards, sometimes chronological and other times thematic. This was a common practice in ancient writing that need not render his gospel as inaccurate.

The Synoptic Problem

The word *synoptic* means "same" and refers to the gospels of Matthew, Mark, and Luke. The "Synoptic Problem" is the technical term for why the Synoptic Gospels are similar in places and different elsewhere. As we delve into this issue, both in this chapter and in the next, you'll begin to see ways to explain many apparent contradictions. What I'm going to illustrate here is sometimes called "harmonization."[12]

Remember, the gospel writers are selective in choosing their material, and they have different goals in mind that dictate their selection and ordering of the material. Let's take the birth stories of Jesus to illustrate. Mark starts his story with the coming of John the Baptist. John starts with Jesus' existence before birth and then jumps to John's ministry. Only Matthew and Luke tell about Jesus' birth.

Matthew	Matthew and Luke	Luke
	Birth	
		Shepherds
		Circumcision
		Naming
Magi		
Egypt		
	Nazareth	

Matthew's and Luke's accounts both start with Jesus' birth, and they both agree that Jesus ends up in Nazareth, but what happened in the meantime? In Luke we read about the shepherds, Jesus' circumcision, and his naming in the temple. In Matthew we read about the coming of the Magi and the trip to Egypt. What actually happened? Is this variation a contradiction? There are clues in the text.

1. When did the shepherds come? Luke explicitly says it was the night Jesus was born (Luke 2:8–12).
2. When was Jesus circumcised? The eighth day after birth (Luke 2:21).
3. When was Jesus named? Luke tells us it was "when the time came for the purification rites required by the Law of Moses" (Luke 2:22). This would have happened forty days after his birth (Lev 12:2–4).
4. Jesus was born "in a manger, because there was no guest room available for them" (Luke 2:7). However, when the Magi came, they found Jesus in a "house" (Matt 2:11). Sorry to ruin your image of the nativity scenes, but the Magi were not with the shepherds and Jesus was not in a feeding trough when they arrived. If Jesus' star rose when he was born (Matt 2:2), the Magi needed time to travel to Bethlehem as they followed the star.

5. In an attempt to kill Jesus, Herod had the soldiers slaughter all the boys two years old and younger (Matt 2:16). We know that Herod had serious mental issues, but even a soldier should be able to tell the difference between a newborn and a two-year-old boy. Why two years? Why not six months?

There are a few other clues as to what happened, and these relate more to the different writers' purposes in writing.

1. One of Luke's dominant themes is that social outcasts have a place in God's kingdom, and there weren't many professions lower than that of a shepherd. God announces the birth of his Son, the coming King, to shepherds. What a glorious picture of Jesus' future theme that the first will be last and the last will be first as the mighty angels announced to the lowly shepherds that the Messiah had arrived.

2. The circumcision and naming events put Jesus in the temple, where we read about Simeon, who says, "For my eyes have seen your salvation, which you have prepared in the sight of all nations: *a light for revelation to the Gentiles*, and the glory of your people Israel" (Luke 2:30–32, italics added). Luke has a prominent theme that the gospel is also for Gentiles, and this account shows the prophecy that Jesus will be a light to the Gentiles.

3. The Magi and the ensuing trip to Egypt allow Matthew to emphasize that Jesus fulfilled prophecy: "Out of Egypt I called my son" (Matt 2:15, referencing Hos 11:1). This is an important detail, since Matthew is writing primarily to a Jewish audience that would see fulfillment of prophecy as significant. Luke is writing to a Gentile audience, and therefore the prophecy wouldn't have been as significant.

4. Matthew sees the killing of the children by the soldiers as another fulfillment of prophecy. "A voice is heard in Ramah,

weeping and great mourning, Rachel weeping for her children and refusing to be comforted, because they are no more" (Matt 2:18, referencing Jer 31:15).

When we put the pieces together, a believable picture emerges. Jesus was born in Bethlehem, and that very night God announced the birth of his son to the lowest in the Jewish social order (Luke's theme). Jesus goes to the temple eight days later to be circumcised, and about thirty-two days later, he returns to be named. Simeon prophesies that Jesus will be a light also to the Gentiles, not just the Jews (another Lukan theme). Given the facts that the people back home in Nazareth may well have been convinced that Mary had had a child out of wedlock, that she had just gone through the pain of childbirth, and that Bethlehem was Joseph's ancestral home, Joseph probably decided to stay in Bethlehem. One to two years later, the Magi arrived and Joseph fled to Egypt to avoid Herod, fully funded by their gifts, and the prophecies of Jeremiah 31:15 and Hosea 11:1 were fulfilled (Matthean themes). Two years later, they returned to Nazareth when Jesus was about four years old.

Can we prove this is precisely what happened? No. Is it believable? Yes. Remember, you don't have to prove every detail of how something happened, but the logic and flow of events do need to be believable. Once you do this, the burden of proof falls on the person who says it could *not* have happened that way.

Dr. George Guthrie, a good friend of mine, is a professor of New Testament at Regent College in Canada. When George teaches on the Synoptic Problem, he begins by asking two of his students to sit in the hall for thirty minutes. George explains the Synoptic Problem to the remaining students, and then he asks one of the students to come back to the classroom and share what happened in the hall for the past thirty minutes. Once that student is finished, he brings in the second student and asks the same question. As the second story unfolds, the students start to giggle and then laugh. They are amazed that two people sitting in the same place for the same time could have had such radically different recollections of what happened in the hall, and yet both accounts are true. Some of the things they remember are the same, but mostly they talk about different things.

Harmonization asks if you can conceive of a situation in which both biblical accounts could be true, despite their obvious differences. It acknowledges that we often tell stories about the same events but from different points of view. We select material to share and arrange it in ways that help us achieve our goals. Perhaps we want to be strictly chronological. Or we want to group similar events together. Maybe we want to compare and contrast two events that are disconnected in time. These different versions are not errors or contradictions. They are simply a reflection of the way we tell stories.

And the existence of these different perspectives makes a positive case that they are legitimate. If there were no differences to be found among the Gospels, we would assume the writers had colluded with each other and produced only one story of Jesus. The variations tell us that each of the gospel writers wrote independently, using some of the same material but being led by their own purposes, exercising the normal freedom we all have to vary some of the details of our stories. This is especially true when we compare Matthew and Luke in the passages where they show a literary dependence on Mark. We see patterns emerging as they have points of agreement with what Mark says, but yet they slightly massage Mark's writing, improving his grammar and style, softening his harsh treatment of the disciples, and making their gospels relevant to their own audiences. As a result, we have four faithful streams of information about Jesus, showing basic agreement but varying in some of the details.

Conclusion

Often we find it all boils down to using common sense as we figure out what really happened and acknowledge that different people can tell the same story from different points of view. When we add to this the freedom felt by the gospel writers to be selective and not necessarily chronological, many apparent contradictions are easily solved.

Notes

1. Craig L. Blomberg, *The Historical Reliability of the New Testament* (Nashville: B&H Academic, 2016); *The Historical Reliability of the Gospels*, 2nd ed. (Downers Grove, IL: IVP Academic, 2007). If you want to go deeper, I strongly recommend you attend his class on the historical reliability of the Gospels at BiblicalTraining.org (https://gk2.me/reliability).
2. Blomberg, *Historical Reliability of the Gospels*, 228.
3. Diana L. Severance, the curator of the Bible museum at Houston Baptist University, has been a great help to me. She wrote me that in 1701 the Church of England adopted the 4004 BC date in its official Bible, and the earliest Bible the museum has with that date was published by Charles Bill in London in 1701.
4. "Supra Idumaeam et Samariam Iudaea longe lateque funditur. pars eius Syriae iuncta Galilaea vocatur, Arabiae vero et Aegypto proxima Peraea, asperis dispersa montibus et a ceteris Iudaeis Iordane amne discrete," http://penelope.uchicago.edu/Thayer/L/Roman/Texts/Pliny_the_Elder/5*.html.
5. See W. M. Ramsay, *The Bearing of Recent Discovery on the Trustworthiness of the New Testament*, 2nd ed. (London: Hodder & Stoughton, 1915); Ramsay, *St. Paul the Traveller and the Roman Citizen* (London: Hodder & Stoughton, 1904). For the effect of archaeology on the New Testament, see Blomberg, *Historical Reliability of the Gospels*, 322–31.
6. Dr. Craig Evans, "True or False: Is the New Testament Historically Reliable?" YouTube, https://gk2.me/evans-mythicism at 8:25.
7. K. A. Kitchen, *On the Reliability of the Old Testament* (Grand Rapids: Eerdmans, 2003); see also Richard Hess's work for evidence showing that Joshua is firmly embedded in the second millennium BC (*Joshua*, Tyndale Old Testament Commentaries [Downers Grove, IL: InterVarsity, 1996], 27–33).
8. Jeffery L. Sheler, *Is the Bible True? How Modern Debates and Discoveries Affirm the Essence of the Scriptures* (New York: HarperCollins, 1999), 59–133; see Iain Provan, V. Philips Long, and Tremper Longman III, *A Biblical History of Israel*, 2nd ed. (Louisville, KY: Westminster John Knox, 2015), 231–61.

9. Walter C. Kaiser, *The Old Testament Documents: Are They Reliable and Relevant?* (Downers Grove, IL: IVP Academic, 2001), 53–182.

10. Blomberg, *Historical Reliability of the New Testament*, 99–148, 189–229, 250–93; Paul Barnett, *Is the New Testament Reliable?* 2nd ed. (Downers Grove, IL: IVP Academic, 2003), 159–64, especially the charts on pages 170–75.

11. J. Ed Komoszewski, M. James Sawyer, and Daniel B. Wallace, *Reinventing Jesus: How Contemporary Skeptics Miss the Real Jesus and Mislead Popular Culture* (Grand Rapids: Kregel, 2006), 71. They also have statistics for Livy, Suetonius, Thucydides, and Herodotus.

12. For an excellent illustration of harmonizing the different events surrounding the empty tomb and Jesus' resurrection, see Grant R. Osborne, *Three Crucial Questions about the Bible* (Grand Rapids: Baker, 1995), 39–41.

Chapter 4

DIGGING DEEPER INTO APPARENT CONTRADICTIONS

Now that we're acquainted with the way the Synoptic Gospels were written and the role of interpretation in solving apparent contradictions, let's examine some of the more complicated issues.

More on the Synoptics

How They Were Written

In the early centuries, people believed Matthew was the first gospel to be written and Mark was an abridgment of Matthew. But for the last couple of centuries, most scholars have agreed that Mark was written first, and Matthew and Luke made use of Mark and other sources when writing their own gospels. This historical process will help us understand some of the similarities and differences among the Synoptics.

There was no such thing as a copyright in the ancient world. Mark did not "own" what he wrote. According to church tradition, the gospel of Mark contains Peter's memoirs; Mark is believed to have written down what Peter remembered about his time with Jesus. After all, Jesus had promised that the coming Holy Spirit "will teach you all things and will remind you of everything I have said to you" (John 14:26). So Peter remembered, and Mark wrote. Later, Matthew and Luke began writing their own accounts, incorporating almost everything from Mark into their own gospels while adding their own material. This explains why all three Synoptics often have the exact or similar wording for the same stories, even when those stories are told in a different chronological order.

It's generally believed there was another collection of Jesus' teachings called "Q"—from the German word *Quelle*, meaning "source." We don't know if it was a single document, a series of documents, oral stories retold by the early church, or some combination of the above. But many passages in Matthew and Luke are word for word the same, or very similar, but the passage is not found in Mark. This has led scholars to suggest that Matthew and Luke both incorporated the teachings from Q into their gospels (about 235 verses). There is also material unique to Matthew—after all, he was one of the twelve disciples—and we cleverly use "M" to refer to that material. And as you would guess, there was material only in Luke called "L." M and L were not necessarily written documents. We don't know how the information was preserved or shared, but M and L help us identify material found only in Matthew and Luke, respectively. So how did Matthew and Luke incorporate these different sources, and how does this help us harmonize differences among the Synoptics?

Personal Tendencies

When Matthew and Luke have the same stories, drawing from Mark or Q, we can compare them and see where they're the same and where they're different, and then try to identify patterns. One of the patterns that emerges is that Mark is less forgiving of the disciples. He is harder on them than the other writers are. When you read the same material in Matthew, you'll see that Matthew has somewhat softened the failures of the disciples. To be clear, he doesn't lie or cover them up; he just softens them.

For example, when Jesus came to the disciples in the boat, walking on the water, we read in Mark, "Shortly before dawn he went out to them, walking on the lake. He was about to pass by them" (6:48). But in Matthew there is no fear of Jesus *passing* them. Matthew writes, "When the disciples saw him walking on the lake, they were terrified. 'It's a ghost,' they said, and cried out in fear" (14:26; likewise John 6:19). Most likely, when Mark writes, "He was about to pass by them," we are getting Peter's personal recollection of his first impression when he saw Jesus. Matthew softens Peter's misunderstanding by omitting that comment.

Common Sense

Sometimes apparent contradictions among the Gospels can be solved by applying a little common sense. To use the example above, Jesus comes walking on the water to the disciples, and in Mark they were "completely amazed" (6:51–52), while in John they were "frightened" (6:19). However, in Matthew, after Peter had walked on the water, we read, "Those who were in the boat *worshiped* him, saying, 'Truly you are the Son of God'" (14:33, italics added). There is perhaps a slight difference between being "amazed" and "frightened," but there is a bigger difference between those emotions and "worship." Is this a contradiction?

There are two keys to unraveling this apparent contradiction. The first is to see that in Matthew, some time had passed from when the disciples first saw Jesus and when they eventually worshiped him. In that time, they had seen Peter walk and sink, and then they had witnessed Jesus saving him. Their initial fear and amazement had apparently turned to worship over time. That makes sense and is not a contradiction.

The second key is to consider the depth of their worship. If their worship was immature or imperfect, the difference between "fright" and "worship" is not as great as we might assume. Did they truly understand who Jesus was and worship him as God, or did they merely respond to the miracle by worshiping Jesus as some sort of divine person? At this time, the phrase "Son of God" certainly didn't mean the second person of the Trinity; that concept hadn't yet been revealed. "Son of God" in this context may mean no more than they thought Jesus was some sort of divine person, but their lack of faith kept them from truly grasping the full significance of the miracle. They didn't fully understand that Jesus was the God who had made and sustains all creation.

Craig Blomberg also points out that two chapters later, we read "Peter's confession."[1]

> "But what about you?" [Jesus] asked. "Who do you say I am?"
>
> Simon Peter answered, "You are the Messiah, the Son of the living God."
>
> Jesus replied, "Blessed are you, Simon son of Jonah, for this was not revealed to you by flesh and blood, but by my Father in heaven."
>
> *Matthew 16:15–17*

Whatever the disciples meant by "Son of God" in Matthew 14, the fuller knowledge that Jesus was the "Messiah, the Son of the living God" in chapter 16 was something that had just been revealed through direct revelation from God. And yet even at chapter 16, Peter will still be firmly rebuked for his lack of understanding about Jesus' coming death. "Get behind me, Satan! You are a stumbling block to me; you do not have in mind the concerns of God, but merely human concerns" (16:23). The point is that faith often unfolds slowly over time. We see in this sequence of stories how the disciples' faith slowly grew, moving them from fear to imperfect worship to the reception of divine revelation, even though they still did not fully understand everything about who Jesus was. There is no contradiction between Matthew 14 and 16, just a growing faith.

Repetition

One of the main techniques used by Jewish teachers was repetition. Jesus was a Jewish teacher, so why would he come up with a good saying and use it only once? And similarly, why must we assume he would use the same saying to mean the same thing every time he used it?

In the Sermon on the Mount, Jesus says, "Blessed are the poor in spirit, for theirs is the kingdom of heaven" (Matt 5:3). In the Sermon on the Plain, Jesus says, "Blessed are you who are poor, for yours is the kingdom of God" (Luke 6:20). Does God's blessing fall on the financially poor (Luke) or on those who recognize their spiritual poverty (Matthew)?

There are several ways to solve this apparent dilemma. Luke could be reflecting the Old Testament teaching of God's blessing on the poor, who because of their financial poverty have learned to rely on God. This is very close to the meaning of "poor in spirit." But it could also be true that the Sermon on the Mount and the Sermon on the Plain are not the same event. Matthew and Mark could be referencing different sermons in which Jesus was making different points, yet using a similar expression: "Blessed are the . . ." In my years of teaching, I have often said the same thing in slightly different ways, sometimes to make a different point.

Paraphrase

Scholars talk about the *ipsissima verba* and the *ipsissima vox*. The *ipsissima verba* refers to "the very words" Jesus spoke; the *ipsissima vox* refers to "the very voice" of Jesus, not so much to the precise words but to the precise meaning of what he said. No doubt we have the *ipsissima verba* of Jesus in a few passages, such as those translated by the gospel writer. Jesus took the hand of the little girl and said, *"Talitha koum!"* to which Mark adds that it means, "Little girl, I say to you, get up!" (5:41). The writer certainly expects us to accept that Jesus actually uttered the two words, *"Talitha koum!"* Perhaps Jesus' last word on the cross was his exact word, τετέλεσται (*tetelestai*), "It is finished"—uttered in Greek for all to hear and understand (John 19:30). And yet we should also remember that Jesus probably spoke mostly in Aramaic, so that what we have recorded in the Gospels is a translation of his words into

Greek, and therefore in most cases we have his *ipsissima vox*. Remember that the ancient world did not have quotation marks and often did not distinguish between direct and indirect speech.[2]

Here's a minor example, but one replicated hundreds of times throughout the Synoptics. The paralyzed man is let down through the roof of the house, and Jesus says,

> "Get up, take your *mat* and *go* home." (Matt 9:6, italics added)
> ἐγερθεὶς ἆρόν σου τὴν κλίνην καὶ ὕπαγε εἰς τὸν οἶκόν σου.

> "Get up, take your *mat* and *go* home." (Mark 2:11, italics added)
> ἔγειρε ἆρον τὸν κράβαττόν σου καὶ ὕπαγε εἰς τὸν οἶκόν σου.

> "Get up, take your *mat* and *go* home." (Luke 5:24, italics added)
> ἔγειρε καὶ ἄρας τὸ κλινίδιόν σου πορεύου εἰς τὸν οἶκόν σου.

Did Jesus say κλίνην (*klinēn*; Matthew), κράβαττόν (*krabbatton*; Mark), or κλινίδιόν (*klinidion*; Luke), all three translated "mat"? The words mean the same basic thing, but they are different words: κλίνη is a bed (or even a couch); κλινίδιον is a small bed, much like a modern stretcher; κράβαττος is a mattress or pallet, specifically a poor person's bed. Also, did Jesus say ὕπαγε (*hypage*) or πορεύου (*poreuou*), telling the man to *go* home? Though ὕπαγε and πορεύου are different words, they mean the same basic thing. As the story was (probably) translated from Aramaic into Greek, different but synonymous words were used, all accurately conveying the "very voice" of Jesus but not the "very [Aramaic] words."

You and I do the same thing today. If my son, Hayden, said, "Mom says it's time to eat," and if my wife, Robin, actually said, "Can you tell Dad that lunch is ready," would you say that Hayden misrepresented what Robin said, even if you used quotation marks in writing his words? I don't think so. We often allow for such paraphrasing, even in direct speech.

If you're uncomfortable with the idea of paraphrase, you'll undoubtedly find an insuperable number of contradictions in the Synoptics. It's better to understand that the authors were intent on retelling what Jesus said with accuracy even while paraphrasing his words in their translations, and to recognize that no one had yet invented the symbol to indicate a quotation, nor was there a perceived need for one.

Approximations

We all use approximations. If you were to ask me how big I am, I would tell you I'm six foot three inches tall and weigh two hundred pounds. But the more precise answer is that I'm slowly shrinking and am now about six foot two inches tall and generally weigh a few pounds over two hundred. Is that an error? Of course not. It's an approximation.

My dad, a well-respected New Testament scholar, wrote an article years ago about a supposed error in the Bible. It concerned the large caldron located in front of Solomon's temple that was called the "bronze Sea." The text says it was ten cubits in diameter and thirty cubits in circumference: "He made the Sea of cast metal, circular in shape, measuring ten cubits from rim to rim and five cubits high. It took a line of thirty cubits to measure around it" (2 Chron 4:2). However, we learned in high school math that you can't express the diameter and circumference of any object in real numbers—you must use *pi*. Did the Chronicler make an error here? Of course not. As my dad argued, it's an approximation.

A condescending author wrote that Dad was wrong and had a deficient view of inspiration, claiming that if you measured the inside circumference of the caldron and the outside diameter, the measurements were exact. Not only was this comment foolish—the numbers still don't add up, and I wonder if the author ever saw a handmade object—but it was cruel. My father was no longer allowed to be a conference speaker at a well-known Christian ministry that my family had been involved with for years, all because this author had concluded that Dad had a low view of Scripture.

My point is that all of us, including the biblical writers, use approximations. These are not errors; they are the way we normally speak. This also explains some of the numbers in the Old Testament, as when we read that "those who died in the plague numbered 24,000" (Num 25:9). Really? Not 24,001? Or 23,999? It's an approximation. Elsewhere, Paul says the number is 23,000 (1 Cor 10:8). Again, an approximation.

Help the Reader

There are other times when apparent contradictions can be solved by recognizing that the biblical writers are trying to help the readers understand. When Mark tells the story of the paralyzed man let down through the roof, he says that the friends "dug through" (ἐξορύσσω, *exsorussō*) the roof, since it would have been a sod roof in Palestine (2:4). In the Gentile world, where roofs were mostly made with tiles, they would have been confused by the verb "dug through," so Luke says they lowered him "through the tiles" (διὰ τῶν κεράμων, *dia tōn keramōn*), an image that makes the passage understandable to his culture (5:19). True, it can't be both; the roof was either sod or tiles. However, you have to decide if you think this is an error or if you can accept this level of accommodation. After all, the structure of the roof is not the issue of the passage, but the fact that a paralyzed man was let down through an opening in the roof and Jesus used the occasion to claim that as the Son of Man he had the right to forgive sins.

Consider also the controversial divorce exception clause. In Mark, Jesus gives the basic rule: "Anyone who divorces his wife and marries another woman commits adultery against her" (10:11). However, it was universally recognized in many cultures that sexual infidelity was the one legitimate grounds for divorce, and hence there was no reason to say, "except for sexual immorality." But in Matthew's gospel, the exception clause is explicitly stated: "I tell you that anyone who divorces his wife, *except for sexual immorality*, and marries another woman commits adultery" (19:9, italics added). Matthew is helping the reader see that Jesus accepted the exception clause, even if Jesus didn't say so here. This is an interpretive position, but one that is widely held and believable, since Paul adds abandonment as another legitimate reason for divorce (1 Cor 7:15). Paul would not have written this if Jesus had absolutely said there were no exceptions. Another solution to this apparent problem is that perhaps Jesus really did utter the exception clause, and Mark gives the generalization, understanding that people would implicitly understand the exception.

While there are passages in the Gospels that appear to contradict each other, they can often be explained by a careful examination of their historical context. While you can't prove a harmonization, it can be comforting to know that it is possible, especially if you accept the basic reliability of the Bible. You may not be able to prove your point to the skeptic who comes to the text with a different set of beliefs, but you can find encouragement in knowing there are answers.

Ancient Writing Standards

In this next section, I'll cover what may well be the most difficult issue we need to address. While some people won't like what I'm going to say, my response is quite simple. Either you accept the reality that ancient writing standards differed from today's standards, or there are contradictions in the Gospels. There is no other sensible way to deal with some of these issues.

When we study the standards of ancient historical writing, we quickly realize they aren't the same as ours. The ancient writers were quite comfortable with simplification, paraphrase, and approximations. They were even comfortable compressing two events into one. Granted, we do the same today, but the ancients were even more willing to compress and simplify a story.

This doesn't mean that ancient historians weren't concerned with truth. It's not as if they thought they could create material out of thin air. Paul Barnett cites the second-century AD historian Lucian (*Quomodo* 47): "Facts must not be carelessly put together, but the historian must work with great labour and often at great trouble make inquiry preferably being present and an eyewitness; failing that he must rely on those who are incorruptible, and have no bias from passion, nor add or diminish anything."[3] Ancient historians understood the importance of being truthful and accurate, but they had greater freedom to simplify and compress their accounts.

Simplification

No one can deny that the stories in the Gospels were simplified and condensed. One simply can't tell the story, the whole story, and nothing but the story without omitting some details and events. And while we simplify stories and leave out facts all the time today, ancient writing standards allowed significantly more simplification.

For example, when Jesus first went to the synagogue in Nazareth, he read the prophecy of Isaiah 61:1–2 and said, "'Today this scripture is fulfilled in your hearing.' All spoke well of him and were amazed at the gracious words that came from his lips" (Luke 4:21–22). What gracious words? Certainly "today this scripture is fulfilled in your hearing" could not be called "gracious words." Obviously, what Jesus said was intentionally omitted between verses 21 and 22.

Or consider another example. The longest sermon in the New Testament is the Sermon on the Mount, found in Matthew 5–7. If you read these three chapters out loud, it will take you about twenty minutes. Is it reasonable to think Jesus originally spoke for less than a half hour? Or what about Peter's preaching at Pentecost (Acts 2:14–40), or Paul's preaching in Athens (17:22–31)? Were these short sermons? Probably not. But the writers did not feel it was important to include more, so the other things Jesus, Peter, and Paul said were omitted and the sermons simplified.

How can the fact of simplification help us with apparent contradictions? Consider the Last Supper. This was a Passover meal, and historically we've believed that four cups were shared in sequence during the meal. But when the story was shortened, Matthew and Mark told of the blessing of the bread and then a (later) cup, while Luke speaks of an (earlier) cup and then refers to the bread breaking (22:19–20). Certainly the meal went on for some time, and what we have is an abbreviated retelling of the events, with different authors referencing different cups, so there is no contradiction.

Compression

The cursing of the fig tree. The fig tree is one of the metaphors used for the people of Israel in the Old Testament. On the day after Jesus' triumphal entry, we read this about him:

> Early in the morning, as Jesus was on his way back to the city, he was hungry. Seeing a fig tree by the road, he went up to it but found nothing on it except leaves. Then he said to it, "May you never bear fruit again!" Immediately the tree withered.
>
> When the disciples saw this, they were amazed. "How did the fig tree wither so quickly?" they asked.
>
> *Matthew 21:18–20*

This is called an "enacted parable." Because the fig tree was unfruitful, Jesus cursed it. Then he went into the temple and debated with the spiritually dead and fruitless Jewish leaders. Jesus' curse on the fig tree was in reality a curse on the Jewish leaders who had not borne spiritual fruit.

However, this story is slightly different in Mark. Jesus cursed the fig tree, then went into Jerusalem and cleared the temple courts, and then on the *next* day we read, "In the morning, as they went along, they saw the fig tree withered from the roots" (11:20). The story is not told by Luke or John.

So which was it? Did the tree wither on that same day or on the next? We should first admit that the fact that the tree withered within twenty-four hours is miraculous. Whether the disciples saw it wither at that very moment or noticed it the next morning, the meaning of the curse was probably not lost on them. But this is where our understanding of ancient history writing also comes into play. Our rules about writing history are more precise and exact today. We would say it is either the first day *or* the second day. It was either 1892 *or* 1893. Either Ed said it *or* Jeff said it. In today's culture, we require a greater level of specificity.

Ancient standards of writing were not as precise as they are today, and to be fair, we can't hold them to our writing standards. This isn't an issue of right or wrong; it's just different. We know from secular ancient writing, for example, that authors could abbreviate an event by combining two events into one. And all of this was acceptable and not seen as deception.[4] So is it possible that Matthew, in an attempt to abbreviate the story, took what was in fact a twenty-four-hour process and simply said, "Immediately the tree withered"?

There may be another way to explain this apparent contradiction. Note that in Mark we read, "In the morning, as they went along, they saw the fig tree withered from the roots." *Withered* is in the perfect tense in Greek, which describes a completed action (and hence in the past), with consequences continuing into the present. So it could be translated "that had withered." All that the text says is the next morning they saw that it had withered; it doesn't say when it withered. And yet Matthew does say, "When the disciples saw this, they were amazed. 'How did the fig tree wither so quickly?' they asked." It sounds like their amazement was immediate, and this is an example of the gospel writer compressing the story.

Jairus's daughter. One of the most difficult passages to harmonize is the story of Jairus's daughter. In Mark, this is how the story is told (compare also Luke 8): "Then one of the synagogue leaders, named Jairus, came, and when he saw Jesus, he fell at his feet. He pleaded earnestly with him, 'My little daughter is dying. Please come and put your hands on her so that she will be healed and live'" (Mark 5:22–23). As Jesus and Jairus were on the way, we read, "While Jesus was still speaking, some people came from the house of Jairus, the synagogue leader. 'Your daughter is dead,' they said" (5:35).

The story is different in Matthew: "A synagogue leader came and knelt before him and said, 'My daughter *has just died*. But come and put your hand on her, and she will live'" (9:18, italics added). In Matthew, there is no account of anyone coming to tell Jairus that his daughter had died, and Jairus doesn't say his daughter is dying but that she has died. So was his daughter dead, or not dead, when Jairus found Jesus?

This is one of those situations in which it's easiest to say that Matthew has condensed the two events into one. Jairus's daughter was close to death when he left, so close that she died possibly a few minutes after he had left. Matthew simplifies the story and simply has Jairus say she has just died. If you read Matthew and compare his writing to Mark and Luke, you'll see that compression is a frequent pattern for Matthew. Again, to our ears, there is a significant difference between "is dying" and "has just died," even if there is only ten minutes between the two assessments. But that's not the case when it comes to ancient historical writing standards.

If you find this technique of compression difficult to accept, let me tell you the story of my mom's death. Her health had been steadily declining for five years, and her body was giving out, even though (we think) her mind was still working. On the morning Mom died, my older brother Mike was reading C. S. Lewis's *The Last Battle* out loud to her, and when he turned to the last page, the only visible sign of life was that Mom was barely breathing. When he finished the page and looked up, she had stopped breathing. So was she still alive at the beginning of the page? Scientifically, yes. Her brain neurons were still (barely) firing. But apart from her slight breathing, there was barely any difference in Mom's condition between the beginning of the page and the end of the page. We can talk about a person being "as good as dead" or even "dead," meaning that while they're scientifically alive, they are, for all practical purposes, dead. Mom was in this sense "dead" at the beginning of the page. There was virtually no difference between Mike calling me to say that Mom "is dying" and that Mom "has died."

Mom's story helps me better understand why and how Matthew

used compression. In Matthew, Jairus says his daughter has "just died" (ἄρτι ἐτελεύτησεν, 9:18). When he left his home, he knew she "was dying" (Luke 8:42, ἀπέθνῃσκεν), that she was in fact "at the point of death" (Mark 5:23 ESV, ἐσχάτως ἔχει). It would be safe to assume he knew that by the time he found Jesus, she would have died, and the news that she had died (Luke 8:49, τέθνηκεν) didn't come as a surprise. In fact, I wonder if "just died" in Matthew reflects Jairus's assumption that by the time he found Jesus his daughter would have in fact died. If I'm right, the compression should be less troublesome.

Even with all of this, I know the issue of compression will be difficult for some to accept. I myself resisted accepting it for many years. But the more I read and studied, the more I came to see how this kind of historical writing was perfectly acceptable in ancient times. It wasn't considered erroneous or deceptive, and it does explain some of the more difficult issues of the Synoptic Problem.

John

When compared to the Synoptics, the gospel of John has its own set of challenges. It's so different from the Synoptics that skeptics wonder how the two pictures of Jesus could possibly be compatible. What Jesus talks about and the way he speaks are different in John. The differences are real, and there is no reason to deny that fact. The real question has to do with the significance and meaning of these differences.

Selection

At least 80 percent of John's content is not found in the Synoptics, and skeptics often mistrust material contained in only one gospel. However, John was probably the last gospel written, and he shows no desire to repeat what the church already knew from the Synoptics. John apparently decided to include material the church wasn't aware of. After all, he was one of the twelve disciples and part of the inner circle with Peter and James. He was privy to much information not generally accessible to others. According to Eusebius, Clement of Alexandria wrote, "But that John, last of all, conscious that the outward facts had been set forth in the Gospels, was urged on by his disciples, and, divinely moved by the Spirit, composed a spiritual Gospel."[5]

We must remember that all four gospel writers have their own purposes that control their selection and arrangement of material. John has a strong evangelistic thrust, and he selected stories and teachings of Jesus that he felt would achieve his goals. Because John's gospel was written in the 90s and was the last gospel written, John had more time to reflect on the life and teachings of Jesus. Perhaps those decades of reflection led him to want to share different stories about Jesus.

Both Craig Blomberg and D. A. Carson and Doug Moo make a strong case that certain teachings in John require a prior knowledge of the Synoptics (or at least the traditions reflected in the Synoptics).[6] This supports the argument that John assumed his readers already had the Synoptic Gospels, and that he wanted his gospel to present new and different material.

Sometimes skeptics charge that John includes stories that, if true, certainly would have been included in the Synoptics; the fact that they are not in the Synoptics suggests to them that they never really happened. The prime example is the raising of Lazarus from the dead (John 11:1–44). This event occurred at the end of Jesus' public ministry, right before he began his final week, and it occurred on the outskirts of Jerusalem. How could the Synoptics omit this story if it was true?

But it's presumptuous to insist what a writer should or should not have included. To us one story may seem essential, but to other writers it may not. Perhaps the raising of Lazarus did not fit with their themes. Perhaps their scrolls were not long enough to include the story. Perhaps the Synoptics wanted to move the story forward to the Passion Week in terms of their literary thrust. I would assume that Jesus performed many stupendous miracles that we would include if we were writing the gospel story, but we aren't, and neither are the skeptics. And remember, the Synoptics do include the resurrection stories of Jairus's daughter (Matt 9:18–26; Mark 5:21–43; Luke 8:41–56) and the son of the widow of Nain (Luke 7:11–17). If the story were essential to the gospel message, such as Jesus' death and resurrection, then this would be a legitimate charge. But the story of Lazarus is not core to the gospel, as spectacular as it was.

We may also ask why Mark failed to include the account of Jesus' birth. Why do Matthew and Mark not tell of Jesus' visit to Jerusalem when he was twelve, given people's natural curiosity about what Jesus was like when he was younger? But these are not helpful questions to ask *because we can't know the answers.* The writers chose what they chose to make the points they wished. That is all we can know.[7]

Writing Style

There is also the issue of differing writing styles. For example, why does Jesus use a different idiom in John from the one used in the Synoptics? The Jesus who said, "God so loved the world that he gave his one and only Son" (3:16), and who uttered the "I Am" sayings (6:35; 8:12; 10:7, 14; 11:25; 14:6; 15:1) does not sound like the Jesus who says, "Whoever wants to be my disciple must deny themselves and take up their cross and follow me" (Mark 8:34). The idioms are different.

This is a difficult issue to resolve, but there is a hint to a solution in what is called the "Johannine Thunderbolt" (Luke 10:21–22, parallel at Matt 11:25–27). This passage in the Synoptics sounds similar to the way Jesus typically speaks in John's gospel:

> At that time Jesus, full of joy through the Holy Spirit, said, "I praise you, Father, Lord of heaven and earth, because you have hidden these things from the wise and learned, and revealed them to little children. Yes, Father, for this is what you were pleased to do.
>
> "All things have been committed to me by my Father. No one knows who the Son is except the Father, and no one knows who the Father is except the Son and those to whom the Son chooses to reveal him."

The suggestion is that Jesus did not always speak the same way. His style varied between what we generally read in the Synoptics and what we read in John (and in the Johannine Thunderbolt). For some reason, John was attracted to Jesus' other style of speech, and as he was translating Jesus' teaching into Greek, this is the style in which John wrote. Remember, John is translating from Aramaic into Greek and remembers events from decades earlier through his Aramaic prism. He is surely free to adopt whatever style he chooses.

Theology

A more significant difference between John and the Synoptics is what appears to be John's more developed theology:

- There is the sense that Jesus' divinity is more pronounced in John's gospel. There is no overt statement of Jesus' divinity in the Synoptics paralleling John's citing of Jesus' affirmation, "I and the Father are one" (10:30), or claiming that Jesus "is himself God" (1:18).
- There is John's doctrine of what scholars call "realized eschatology," which means that John brings the reality of the future into the present: "Whoever believes in him [Jesus] is not condemned, but whoever does not believe *stands condemned already* because they have not believed in the name of God's one and only Son" (3:18, italics added). The condemnation belongs to the future judgment, but what is future has, in essence, intruded into the present.
- There is also a strong dualism in John that has no direct parallel in the Synoptics: "This is the verdict: Light has come into the world, but people loved darkness instead of light because their deeds were evil" (3:19).

This apparent difference in theology is partially solved by realizing that John has had decades to think through Jesus' teaching and is summarizing and paraphrasing, using his own words and style that he may have learned from Jesus. He has had decades of time in which the Holy Spirit has helped him remember (and understand) the teachings of Jesus (14:26; 15:26), and this deeper knowledge is reflected in his gospel. John's theology is more developed in the sense that he makes *explicit* what was *implicit* in its original context. He takes what the disciples understood, or should have understood, and makes it clear. John is not changing Jesus' instruction; he is clarifying it.

However, the theological differences between the Synoptics and John should not be overemphasized. First of all, they are not contradictory but compatible. D. A. Carson and Doug Moo give an extensive list of statements in the Synoptics that affirm Jesus' deity to the same degree that John's gospel does.[8] Like John, the authors of the Synoptics do assert the divinity of Christ.[9] Like John, the Synoptics do teach the certainty the believer has before the throne of judgment.[10] Like John, they recognize that there are two realms at war—the realm of Satan and the kingdom of God.[11]

The Cleansing of the Temple

One of the most notable differences between John and the Synoptics is the timing of the temple cleansing. In John's gospel, at the *beginning* of his ministry, Jesus goes into the temple courts, makes a whip, and drives out of the temple courts the people selling animals for sacrifice. He went to the people exchanging foreign money for the Jewish currency that could be used in the temple and flipped over their tables, declaring that they must "stop turning my Father's house into a market!" (2:16). The apparent contradiction is that in the Synoptics, Jesus does this at the *end* of his ministry, immediately after his triumphal entry (Matt 21:12–13; Mark 11:15–17; Luke 19:45–46).

In both cases, the "cleansing" is an act of judgment on a fruitless religious system. In John, the enacted judgment at the beginning of Jesus' ministry gives a clear picture of what he will be like. In the Synoptics, it summarizes the Jewish failure to heed Jesus' teachings.

Some argue that John has moved the cleansing to the beginning of Jesus' ministry to emphasize Jesus' intentions from the very beginning. To us, this may sound like excessive freedom with the facts, but in ancient historical writing, this level of freedom was accepted.

Another solution is that Jesus "cleansed" the temple twice, at the beginning and the end of his ministry. Leon Morris enumerates all the differences between the two accounts.[12] Although there are obvious similarities, there are enough differences that allow us to see Jesus beginning and ending his ministry on the same note of judgment. Remember what I said earlier. If we accept the basic reliability of the Bible, we don't have to prove this is what happened. All we have to do is find a believable scenario, recognizing that the skeptic cannot prove that Jesus only cleansed the temple once.

The Timing of the Last Supper

The other major apparent contradiction between John and the Synoptics is the timing of the Last Supper. In the Synoptics, Jesus' last meal was the Passover meal, eaten on Thursday night, the first day of the weeklong festival. Later that night, he was arrested, went through a pretrial examination, was brought to Pilate on Friday morning, and was crucified Friday midday. Since the next day was Sabbath (Saturday), which started at sunset on our Friday, the Pharisees wanted Jesus' body taken down from the cross before the beginning of Sabbath. Therefore, in the Synoptics, the meal was "on the first day of the Festival of Unleavened Bread," which was Passover (Matt 26:17–19; Mark 14:12–16; "day of Unleavened Bread," Luke 22:7–13) —on Thursday.

Several verses in John can create confusion. When Pilate is about to condemn Jesus (the day after the meal in question), John says "it was the day of Preparation of the Passover" (19:14; cf. vv. 31, 42), which sounds like it was the day *before* the Passover meal—on Wednesday. But if you work backward through the events of the passion of Jesus, you see that all four gospels agree that Jesus died on Friday afternoon, since the Jewish leaders wanted his body taken down from the cross before Sabbath. This means his trial before Pilate must have been Friday morning, the Jewish examination late Thursday into early Friday morning, and the meal with his disciples Thursday evening—the Passover meal. Whatever John means by "day of Preparation," it still must refer to Friday. The Greek word behind *Preparation* is the name of the day we call "Friday," and it would have been the day of preparing for the coming week of festivities, not the day of preparing for the Passover meal (Thursday). John 13:1 confirms that the upper room discourse started "just before the Passover Festival," and the following meal was therefore the Passover meal (v. 2).

It seems clear that John is portraying the last meal as the same Passover meal we read about in the Synoptics, since they both include references to Judas's betrayal and Peter's denial. In John 18:28, when the Jewish leaders refused to enter the palace of the Roman governor "because they wanted to be able to eat the Passover," it probably means they wanted to eat the next day's lunch, called the *hagigah*. It was the second most important meal of the weeklong festivities.

Leon Morris offers a different solution. He argues that two different calendars were being followed. While the people followed one calendar, the temple authorities followed another, and there was a difference of one day between them. This would also explain the confusion.[13]

Yes, the gospel of John has distinct differences from the Synoptics. But if you allow for the flexibility of ancient historical writing and for the freedom of John to do what the other writers do—translate, summarize, compress, and paraphrase—there are no insurmountable problems.

John had six decades of ministry to reflect on the teachings of Jesus, six decades to let the truths of what Jesus said and did sink in and be clarified by the Holy Spirit, and out of those sixty years of reflection to draw out what was implicit in the Synoptic Gospels and make those truths explicit without merely repeating the teachings of the Synoptics. This is a believable scenario.

Miracles

Finally, we must talk about miracles. The Bible says that God is the creator and sustainer of all things. As such, he can perform any miracle he wishes. He can set aside the rules of nature, which he created, and make water firm enough for his Son to walk on. He made people, and he can heal their infirmities. He is Lord over all, and therefore he can command the demonic world. He can give life to a virgin's womb and life to his Son's dead body in the grave. He is sovereign, and he works all things in accordance with his will.

But what if you don't believe there is a God, or you believe that God is unable to intervene in his creation? What if you believe that God or his Son can't do miracles? Then the only possible result of these presuppositions, these faith beliefs, is that the Bible is inaccurate and unreliable, and you have to create a scenario in which someone changed the Bible, or you have to conclude that the Bible is simply wrong.

Of course, an anti-supernatural bias is simply that—a bias. It's a faith position that can't be proven. It's by faith that a person says that miracles are contrary to nature; the laws of nature can't be broken; there are no miracles. It's by faith that scientific naturalism insists that all effects must have a natural cause. So if a person says the Bible is unreliable because it contains accounts of the miraculous, an honest person will admit this has more to do with their own faith system than the reliability of the Bible. In light of the widespread evidence for miracles, it's not up to you or me to prove miracles can happen; I think it's up to the skeptics to prove they can't.

New Testament scholar Craig Keener has written a massive, two-volume study of miracles in Africa.[14] These are documented miracles either that he has seen or that have been researched and confirmed. In these two volumes, he documents thousands of miracles. Those of us who know Craig have no doubts that he is a world-class scholar with impeccable credentials, and he writes about what he knows. If you personally struggle with the possibility of miracles, I encourage you to read his books and reexamine your presuppositions.[15]

People will say they have never seen a miracle, and therefore they don't believe miracles can occur. But I haven't seen the other side of the moon, yet I believe it exists. I have never experienced what it's like to climb to the top of Mount Everest, and I can't imagine the stamina and strength required to do so, especially without oxygen, but I believe others have made the ascent. I will never understand how each cell of my body contains hundreds of thousands of genetic instructions coded into a single strand of DNA that determines the color of eyes, my intelligence, my athletic ability, and whether or not I will remember my dreams when I wake up (just to pick a silly example). The fact that I haven't experienced something or don't understand something has nothing to do with whether or not it's real. If you were born and raised in the United States, all you have to do is visit some churches where visible, external, verifiable healings have taken place, or travel to Africa or India where you will encounter an entirely different worldview. In many non-Western countries, there is no presupposition against the miraculous.

As with most things we discuss in this book, the question of miracles is a topic with hundreds of books written on it. But the core issue is that many people won't accept miracles because of a prior bias against the supernatural. If a person doesn't believe the rules of the physical universe can be set aside, no amount of arguing about miracles can change their mind. But we must always remember that this is a belief, not a provable fact. No amount of science can prove what *must* happen. Science can only attempt to explain what *did* happen, and what *might* happen in the future given the same set of factors.

Another approach to miracles is to argue that many other miracle workers lived in the ancient world, and the myth of Jesus doing miracles is just a borrowing from other superstitions. There are two responses to this accusation. First, no person in history claims to have done thousands of miracles. For the most part, one or two miracles have been attributed to a person. Second, these supposed parallels need to be read carefully. Craig Blomberg points out these three (among many):[16]

- Julius Caesar is said to have performed miracles, but actually just one. The miracle is that he prayed and was kept safe in a storm. He didn't calm the storm; he prayed that he would be safe.
- Honi the Circle Maker was a first-century Jewish miracle worker, so it's claimed. He drew a circle around himself and said he wouldn't leave until God made it rain. He prayed; he did not perform a miracle.
- Apollonius of Tyana was a first-century Greek miracle worker. Among other miracles, Apollonius supposedly raised the dead. But if you read the account, the biography actually says he knew the person wasn't really dead.

Most of these supposedly parallel miracle stories come from *after* the time of Jesus, even if the person they speak about lived before Jesus, and skeptics should acknowledge the possibility that ideas and terminology could be borrowed from Christianity. For example, Apollonius of Tyana actually lived in the middle to late *first century AD*, and Philostratus wrote about him in the early *third century AD*. Who's borrowing from whom? My PhD dissertation examined the frequent academic assertion that the idea of rebirth was borrowed by Christianity from the mystery religions. If we filter out the false parallels (where rebirth has nothing to do with cultic initiation) and confirm the dates, it's easily proven that the mysteries borrowed from Christianity. The concept of rebirth was widely used by the church as a metaphor for baptism, and Mithraism (among others) clearly borrowed the term to describe its own cultic ceremonies.[17]

The truth is that there is no one like Jesus in ancient literature, someone who claims to have performed thousands of miracles. Christianity is not borrowing from other faith systems.

Conclusion

There are significant similarities and differences among the Synoptics, and between the Synoptics and John. If you allow the authors to write according to the historical standards of their day, which include simplification, paraphrase, and approximations; if you see how they used written sources and their personal memories; and if you understand their process of translating Jesus' words and deeds into Greek, then many of the apparent contradictions can be easily explained.

Skeptics believe the Bible is generally unreliable, so they don't give it the benefit of the doubt. As for me, I have decided that the Bible is reliable and has earned my trust. I encourage you to think through the issues and decide for yourself.

For Further Reading

Blomberg, Craig L. *The Historical Reliability of the Gospels*. 2nd ed. Downers Grove, IL: IVP Academic, 2007.

———. "The Historical Reliability of the Gospels." Biblical Training Institute, https://gk2.me/reliability.

———. *The Historical Reliability of the New Testament: Countering the Challenges to Evangelical Christian Beliefs*. Nashville: B&H Academic, 2016.

———. "Why We Trust Our Bible." Lectures 6–11. Biblical Training Institute, https://gk2.me/we-trust.

Roberts, Mark D. *Can We Trust the Gospels? Investigating the Reliability of Matthew, Mark, Luke, and John*. Wheaton, IL: Crossway, 2007.

Williams, Peter J. *Can We Trust the Gospels?* Wheaton, IL: Crossway, 2018.

Notes

1. Craig Blomberg, *The Historical Reliability of the New Testament* (Nashville: B&H Academic, 2016), 84.
2. See Darrell L. Bock, "The Words of Jesus in the Gospels: Live, Jive, or Memorex?" in *Jesus Under Fire: Modern Scholarship Reinvents the Historical Jesus*, ed. Michael J. Wilkins and J. P. Moreland (Grand

Rapids: Zondervan, 1995), 73–100. Peter Williams says that quotation marks did not originate until the sixteenth century (*Can We Trust the Gospels?* [Wheaton, IL: Crossway, 2018], 98).

3. Quoted in Paul Barnett, *Is the New Testament Reliable?* 2nd ed. (Downers Grove, IL: InterVarsity, 2007), 13; fuller citation in Craig A. Evans, *Jesus and the Manuscripts* (Peabody, MA: Hendrickson, 2020), 11.

4. See Craig Blomberg, "Literary Genre of the Gospels," in "The Historical Reliability of the Gospels," Biblical Training Institute, https://gk2.mc /genre-gospels.

5. Quoted in Eusebius, *Ecclesiastical History* 6.14.7; quoted in D. A. Carson and Douglas J. Moo, *An Introduction to the New Testament*, 2nd ed. (Grand Rapids: Zondervan, 2005), 231.

6. Blomberg, *Historical Reliability of the New Testament*, 165–68; Carson and Moo, *Introduction to the New Testament*, 258–60.

7. Blomberg (*Historical Reliability of the New Testament*, 176) summarizes the work of Philipp Bartholomä, who "demonstrates that only thirty out of the 322 discrete propositions [in John] have neither verbal nor conceptual parallels in the Synoptics (only 9.4 percent), while a full 166 (or 51.5 percent) contain not merely conceptual but also verbal parallelism of some significance." Perhaps the differences between John and the Synoptics are not as great as they seem to some.

8. Carson and Moo, *Introduction to the New Testament*, 261–63.

9. One of Mark's themes is to show Jesus doing and saying things that God alone can do (e.g., 2:7). When Jesus refers to himself in words that echo the prophecy of Daniel 7, the high priest says he is blaspheming (Matt 26:65). How different is this from the Johannine "I am" sayings?

10. While the Synoptics emphasize a "promise and fulfillment" motif, an "already but not yet" view of eschatology, John is merely stressing that the future is in some ways present.

11. Luke wrote, "But if I [Jesus] drive out demons by the finger of God, then the kingdom of God has come upon you" (11:20), and "I [Jesus] saw Satan fall like lightning from heaven" (10:18).

12. Leon Morris, *The Gospel According to John*, New International Commentary on the New Testament (Grand Rapids: Eerdmans, 1971), 188–91.

13. See Morris, *John*, 774–86.

14. Craig S. Keener, *Miracles: The Credibility of the New Testament Accounts*, 2 vols. (Grand Rapids: Baker, 2011).

15. See also Grant Osborne, *Three Crucial Questions about the Bible* (Grand Rapids: Baker, 1995), 53–59. For a fuller discussion of miracles, see Craig Blomberg, "Miracles," chap. 3 in *The Historical Reliability of the Gospels*, 2nd ed. (Downers Grove, IL: IVP Academic, 2007), 104–51; Blomberg, "The Problem of Miracles," part 6 in *Historical Reliability of the New Testament*, 663–715; Blomberg, "Don't All the Miracles Make the Bible Mythical? chap. 6 in *Can We Still Believe the Bible? An Evangelical Engagement with Contemporary Questions* (Grand Rapids: Brazos, 2014), 179–212.

16. For these "miracles" and others, see Craig Blomberg, "The Unique Problem of Miracles (Part 2)," (https://gk2.me/blomberg-miracles); *Historical Reliability of the Gospels*, 112–27; *Historical Reliability of the New Testament*, 678–85.

17. William D. Mounce, *The Origin of the New Testament Metaphor of Rebirth* (Aberdeen: University of Aberdeen, 1981); see also the section "Stealing Thunder: Did Christianity Rip Off Mythical Gods?" in J. Ed Komoszewski, M. James Sawyer, and Daniel B. Wallace, *Reinventing Jesus: How Contemporary Skeptics Miss the Real Jesus and Mislead Popular Culture* (Grand Rapids: Kregel, 2006), 219–58.

THE CANON
Canonicity: Why We Have the Books We Do

Challenge

I met Tim when I started attending Western Kentucky University in 1975. He was a leader in CRU (formerly Campus Crusade for Christ) and Navigators and was president of the Baptist Student Union. Tim was one of the more public leaders within the Christian university ministries.

In my second year, I noticed that Tim was no longer attending our weekly meetings and had even stopped attending classes. I wondered where he was—whether he had dropped out of school or had become too busy for extracurricular activities. Never did I suspect he was having a crisis of faith.

I ran into him several months later and asked where he had been and why he wasn't attending our meetings anymore. "I'm not even sure if I still believe that Christian stuff," he replied. "Why?" I asked. Tim proceeded to share that one of his professors had raised the issue of the books that are in the Bible, telling Tim that the books we have are not the right ones. He asserted that several good books were left out of the Bible due to the caprice of a few academic church leaders, and several wrong ones were included instead. As a result, Tim felt he couldn't trust his Bible. I assumed Tim had other issues of faith that he was struggling with as well, but it was the issue of the "canon" that was the proverbial straw that broke the camel's back.

We've seen books written by the New Testament scholar Bart Ehrman and novel fabrications like Dan Brown's *The Da Vinci Code* that have deceived thousands of university students who, like Tim, have abandoned their Christian faith.[1] My friend Craig Blomberg told me his daughter came home from university one day and shared that her history professor was using *The Da Vinci Code* as a historical document, even though Brown clearly states that his book is fiction.

So here is the challenge we'll consider next: Do we have the right books in the Bible? Were good ones left out? Who made these decisions, and why? Can we trust the books we do have in our Bible? Note: Discussion of the Old Testament canon is reserved for chapter 13.

Notes

1. Bart Ehrman, *Lost Scriptures: Books That Did Not Make It into the New Testament* (Oxford: Oxford University Press, 2003); Dan Brown, *The Da Vinci Code* (New York: Doubleday, 2003).

Chapter 5

WHY DO WE HAVE THE TWENTY-SEVEN BOOKS IN THE NEW TESTAMENT?

In this chapter, we will look at the historical process of canonization, the three criteria a writing had to meet to be included in the canon, and why the Gospel of Thomas is not, and should not be, in the canon.

Let's Start by Defining Our Terms

- *Canon* refers to a rule, the standard by which something is judged to be true or false.
- In biblical terms, *canon* refers to the books that Christians accept as authoritative. We have an Old Testament canon and a New Testament canon.
- *Canonization* is the process by which the church recognized which books were authoritative and therefore belonged in the New Testament.
- The Old Testament *Apocrypha* are the books (such as 1 Maccabees and 2 Esdras) that are not accepted by Protestants as part of

the Old Testament but are accepted by Roman Catholics. These books are sometimes called "the deuterocanonicals."

- The New Testament Apocrypha are the books not accepted by the church as part of the New Testament, such as the Gospel of Thomas.
- The Old Testament *Pseudepigrapha* and the New Testament Pseudepigrapha are catch-all phrases for the writings that were not accepted as authoritative by mainstream Judaism or Christianity.[1] Many, if not most, of these claimed to be written by people who never wrote them, hence the title "pseudepigrapha," or "false writings."

First Question

When you meet someone like my university friend Tim, someone who questions why we have the books that are in the Bible today, my recommendation is to ask a simple question: "Have you read the book or books you think should be in the New Testament?" Or alternately you could ask, "Which book or books do you think should be in the New Testament canon?" And again, this could trigger a similar question: "Which book or books of the New Testament do you think should *not* be in the Bible?"

The vast majority of people will not be able to answer the first question with a yes. While some people may say they think the Gospel of Thomas should be included, it's highly doubtful they've ever read it. You may also find people who don't like a certain verse or a specific theological theme in one of the twenty-seven accepted books, but I doubt anyone will be able to formulate an argument as to why an entire book should be omitted.

This is an important line of questioning. In my personal experience, the majority of people, if they're honest, don't have an academic issue with the canon. They have never read the extrabiblical books ("extrabiblical" means they're outside of the canonical books), nor have they considered which biblical books should be rejected. The issue of canon is, yet again, a smoke screen for their real objections, which are to the teachings of the Bible itself. I say this because if you try to answer their questions about canon, you may not be dealing with the real issues that concern this person.

If on a rare occasion you meet someone who *has* read the extrabiblical books and thinks one or more should be included in the canon, then this chapter will help you know how to interact with them. These are more likely to be honest inquirers, and we should walk graciously with them on their spiritual journey.

The Facts

Let's start with a few facts. These are undeniable historical facts with no historical evidence to the contrary.

Neither Emperor Constantine nor the Council of Nicaea determined the canon—the twenty-seven books we accept as the authoritative New Testament. Constantine called the Council of Nicaea in AD 325 because he was concerned about a group within the church called the Arians and the possible split they could cause in his kingdom. The Arians were followers of a man named Arius, who taught that Jesus was not fully God. Church leaders from around the world were called to Constantinople—both those representing the long-held, traditional belief that Jesus was fully God and fully human, and those representing the Arian position (including Arius himself). As far as the historical evidence shows, neither Constantine nor his mother played any role in the debates. They exerted no influence over the canon at this gathering, nor was the canon something Constantine was even considering. His concern was political unity.

After the various positions were debated, the majority position easily won out, and the participants wrote what is now called the Nicene Creed. This creedal statement affirms the long-held orthodox position that Jesus was fully God and fully human and clarifies the nature of the relationship between God the Father and Jesus.[2]

It's worth emphasizing that the decision about which books belonged in the canon was not made in secret by a group of academics living in an ivory tower—as is often portrayed. The topic was never discussed in Nicaea. In fact, not a single council was ever called whose primary purpose was to settle the issue of the canon—not until the Council of Trent met in 1545–1563, which ratified the Old Testament Apocrypha as part of the Roman Catholic canon. The process of how the canon came about was rather different and involved the church as a whole.

Let me repeat this again. Despite conspiracy theories floated by fiction writers and internet bloggers, these are the facts of historical inquiry, and there are no historical facts to the contrary.

Historical Developments

What gave rise to the New Testament canon? Why was a canon even developed? And what determined which books should be included? The church faced three challenges that led to the formation of an official canon.

1. A canon became necessary following the death of eyewitnesses and apostles. As long as the twelve apostles, as long as the original group of disciples who had traveled with Jesus, and as long as Paul were alive, they were able to determine what was true about Jesus and what was not.

The first debate of the early church was whether a non-Jewish person had to be circumcised in order to become a Christian. Paul and Barnabas's missionary journey to Gentile lands raised the issue. In Acts 15, we read that Paul and Barnabas came to Jerusalem, met with the apostles and elders and the church as a whole, and shared everything the Lord had been doing among the Gentiles. The leadership concluded that the Gentiles did not have to be circumcised but that they should restrain from certain practices (such as eating meat that still had the blood in it) so as not to offend Jews and hinder the spread of the gospel.

The important point here is that the leaders of the church, many of whom were personally part of Jesus' ministry, were publicly asked to provide the checks and balances as to what was orthodox Christian doctrine. However, when persecution or old age removed these eyewitnesses, the church needed a new set of checks and balances—hence the need for an authoritative canon.[3]

2. The rise of persecution of Christians spurred on the process of canonization. Persecution of the church began as early as Acts 4, when Herod executed James, the brother of John (Acts 12:2). By the time of Emperor Diocletian (AD 303–312), it was illegal even to own copies of the Bible. So imagine living in 303. A soldier is searching your house, and you have a copy of the book *Shepherd of Hermas*. Would this be illegal? The book is orthodox in its teaching, but is it canonical?

3. The rise of false writings and teaching made a canon necessary to distinguish the real from the fake. The rise of heresy and false writings was already happening in Paul's day. The church in Thessalonica had received a letter that claimed to be from Paul, teaching that "the day of the Lord has already come" (2 Thess 2:2). It's possible that Paul signed his letters with a large signature to show their authenticity (Gal 6:11).

But once these eyewitnesses were gone, there were fewer checks and balances against false writings and their false teachings. Gnosticism was primarily a second-century heresy that also reached back into the first century. If your church was reading a Gnostic document, you needed to know if it was true or not. Hence, the church needed to know which books belonged in the canon.

Three Criteria of Authenticity

It seems there were three criteria by which the church recognized which New Testament books were authoritative. These three were never codified in an official church statement, but they best explain the historical data. Most of the questions about authenticity surround the General

Epistles, and there was little question about the other remaining books, sometimes called the "core" of the New Testament canon.

Keep in mind that these criteria don't create the canon, nor do they give authority to a book. Apostles bear the authority of Christ; their writings—and those of close associates Mark, Luke, James, and Jude—bear the apostles' authority. The apostles and their teachings are the foundation of the church, so they didn't need the church's later approval.

1. Apostolicity

The primary criterion for inclusion in the canon is *authorship*. Who wrote the book or letter in question? This criterion is to be expected, since the writing naturally carries the authority of the author. In the case of the apostles, the church recognized that they carried the authority of Christ himself, which is why the gospel of Matthew, the gospel of Mark (who according to church tradition wrote down what Peter said), 1 Peter, 1 John, and all of Paul's thirteen epistles were seen as authoritative the minute they were composed.

It also seems to be the case that being a close associate of an apostle carried the same weight. The author Luke was closely connected with the apostle Paul, and hence his gospel and the book of Acts were inherently authoritative. In fact, it's somewhat surprising to see how little debate there was on the canonicity of his two books, since Luke was not an apostle.

The letter to the Hebrews struggled to be recognized as authoritative because its authorship was unknown. Even as late as the time of Eusebius, the church in the West (i.e., Rome) was not committed to its inclusion. However, the church in the East viewed the book as Pauline and accepted it into their canon. Despite the letter's ambiguous status, many of the church fathers quoted from it as an authority.[4]

Second Peter was not always seen as authoritative either, probably because the Greek is so different from the Greek of 1 Peter, in both grammar and style, that it raised the issue of authorship; some people feared it was a forgery. Likewise, Jude was not always seen as authoritative because so much of it is contained in 2 Peter and because Jude alludes to a noncanonical book in verse 9 (*Testament of Moses*) and another one in verses 14–15 (*First Enoch*). Presumably, knowledge of their authorship overcame these hesitations. Both of these letters are also short and may not have been widely distributed (see section below on "Catholicity").

The recognition of Revelation as authoritative happened in reverse order compared to most of the disputed books. Initially, Revelation was widely accepted, and it wasn't until later centuries that its canonical standing was questioned in the East. But this questioning was short-lived.

The process of accepting apostolic writings as authoritative began in the New Testament itself. Jesus had promised to send the Spirit to help the apostles remember all he had taught them (John 14:26) and to guide them into all truth (John 16:13). The apostles taught with Christ's authority (1 Cor 14:37; 7:10–12; Gal 1:1; 1 Thess 2:13; 2 Pet 3:2; Rev 1:1–2), and therefore the church accepted their writings to be as authoritative as the actual sayings of Jesus. Paul quotes both Deuteronomy 25:4 and Luke 10:7 as "Scripture" (1 Tim 5:18). Paul can list instructions from Jesus (1 Cor 7:10) and his own (1 Cor 7:12) as having equal authority. Peter viewed Paul's writings as "Scripture" (2 Pet 3:15–16). I suspect Paul would be surprised to hear the modern claim that he did not know he was writing authoritative documents. If not authoritative, what were they? Opinion? Did he see the letters as Scripture in the sense of being part of a canon? Perhaps not. Did he see himself writing with the full authority of Christ? Absolutely.[5]

Looking beyond the New Testament, we see how the church fathers (second century) quoted from a wide selection of writings, indicating that they accepted the writings of the apostles as authoritative.[6]

- Polycarp (d. 155) was the bishop of Smyrna; he knew the apostle John personally and quoted Paul's writings as "Scripture" (*To the Philippians* 12.1).

- Clement of Rome (d. 96) wrote that God sent Christ, and Christ sent the apostles (First Epistle of Clement 47:1–3; cf. 42:1–2).
- Ignatius (d. 107) said that the apostles were the mouthpiece of Christ (*To the Magnesians* 7.1).[7]
- Justin Martyr (d. 165) taught that the apostles were sent by God (*First Apology* 39).
- Irenaeus (d. 200) taught that the apostles handed down the gospel "in the Scriptures, to be the ground and pillar of our faith" (*Against Heresies* 3.1.1).[8]

The value placed on apostolic authorship can also be seen in how the church handled forgeries. Once the letter was recognized as a forgery, it was always thrown out, even if its teaching was orthodox. The Muratorian Canon says the pseudepigraphical *Epistle to the Laodiceans* (cf. Col 4:16) was good to read but wasn't Scripture, since it was written "in our time."

A forgery called *3 Corinthians* was supposedly written out of "love" for Paul; however, when it was discovered that the author was not Paul, this forgery was thrown out and the writer removed from his ecclesiastical office.[9] Serapion of Antioch (late second century) says this: "For our part, brethren, we receive both Peter and the other apostles as Christ, but the writings which falsely bear their names we reject, as men of experience, knowing that such were not handed down to us."[10] Authorship mattered to the early church.

One of the other aspects of the debate has to do with the time when the canon was considered "closed," that is, when the church concluded that the twenty-seven books, and only those twenty-seven, were the sum total of authoritative New Testament writings. We'll look at this closely in the next chapter, but it's important here to know that the majority of the canon was "formed" as soon as the apostles wrote their books and letters, and this would have happened by the middle to end of the first century. In other words, the church didn't waffle for hundreds of years trying to decide which books were authoritative, only coming to a decision after several centuries had passed. If this were the case, we might struggle with their decision. This is also why we say the canon was not "formed"; rather, the inspiration of apostolic writings was "recognized" as having the same authority as did their authors.

Here is the core of the canon, the twenty-one books that were *always* recognized as authoritative.

- The four gospels (Matthew, Mark, Luke, John)
- Acts
- Paul's thirteen epistles[11]
- 1 Peter
- 1 John
- Revelation[12]

Such was the strength of apostolic authorship.

2. Orthodoxy

The second test that a book or letter had to pass was the test of orthodoxy ("right belief"). Were its teachings consistent with the teachings of the books already accepted as authoritative? Fortunately, ever since the mid-60s the church had all of Paul's writings (32,471 words in today's Greek text) and probably the gospel of Mark (11,314 words). These fourteen books contain 43,785 of the total 138,213 words in our New Testament canon and provided a strong basis on which to judge other writings as orthodox or unorthodox. If the gospel of Luke (19,497) was written before Acts, and since Acts (18,472) ends before Paul's trial, these two books were also part of the core of the canon by the 70s. These sixteen books contain 81,754 of the total 138,213 words in our canon, or 59 percent. Matthew would add another 18,365 words (72 percent). Because the core of the canon is first century and constitutes a majority of the final canon, plenty of teaching existed by which to judge whether or not other writings were orthodox.

In fact, it was the test of orthodoxy that led some to question the canonicity of the letter of James. Both Paul (Rom 4:3; Gal 3:6) and James (2:23) use Genesis 15:6 to prove what appear to be opposite conclusions. Was Abraham justified by faith (Paul) or by works (James)? We dealt with this apparent contradiction in chapter 3, and as you might have guessed, the church also concluded these teachings weren't contradictory either. They accepted James as canonical, partially based on its author being the brother of Jesus.[13]

Because the church possessed a significant amount of material that was considered orthodox at an early date, it was able to withstand two second-century heretical movements, one led by a man named Marcion and the other a broad movement called Gnosticism. Marcion taught that the wrathful God of the Old Testament and the loving God of the New Testament were not compatible. He rejected the Old Testament and kept only the Pauline writings and a modified version of Luke's gospel. Gnosticism held a dualistic view of the world in which all that is material is evil, and salvation is about freeing the immaterial spirit. Because there was an orthodoxy at an early date, the early church was able to judge and defeat these alternative theologies. This defeat was possible only because of a widely held agreement on the core of the canon.

Again, I want to emphasize a nuance that's easy to miss. There is a difference between the church *recognizing* a book as authoritative and *bestowing* canonicity on a book. In the next chapter, we will look more closely at Michael Kruger's distinction between the exclusive, functional, and ontological definitions of the canon. Here I'll simply repeat what I mentioned earlier—namely, that the church does not bestow canonicity on a book. An apostolic book was authoritative the moment it was written, while the church's acceptance of the book was certainly important but secondary and happened over time.

3. Catholicity

The third test a book or writing had to pass was based on its usage in the church as a whole. Here we're using the word *catholicity* to describe the universality of acceptance (without reference to the Roman Catholic Church). The widespread or universal usage of these writings means that decisions of canonicity were not made by a few individuals in isolation, nor by a political power such as the emperor Constantine. Instead, the church as a whole recognized a book's divine origin or rejected a book if it was of human origin. What made this process somewhat complicated and time-consuming is that the New Testament books were written and circulated independently of each other. This means it would have taken considerable time for these books to circulate throughout the known world and to be accepted by the wider church.

With this in mind, you can see why the letter to Philemon and the last two letters of John may have caused some concern. Philemon is a letter to a single person, and John's last two letters are written to individual churches. It doesn't require much imagination to see why these three were not accepted instantly as authoritative—very few people would have read them! Yet eventually, as they spread throughout the universal church, their apostolic origin was seen and the authority of the books recognized.

In AD 303, the emperor Diocletian outlawed Christianity. He destroyed churches, burned Bibles, and threatened Christians, making possession of a Bible an act of treason. It's remarkable, and even providential, that any manuscripts survived this period. But they did, and we are able to see which New Testament books were known throughout the empire at this time.

But how do we know which books were recognized as authoritative by the church *as a whole*? We'll dig into this in more detail in the next chapter, but there are several things we look for. Were the books included in the lists of canonical books over a wide range of dates and locations? Did a wide range of church fathers quote from them? By asking questions such as these, we can conclude whether a book was recognized by the church as a whole.

Test Case: The Gospel of Thomas

Let's look at the Gospel of Thomas as a test case. How does this "gospel" fare in relation to the three criteria I've outlined? The Gospel of Thomas is a gnostic text discovered as part of the Nag Hammadi library in Egypt in 1945. I place "gospel" in quotes because it's a misnomer to call it a gospel. It's nothing more than a collection of sayings supposedly spoken by Jesus.[14]

- It fails the test of apostolicity because it's generally dated from AD 175 to 180, possibly as early as AD 140. Thomas never wrote it.
- It fails the test of orthodoxy because Gnosticism was heretical. The last of the 114 sayings illustrates the point:

> Simon Peter said to them [the apostles], "Make Mary leave us, for females don't deserve life." Jesus said, "Look, I will guide her to make her male, so that she too may become a living spirit resembling you males. For every female who makes herself male will enter the kingdom of Heaven."[15]

Is there any chance this misogynist view of women belongs in the canon? Eusebius called Gnosticism "the fictions of heretics," and yet the Jesus Seminar published five gospels—with Thomas as the fifth, which has more red-letter print in it than does the Gospel of John.[16]

- It fails the test of catholicity. Because it was discovered in 1945, it was never read, much less acknowledged, by the worldwide church. It was merely the writing of a heretical sect. Origen says the Gospel of Thomas was never accepted by the church (*Homilies on Luke* 1.2).

I will never forget walking in downtown Pasadena, California, during my years in seminary. One day I turned a corner, and in the window of a bookstore was a large ad for a book claiming to contain writings that the leaders of the church had removed and hidden for theological and political reasons. I wish I had taken a picture of that poster. It seems that almost every decade someone else resurrects the same false claims referencing the same apocryphal and pseudepigraphical works of fiction. There is rarely anything new under the sun.

Through the combination of these three criteria, the church was able to recognize which books were from God. A book could be apostolic and orthodox, but it might not pass the test of catholicity because it was not preserved (e.g., two of the four letters Paul wrote to the Corinthian church). A book could be orthodox and widely used but not apostolic and not accepted as canonical (e.g., *Shepherd of Hermas*). It was only in the combination of all three criteria that divine authorship was recognized.[17]

Eusebius's Categories

The church father Eusebius had a helpful way of looking at the canonical and noncanonical writings.[18] Eusebius was patriarch of Constantinople and a key leader in the fourth-century church. He played a central role in the Council of Nicaea, and his writings are invaluable in helping us understand the nature of the church in his lifetime.

Eusebius said there were four categories of books.

1. **Undisputed.** This includes twenty-one of our twenty-seven books. Eusebius is confusing at this point as he includes Revelation in both the "undisputed" and the "spurious" groups. Eusebius writes:

> At this point it seems appropriate to summarize the writings of the New Testament which have already been mentioned. In the first place must be put the holy

quaternion of the Gospels, which are followed by the book of the Acts of the Apostles. After this must be reckoned the Epistles of Paul; next in order the extant former Epistle of John, and likewise the Epistle of Peter must be recognized. After these must be put, if it really seems right, the Apocalypse of John, concerning which we shall give the different opinions at the proper time. These, then, [are to be placed] among the recognized books.[19]

2. **Disputed.** These include James, Jude, 2 Peter, 2 and 3 John. Eusebius doesn't list Hebrews anywhere. Eusebius's use of the disputed category doesn't mean he personally had concerns about these books. He is simply acknowledging that some people had questions about them. He writes:

> Of the disputed books, which are nevertheless familiar to the majority, there are extant the Epistle of James, as it is called; and that of Jude; and the second Epistle of Peter; and those that are called the Second and Third of John, whether they belong to the evangelist or to another of the same name.

3. **Spurious.** These are books that were often orthodox in their theology and were helpful to read, but they were seen as noncanonical. For example, the book you're currently reading would fit in this category—something that's helpful to read but not equal in authority to the canonical books. Ancient books in this category include *Shepherd of Hermas* (written AD 90–140) and the *Didache* (written AD 70–110). Eusebius confusingly includes Revelation in this category as well. Eusebius writes:

> Among the spurious books must be reckoned also the Acts of Paul, and the Shepherd, as it is called, and the Apocalypse of Peter; and, in addition to these, the extant

Epistle of Barnabas, and the Teaching of the Apostles [*Didache*], as it is called. And, in addition, as I said, the Apocalypse of John, if it seems right. (This last as I said, is rejected by some, but others count it among the recognized books.) And among these some have counted also the Gospel of the Hebrews, with which those of the Hebrews who have accepted Christ take a special pleasure.

4. **Heretical.** These are books that fail the tests of canonicity and should not be read. This category includes the Gospel of Thomas. Eusebius writes:

> Now all these would be among the disputed books; but nevertheless we have felt compelled to make this catalogue of them, distinguishing between those writings which, according to the tradition of the Church, are true and genuine and recognized, from the others which differ from them in that they are not canonical, but disputed, yet nevertheless are known to most churchmen. [And this we have done] in order that we might be able to know both these same writings and also those which the heretics put forward under the name of the apostles; including, for instance, such books as the Gospels of Peter, of Thomas, of Matthias, or even of some others besides these, and the Acts of Andrew and John and the other apostles. To none of these has any who belonged to the succession of ecclesiastical writers ever thought it right to refer in his writings. Moreover, the character of the style also is far removed from apostolic usage, and the thought and purport of their contents are completely out of harmony with true orthodoxy and clearly show themselves that they are the forgeries of heretics. For this reason they ought not to be reckoned among the spurious books, but are to be cast aside as altogether absurd and impious.

Not only are Eusebius's categories helpful as we think through the issue of canonicity, but they also illustrate that the early church was careful in what it accepted and discerning in what it rejected. For example, Clement of Alexandria quotes from a wide range of books, both canonical and noncanonical (such as *Gospel of the Egyptians* and the *Gospel of the Hebrews*). But this doesn't mean he thought these two were canonical; it simply means he found their teaching helpful, in the same way we might quote books other than the Bible that we find helpful but are nevertheless not inspired.

Conclusion

Well before the end of the first century, the core of the New Testament *canon* was fixed because the books were written by the authoritative apostles or by Luke (apostolicity). These provided the test of *orthodoxy* for the remaining books, most of which were seen as canonical by the middle of the second century (*catholicity*).

Let me conclude by reiterating what I said at the beginning of this chapter. If someone wants to add new books into the New Testament canon, ask them which one and why it should be included. Ask them who wrote it, how it agrees with the rest of the canon, and why the church did not include it in the canon. Ask for specifics. Keep in mind that as long as you stay in a discussion of the canon, you probably aren't dealing with the true issues in that person's life. That's why asking questions is helpful. You want to talk about the things that really matter to a person, not simply debate things they don't really care about.

Notes

1. First Enoch is canonical in the Ethiopian Orthodox Church.
2. To read this creed, go to "Nicene Creed," Biblical Training Library, https://gk2.me/nicene-creed.
3. Michael J. Kruger discusses this issue in detail, emphasizing that written texts could go further and last longer than an apostle's personal visit

(*Canon Revisited: Establishing the Origins and Authority of the New Testament Books* [Wheaton, IL: Crossway, 2012], 210–25).

4. See the references in Paul D. Wegner, *The Journey from Texts to Translations: The Origin and Development of the Bible* (Grand Rapids: Baker, 1999), 140.

5. This may seem overly technical, but it's an important distinction. Paul saw his writings as fully authoritative. For example, there is no room for disagreement when he says, "This is the rule I lay down in all the churches" (1 Cor 7:17), or, "Warn a divisive person once, and then warn them a second time. After that, have nothing to do with them" (Titus 3:10). But it's something different to say that he (not the church) viewed his writings as "Scripture" on a par with the Hebrew Bible. For more on this topic, see Michael J. Kruger, *The Question of Canon: Challenging the Status Quo in the New Testament Debate* (Downers Grove, IL: IVP Academic, 2013), 119–54.

6. For the following, see Kruger, *Canon Revisited*, 210–25, and Kruger, *Question of Canon*, 67–69.

7. See Kruger's summary in *Question of Canon*, 68.

8. Elsewhere Irenaeus says that "Polycarp ... departed this life, having always taught the things which he had learned from the apostles, and which the Church has handed down, and which alone are true" (*Against Heresies* 3.3.4).

9. See Tertullian, *On Baptism* 17.

10. Quoted in Eusebius, *Ecclesiastical History* 6.12.3.

11. The books of 1 and 2 Timothy and Titus were omitted only by the Muratorian Fragment, but probably because the end of the list was lost.

12. As I said earlier, the question of Revelation's canonical status came centuries later. It was initially, and eventually, seen as canonical.

13. See Kruger, *Canon Revisited*, 269, for patristic evidence.

14. For more on the Gospel of Thomas, see Craig L. Blomberg, *Can We Still Believe the Bible? An Evangelical Engagement with Contemporary Questions* (Grand Rapids: Brazos, 2014), 70–74, Blomberg, *The Historical Reliability of the New Testament* (Nashville: B&H Academic, 2016), 570–79; Darrell L. Bock and Daniel B. Wallace, *Dethroning Jesus: Exposing Popular Culture's Quest to Unseat the Biblical Christ* (Nashville: Nelson, 2007), 105–30; Darrell L. Bock, *The Missing Gospels: Unearthing the Truth Behind Alternative Christianities* (Nashville:

Nelson, 2006). Higher academic studies include Simon Gathercole, *The Gospel of Thomas: Introduction and Commentary* (London: Brill, 2014), and Craig A. Evans, *Jesus and the Manuscripts: What We Can Learn from the Older Texts* (Peabody, MA: Hendrickson, 2020), 130–203.

15. Robert J. Miller, *The Complete Gospels: Annotated Scholars Version*, rev. ed. (Sonoma, CA: Polebridge, 1994), 322.

16. The Jesus Seminar claimed that only 18 percent of Jesus' words and 16 percent of the description of his deeds are reliable (Blomberg, *Historical Reliability of the New Testament*, xxviii n. 31). For a description and critique of the skeptics' arguments, see Mark Strauss, *Four Portraits, One Jesus*, 2nd ed. (Grand Rapids: Zondervan, 2020), 435–39.

17. Helpful also is Michael Kruger's discussion of the "self-authenticating" nature of the canonical books, which looks at "attributes of canonicity": divine qualities, corporate reception by the church, and apostolic origins (*Canon Revisited*, 88–122).

18. For further discussion, see Edmon L. Gallagher and John D. Meade, *The Biblical Canon Lists from Early Christianity* (Oxford: Oxford University Press, 2017), 99–110.

19. Eusebius, *Ecclesiastical History* (3.25.1–7; see "The Development of the Canon of the New Testament," www.ntcanon.org/Eusebius.shtml). It's common to say there were twenty undisputed books, which would omit Revelation, but its canonical status was not in question at first.

Chapter 6

DIGGING DEEPER INTO THE CANON

In the previous chapter, I covered the basics of canonicity. In this chapter, we'll dig a little deeper to look at some of the more difficult questions related to this topic.

When Was the Canon Closed?

A common question asked is, "When was the canon *closed*?" In other words, when did the debate over which books are authoritative stop and the church universally recognize the twenty-seven books we have today? The question can be answered in several ways, depending on how we define the word *canon*. Michael Kruger has an excellent discussion on this topic, and in what follows I've summarized some of his work.[1]

The *exclusive* view of the canon says that the canon was formed when there was no longer any serious debate about which books were canonical. By this definition, we would date the closing of the canon at AD 367 with the Easter Letter written by Athanasius, who was the first person to authoritatively list the twenty-seven books, and only the twenty-seven books, we now consider canonical. Yes, there continued to be some debate on the fringes of Christianity, but this is a fair date for affirming that serious debate had ceased. The limitation of this approach is that it obscures the fact that the core of the canon was settled as soon as the books were written. While the edges of the canon were fuzzy and the canonicity of some of the General Epistles continued to be debated, the core twenty-one books were well established by the end of the first century.[2]

The *functional* definition argues that the canon was established when the church started using the books as authoritative books. By this definition, we can speak of the core of the canon being established by the middle of the second century. The limitation of this definition is that it makes an external process—the church's decision—superior to the inherent authority of the books. This means that a book was not canonical until the church said it was authoritative, when in fact a book was authoritative as soon as the apostle wrote the book.

Finally, there is the *ontological* definition, which says that the canon is comprised of the books God gave to the church and carried his authority. In this view, the canon was closed as soon as the last authoritative book was written, probably Revelation in the late 90s. Kruger cites J. I. Packer's comment: "The Church no more gave us the New Testament canon than Sir Isaac Newton gave us the force of gravity. God gave us gravity . . . Newton did not create gravity but recognized it."[3]

I raise all of this to clarify that when I speak of the canon, I'm primarily thinking of the ontological definition. The books we today call the New Testament were authoritative as soon as they were written, even if it took a while for them to be widely disseminated and recognized by the church as authoritative. The canon was closed when the last book was written.

Historical Evidence

Is there any historical evidence for what I have been arguing? This is a complicated issue, to be sure, but we can draw from two historical sources for help.

1. Canonical Lists

Much of our understanding of the process of canonization comes from lists of canonical books we have from writings that date to the early centuries of the church. In the following charts, ✓ means the book was included in the list, and "D" means the book's inclusion was debated.

	Muratorian	Origen	Eusebius
Matthew	✓	✓	✓
Mark	✓	✓	✓
Luke	✓	✓	✓
John	✓	✓	✓
Acts	✓	✓	✓
Romans	✓	✓	✓
1 Corinthians	✓	✓	✓
2 Corinthians	✓	✓	✓
Galatians	✓	✓	✓
Ephesians	✓	✓	✓
Philippians	✓	✓	✓
Colossians	✓	✓	✓
1 Thessalonians	✓	✓	✓
2 Thessalonians	✓	✓	✓
1 Timothy	✓	✓	✓
2 Timothy	✓	✓	✓
Titus	✓	✓	✓
Philemon	✓	✓	✓

(continued)

	Muratorian	Origen	Eusebius
Hebrews		$\checkmark^4$	$\checkmark^5$
James		$\checkmark$	D
1 Peter		$\checkmark$	$\checkmark$
2 Peter		$\checkmark$	D
1 John	$\checkmark$	$\checkmark$	$\checkmark$
2 John	$\checkmark$	$\checkmark^6$	D
3 John	$?^7$	$\checkmark$	D
Jude	$\checkmark$	$\checkmark$	D
Revelation	$\checkmark$	$\checkmark^8$	$\checkmark^9$

Remember, just because a book was listed as disputed did not mean the author of the list thought it should or should not be in the canon. They were simply being honest in relating that some people disputed the inclusion of that book.[10] Several noncanonical books were part of the discussion at various points, but they were all eventually rejected. These include the *Didache*, *Shepherd of Hermas*, *Epistle of Barnabas*, *Apocalypse of Peter*, *Acts of Paul*, and *Wisdom of Solomon*.

The Muratorian Canon (ca. AD 180) is a fragment of a late second-century list preserved in an eighth-century Latin manuscript. It lists twenty-two books in total.[11] The beginning of the manuscript has been lost, but what we have declares that Luke is the "third" gospel, implying that Matthew and Mark were originally included as well. This list affirms twenty-two of the books as clearly canonical, while specifically stating that the *Shepherd of Hermas* was not canonical since it was recently written, and the *Epistle to the Laodiceans* was "forged." It does list *Wisdom of Solomon* and the *Apocalypse of Peter* (with concerns), but the fact that they're listed at the end may suggest they were disputed. The combined witness of this fragment and the writing of Irenaeus (which we will look at soon), both coming from the same time frame, is a strong argument for the core of the canon having been set by the end of the second century (the functional definition of *canon*).

Origen (d. AD 254) was an apostolic father who traveled widely to learn which books were being used in which locations, separating them into those that were universally accepted and those that were disputed. Of the books he listed as disputed, he came to accept all except for 2 and 3 John, though in time he accepted their canonicity as well. He also mentions others as disputed that were not accepted into the canon.[12]

Eusebius (d. AD 340) is an important church father and historian. He lists the twenty-seven books in our canon and argues against many of the disputed books. He specifically states that the Gospel of Thomas is heretical.[13]

Athanasius (d. AD 373), the bishop of Alexandria, wrote an Easter letter to his church in 367 (*Festal Letters* 39.187), which is the first list of our twenty-seven books (and only the twenty-seven).[14]

In the fourth to fifth century AD, synods and councils basically reaffirmed Athanasius's list,[15] specifically the Synod of Laodicea (363), but omitted Revelation (as was true for the Eastern church).

While a council never took place to officially ratify the canonical list, the councils did acknowledge the twenty-seven books. It wasn't until the Counter-Reformation and the Council of Trent in 1546 that a church council took official action on the question of the canon. That decision by the Roman Catholic Church was to include the Old Testament Apocrypha in the existing Roman Catholic canon.

In conclusion, we should note that there was never any real question about twenty-one of the twenty-seven books and letters (Matthew–John, Acts, Romans–Philemon, 1 Peter, 1 John, Revelation). To state this another way, out of the 7,968 verses in the Greek New Testament, the authority of 7,417 verses was never seriously debated.

2. Authoritative Citations

When a church father quoted a passage from a book as an authoritative statement, this usually (but not always) meant he believed the book was authoritative. Three of the canonical books—Philemon, 2 Peter, and 3 John—are not cited at all by Clement of Alexandria, Tertullian, and Irenaeus. There may be several reasons for this omission. Two of these books are very short, for example. The lack of a reference doesn't necessarily mean the writer denies their authority.[16]

Clement of Alexandria (d. AD 215) wrote commentaries on most of the books in our canon, as well as seven books that eventually were not accepted as canonical. Just because Clement, or any church father, cites a book doesn't mean he necessarily views the book as canonical. Clement references the *Gospel of the Egyptians*, but then he explicitly asserts that it's not canonical (*Stromata* 3.13). All canonical books are orthodox, but not all orthodox books are canonical. As a result, citations are just one of several sources for determining a book's canonicity.

Tertullian (d. AD 220) quotes from all the canonical books except for Philemon, 2 Peter, and 3 John, and he also quotes from *Wisdom of Solomon* and *Shepherd of Hermas*.

Irenaeus (d. AD 200) is an especially important witness. He was the bishop of Lyons, and his teacher was Polycarp, who knew the apostle John personally, so he is two generations removed from an apostle. Irenaeus quotes from all the canonical books except for Philemon, 2 Peter, 3 John, and Jude. Michael Kruger writes that Irenaeus's most notable affirmation is that "the four Gospels were so certain that their existence is entrenched in the very structure of creation"[17] Tatian, a pupil of Justin Martyr, compiled a harmony of the four gospels in ca. AD 160 called the *Diatessaron*; no one was debating the acceptance of the four gospels by this time.

Irenaeus cites the Apostolic Writings as "Scripture."[18] Kruger points out that when we examine the way in which Irenaeus cites the Apostolic Writings, we see he is not inventing a new idea or trying to establish a canon, but simply and naturally citing passages he expects his readers to know and whose authority he expects them to accept.[19] Irenaeus did not invent the idea of a canon; rather, he *assumed* his readers' acceptance of the canonical writings as authoritative.

In summary, when we look at both of these sources—lists and citations—we can confidently conclude that the core of the canon was firmly in place as soon as the books were written in the first century. The apostles taught with Christ's authority; their writings carried their authority; and this authority was recognized by the church fathers from the beginning of the second century as evidenced by their willingness to quote from the Apostolic Writings and include them in the canonical lists.

Winners and Losers

Some skeptics argue that there were divergent canons representing different "orthodoxies," concluding that the canon we presently have simply represents the political and theological force that "won" the debate.[20] This is related to the charge we discussed earlier that there were different theologies, and what we have represents only the theology that won the debate and hence became "orthodoxy." But this is an incorrect reading of history on several levels and for at least five key reasons:

1. It's clear that there always was a core of the canon as soon as the books were written, and the historical debates were focused on the General Epistles. It's not as if there were multiple cores.
2. It's difficult to see how any of the books not categorized as part of the core could possibly represent their own orthodoxy that would be in contrast to the accepted core. What is the core orthodoxy of 2 Peter or 3 John that competes with the accepted core?
3. Craig Blomberg makes the excellent argument that the heresies of the first two centuries did not develop on their own but were always positioned in contrast to the existing orthodoxy.[21] There were not competing orthodoxies, only perversions of the core orthodoxy.

4. The fact that the lists continued to be discussed through the first six centuries shows that the orthodox position was not sufficiently powerful to squelch *all* debate. There was no grand conspiracy.
5. The mere existence of heresy doesn't mean there was no orthodoxy. Actually, it's quite the reverse. There can be no heresy unless there is a standard of truth against which to compare it and determine it to be heretical.

While Peter and Paul are often placed at odds with each other by modern skeptics, it's difficult, if not impossible, to construct significantly different theologies that truly could not coexist.

Use of Apocryphal Writings

Another challenge often made suggests that the use of apocryphal gospels by some of the early church fathers proves that the church had not yet accepted the fourfold canon of Matthew, Mark, Luke, and John. The Achilles' heel of this challenge is something we've noted before: it doesn't distinguish between using an apocryphal gospel and treating the apocryphal gospel as authoritative. Clement of Alexandria and Origen were both well-read and well-educated. It's certainly possible that they quoted material without giving the entire book an authoritative status. Even in the New Testament we see this happening. Paul quotes Epimenides when he tells Titus, "One of Crete's own prophets has said it: 'Cretans are always liars, evil brutes, lazy gluttons.' This saying is true" (Titus 1:12–13). But in quoting Epimenides Paul is surely not claiming canonical status for all that Epimenides said. The statement is true, not because Epimenides said it, but because Paul affirmed it. To give a more recent example, I could quote something the Artful Dodger says in the novel *Oliver Twist*, but that doesn't mean I base my theology on Charles Dickens.

Serapion, the bishop over the church of Rhossus, found the church using and reading the Gospel of Peter. In response, Serapion expressly says that the Gospel of Peter was not one of the scriptural books "handed down to us."[22] If the book was not heretical, people could still read it, even though it was not authoritative. Likewise, Clement quotes from the Gospel of the Hebrews while at the same time saying it's not one of the canonical four gospels (*Stromata* 3.6–13). Origen also quotes from a wide range of "gospels" while at the same time affirming there are only four authoritative gospels.[23]

What If We Were to Find More?

Another common question raised concerns a hypothetical situation. What would happen if we found other authentic writings? Would they be accepted into the canon? For example, we know that Paul wrote four letters to the Corinthian church, and what we call 1 and 2 Corinthians are really 2 and 4 Corinthians. What would happen if we found the first or third letter? What would happen if we found Paul's letter to the Laodiceans referenced in Colossians 4:16?

The answer is that I doubt they would ever be part of the canon. Remember, there are three criteria, and even if apostolic authorship could be proven, and even if the theology was orthodox, the book would fail the third test of catholicity—reception by the church as a whole. Consequently, it would never be part of the canon. Jesus Christ is the end of the canon (Heb 1:1–2), and the church is built on the foundational work of the apostles. There is nothing left to be said.

My guess is that this will never happen. God preserved the documents he wanted the church to have, and he allowed the others to be lost.[24]

Conclusion

The historical evidence is overwhelming that the Gospels, Acts, Paul's thirteen letters, 1 Peter, 1 John, and Revelation were viewed as authoritative and therefore canonical as soon as they were written. They carried their authors' authority and were quickly recognized as such by the church. While other books were read and cited, the church was careful to distinguish between canonical and noncanonical writings. The fuzziness around the edges began to disappear by the middle of the second century, and the process was finalized by the end of the fourth century.

Because there was an orthodoxy from the Apostolic Writings, there weren't competing canons. The core provided an authoritative standard, and of the six books that struggled to be accepted, none of them contain a full-orbed, competing theology.

For Further Reading

Blomberg, Craig L. "Textual Transmission and the Formation of the Canon," in *The Historical Reliability of the New Testament: Countering the Challenges to Evangelical Christian Beliefs*. Nashville: B&H Academic, 2016, chapter 13.

———. "Wasn't the Selection of Books for the Canon Just Political?" in *Can We Still Believe the Bible? An Evangelical Engagement with Contemporary Questions*. Grand Rapids: Brazos, 2014, chapter 2.

Bock, Darrell L. *The Missing Gospels: Unearthing the Truth behind Alternate Christianities*. Nashville: Nelson, 2006.

Bruce, F. F. *The Books and the Parchments: How We Got Our English Bible*. 3rd ed. Old Tappan, NJ: Revell, 1984, chapter 13.

———. *The Canon of Scripture*. Downers Grove, IL: IVP Academic, 1988.

———. *The New Testament Documents: Are They Reliable?* 6th ed. Grand Rapids: Eerdmans, 1981.

Hill, Charles E. *Who Chose the Gospels? Probing the Great Gospel Conspiracy*. Oxford: Oxford University Press, 2010.

Komoszewski, J. Ed, M. James Sawyer, and Daniel B. Wallace. "Did the Early Church Muzzle the Canon?" in *Reinventing Jesus: How Contemporary Skeptics Miss the Real Jesus and Mislead Popular Culture*. Grand Rapids: Kregel, 2006, part 3.

Kruger, Michael J. *Canon Revisited: Establishing the Origins and Authority of the New Testament Books*. Wheaton, IL: Crossway, 2012.

———. *The Question of Canon: Challenging the Status Quo in the New Testament Debate*. Downers Grove, IL: IVP Academic, 2013.

———. "Why We Trust Our Bible." Lectures 12–21. Biblical Training Institute, https://gk2.me/we-trust.

———. Visit michaeljkruger.com for more.

Osborne, Grant. *Three Crucial Questions about the Bible*. Grand Rapids: Baker, 1995.

Wegner, Paul D. *The Journey from Texts to Translations: The Origin and Development of the Bible*. Grand Rapids: Baker Academic, 1999.

Advanced

Gallagher, Edmon L., and John D. Meade, *The Biblical Canon Lists from Early Christianity: Texts and Analysis*. Oxford: Oxford University Press, 2017.

McDonald, Lee M., and James A. Sanders, eds. *The Canon Debate*. Grand Rapids: Baker Academic, 2002.

Metzger, Bruce. *The Canon of the New Testament: Its Origin, Development, and Significance*. Oxford: Clarendon, 1997.

Notes

1. See Michael J. Kruger, *The Question of Canon: Challenging the Status Quo in the New Testament Debate* (Downers Grove, IL: IVP Academic, 2013), 27–46.

2. Kruger uses the term *core* to describe the state of the canon in the mid-second century. I use it differently here to refer to the middle to the end of the first century.

3. Quoted in Michael J. Kruger, *Canon Revisited: Establishing the Origins and Authority of the New Testament Books* (Wheaton, IL: Crossway, 2012), 45.

4. Origen refers to Paul's "fourteen" letters, apparently including Hebrews, although there is some debate as to whether the number was original since Origen does not list Hebrews in his catalog of New Testament books (Eusebius, *Ecclesiastical History* 6.25). For Origen's text see Edmon L. Gallagher and John D. Meade, *The Biblical Canon Lists from Early Christianity* (Oxford: Oxford University Press, 2017), 92.

5. Hebrews is not listed in Eusebius's catalogue (*Ecclesiastical History* 3.25.23), but in 3.3.5 he speaks of Paul's "14" letters, which would include Hebrews.

6. Origen refers to the letters of John in the plural, so presumably he means both 2 and 3 John.
7. There is some debate as to whether or not the Muratorian Canon includes 3 John. See Kruger, *Canon Revisited*, 230 n. 178.
8. Origen doesn't include Revelation in his lists, but he accepts it as authoritative elsewhere in his writings.
9. Eusebius also includes Revelation in the disputed group; see Gallagher and Meade, *Biblical Canon Lists*, 101 n. 126.
10. For a comprehensive listing of the thirty canonical lists through the sixth century, see Lee McDonald, "Lists and Catalogues of New Testament Collections," in *The Canon Debate*, ed. Lee M. McDonald and James A. Sanders (Grand Rapids: Baker Academic, 2002), 591–97; see also Gallagher and Meade, *Biblical Canon Lists*.
11. The fragment is cited in full by Paul D. Wegner, *The Journey from Texts to Translations* (Grand Rapids: Baker Academic, 1999), 147–48, and Gallagher and Meade, *Biblical Canon Lists*, 178–82.
12. See Eusebius, *Ecclesiastical History* 6.25.23–14; see also Gallagher and Meade, *Biblical Canon Lists*, 83–99.
13. Eusebius, *Ecclesiastical History* 3.25.6.
14. Included in Gallagher and Meade, *Biblical Canon Lists*, 123–25.
15. On the difference of the canon between the East and the West, see Wegner, *Journey from Texts to Translations*, 145–46.
16. See Wegner, *Journey from Texts to Translations*, 141–45. In addition, Paul Barnett lists the biblical books referenced by three writers from the early second century (Polycarp, Ignatius, and Clement), showing which books they accepted as authoritative (*Is the New Testament Reliable?* [Downers Grove, IL: IVP Academic, 2003], 41).
17. Kruger, *Question of Canon*, 157; Irenaeus's full citation (*Against Heresies* 3.11.8) can be found in Alexander Souter, *The Text and Canon of the New Testament* (New York: Scribner, 1913), 170–73: "It is not possible that the Gospels can be either more or fewer in number than they are. For, since there are four zones of the world in which we live, and four principal winds, while the Church is scattered throughout all the world, and the pillar and ground 1 Timothy 3:15 of the Church is the Gospel and the spirit of life; it is fitting that she should have four pillars, breathing out immortality on every side, and vivifying men afresh. From which fact, it is evident that the Word, the Artificer of all, He that sits upon the cherubim, and contains all things, He who was manifested to

men, has given us the Gospel under four aspects, but bound together by one Spirit. As also David says, when entreating His manifestation, You that sits between the cherubim, shine forth. For the cherubim, too, were four-faced, and their faces were images of the dispensation of the Son of God . . . And therefore the Gospels are in accord with these things, among which Christ Jesus is seated . . . Afterwards, being made man for us, He sent the gift of the celestial Spirit over all the earth, protecting us with His wings. Such, then, as was the course followed by the Son of God, so was also the form of the living creatures; and such as was the form of the living creatures, so was also the character of the Gospel. For the living creatures are quadriform, and the Gospel is quadriform, as is also the course followed by the Lord."

18. See references in Kruger, *Canon Revisited*, 228 n. 167.

19. Kruger, *Question of Canon*, 159; Kruger, *Canon Revisited*, 229.

20. See, for example, Bart Ehrman, *Lost Christianities: The Battles for Scripture and the Faiths We Never Knew* (Oxford: Oxford University Press, 2002).

21. Craig L. Blomberg, *Can We Still Believe the Bible? An Evangelical Engagement with Contemporary Questions* (Grand Rapids: Brazos, 2014), 59–60.

22. See Eusebius, *Ecclesiastical History* 6.12.3.

23. See Eusebius, *Ecclesiastical History* 6.25.3.

24. For a historical survey of this question see Kruger, *Canon Revisited*, 280–87.

TEXTUAL CRITICISM
Greek Manuscripts
through the Centuries

Challenge

Don wrote me the other day about his concern over differences in the Bible. He knows that the scribes who made copies of the original New Testament documents made changes to the text. These changes bother him. If an unknown scribe could change Jesus' reaction from being "compassionate" to being "indignant" toward the man with leprosy (Mark 1:41), why would we trust other changes, like the different endings of Mark (16:9–20) or the story of the woman caught in adultery (John 7:53–8:11)? Don grew up as a conservative Christian with a high view of Scripture, but now he is wondering if the story of Jesus' resurrection could be due to a scribe's imagination.

Many people have similar concerns. One scholar emphasizes that we do not have the original writings of the New Testament—and not only that, but we don't have "copies of the copies of the copies" of the originals. In fact, he claims there are more differences among the Greek New Testament manuscripts (about 400,000) than there are words

(138,213). He also claims that the scribes of the first two to three centuries were sloppy and biased, injecting their own ideas into the text, such as Jesus' divinity.[1]

If these claims were true, they would be devastating to the Christian faith. It would do no good to talk about the historical reliability of the Gospels and canonization if the scribes so heavily altered the contents of the Bible that we couldn't get back to the originals. Why should we think Jesus is divine if in fact the doctrine was created by the Council of Nicaea in AD 325 and inserted into the biblical texts?

In these three chapters, we will focus on the text of the New Testament. I am indebted to New Testament scholar Daniel Wallace, one of the leading experts in this field, for much of my understanding of textual criticism, both from his debate with Bart Ehrman and from our friendship and personal communication. If you want to go deeper into this topic, I strongly recommend you attend his thirty-five-lecture class at the Biblical Training website (biblicaltraining.org).[2]

Notes

1. See Bart D. Ehrman, *Misquoting Jesus: The Story behind Who Changed the Bible and Why* (San Francisco: HarperOne, 2005).
2. Daniel Wallace, "Textual Criticism: The History of the Greek Text behind Modern Translations," Biblical Training Institute, https://gk2.me/textual-criticism. For a shorter version, go to lecture 22 ("Challenges") in the "Why We Trust Our Bible" course at the Biblical Training website, https://gk2.me/trust-wallace.

Chapter 7

ARE THE GREEK TEXTS HOPELESSLY CORRUPT?

In this chapter, we will look at the issues of the Greek manuscripts that relay the original writings throughout the centuries, the differences among them, and whether or not those differences are significant.

Nature and Significance of Textual Differences

Historical Process

Let's start by agreeing with what is right about this challenge. It is true: we don't have any of the original documents penned by the New Testament authors. And it's true: all copies of the originals were made by hand, and the scribes did make mistakes, some intentionally and some unintentionally. And it is also true: there are approximately 400,000 differences among all our Greek manuscripts. And we have no manuscripts from the first and very few from the second century, and what we do have is fragmentary—a verse here and a paragraph there. So these are all true statements.

But the real question is, *How are these facts significant?* At first glance, they seem to create an impenetrable barrier to accepting the claims of Christianity and lead to the inevitable conclusion that the original words written by the New Testament authors have been lost forever. But with a little investigation, we can see that this barrier is not as high as we thought at first glance. I'll begin by laying out several historical realities so the answers to the challenges will make sense.

First, let's define a few terms. We use the term *autograph* to refer to the original document written by the author. In most cases, it would have been dictated and written down by an "amanuensis"—that is, a secretary. Paul used Tertius to write Romans (Rom 16:22), and Peter may have used Silas (also named Silvanus) to write 1 Peter (1 Pet 5:12). I'm convinced that Paul used Luke to write 1 Timothy and perhaps 2 Timothy and Titus.[1]

As a general rule, the amanuensis would have been given some freedom as to what he wrote—word choice, grammar, style. This would explain the unusual frequency of medical imagery in 1 and 2 Timothy, since Luke was a physician. The author would have proofread the written document and, if necessary, made corrections. We also believe that in many cases a copy would have been made by the amanuensis.[2] One of these manuscripts would then be sent to the recipient, and the second kept as a backup.

You can imagine the church in Rome receiving Paul's letter and then instantly desiring copies, or what we call "manuscripts" (often abbreviated "ms" or in the plural "mss" in the footnotes in your Bibles). Wealthy Christians may have wanted their own copies, or perhaps a church in another city had heard about the letter and wanted a copy (Col 4:16). In the pre-Gutenberg era (prior to 1516), all of these copies would have been made by hand. We know that some of the scribes copied one or two letters at a time; we know that other scribes copied one or two words at a time, or more. Both methods reflected the desire for accuracy on the part of the scribe. While most of the people in the first century were illiterate, unable to read or write, there were enough literate people to produce the copies needed. Most were not professional scribes who were trying to create a work of art; rather, they were trying to make accurate copies of the manuscript.

Despite their best efforts, they made mistakes. Sometimes they made an unintentional mistake, such as skipping a word or transposing letters. Other times they made intentional changes, usually for good reasons, such as correcting misspellings or poor grammar. We also know that scribes added notes to the margins, perhaps explaining a word or adding background information they were aware of. We know this happened because we can look directly at these manuscripts and see marginal notes.

The differences between the texts are called "variants." Sometimes we talk about a manuscript having a certain "reading." A variant is any variation among the manuscripts. This includes differences in wording (additions, omissions, changes), word order, and spelling. It doesn't matter if a variant occurs in one manuscript or a thousand, or if a variant occurs in the second century or the tenth—it's still counted as one variant. There are about 400,000 variants in the approximately 5,600 Greek manuscripts of the New Testament. To state it another way, we have so many variants because we have so many manuscripts.

Principles of Textual Criticism

With all these variations in the text, how do we decide which of the variant readings is most likely to be original, i.e., to reflect what the author wrote? In academic circles, this field of study is called "textual criticism," and it is extremely complex. Most of our textual critics have devoted their entire careers to the discipline. It takes dedication and intelligence to get a handle on 5,600 manuscripts and a deep knowledge of Greek and three or four other ancient languages.

One criterion textual critics use to determine what is original is *external evidence*, which means they look at the manuscripts as a whole, including how old they are. A manuscript that was copied in the fifth century will, by default, be more trustworthy than a manuscript copied in the eleventh century. The fifth-century manuscript was copied less than five hundred years after the writing of the original, and the eleventh-century manuscript has had an entire millennium for errors to creep into the "copies of the copies of the copies." Of course, the manuscript (the "exemplar") copied by the eleventh-century manuscript may be more accurate than the exemplar copied by the fifth-century manuscript, in which case the eleventh-century manuscript may be more reliable than the fifth. Examining the external evidence can get quite complicated.

To make things even more complex, we don't always know how many copies existed between the autograph and each of these manuscripts. The manuscript from AD 300 could be a copy, or a copy of a copy, of the original, but we are virtually guaranteed that an eleventh-century manuscript is a copy of a copy of a copy. However, an eighth-century manuscript could be just a copy of a copy of the original. We now know that a manuscript could survive 150 to 200 years as a norm, so how many iterations of manuscripts there were between the autograph and the manuscript we possess is unknown. As I said, textual criticism can get complicated, and textual critics have to make a lot of judgment calls.

The other criterion is *internal evidence*. The basic rule here is that the reading that best explains the others is more likely to be original. This is called the "harder reading." The corollary rule is that the shorter reading tends to be preferred. Consider Mark 9:29 as an example. The disciples are unable to drive out a demon, so Jesus performs the exorcism. In private, the disciples ask him why they were not able to do so, and Jesus responds, "This kind can come out only by prayer" (NIV). But in the KJV we read, "This kind can come forth by nothing, but by prayer *and fasting*" (italics added). The additional words raise a question: Is fasting required for especially difficult exorcisms?

Looking at the internal evidence, the textual critic would ask if it is more likely that "and fasting" was added or omitted. If Jesus had said "prayer and fasting," what possible motivation would there be to drop "and fasting"? None. We also know that later centuries saw an increasing emphasis on spiritual practices like fasting, and so it is quite plausible that a scribe might add it into the text. So the reading that only has "prayer" easily explains the other reading ("prayer and fasting"), and we consider "prayer" to be the shorter and the "harder" reading. Rules like these are based on observation and careful reasoning. We know from looking at thousands of variants that scribes were hesitant to drop words out of the Bible but were willing to add them in, so we can be certain that the words "and fasting" were added.

This is especially evident in the scribal practice of harmonization. There is no evidence that the scribes had nefarious motives, wanting to alter the meaning of the biblical texts. Rather, one of the most common intentional changes was the attempt to make parallel passages agree. This would happen when a scribe was aware of a parallel passage to the one he was currently copying. In Matthew 20:22, Jesus asks, "Can you drink the cup I am going to drink?" In Mark 10:38, the same question is, "Can you drink the cup I drink *or be baptized with the baptism I am baptized with*?" (italics added). A variant of Matthew 20:22 harmonizes the two by adding to Matthew and saying, "Can you drink the cup I am going to drink or be baptized with the baptism with which I am baptized?" The harmonization is so obvious that only the Christian Standard Bible and the New English Translation list the variant in a footnote.

Fortunately, we have a gifted group of textual critics who have done an excellent job of looking at all the manuscripts, applying the principles of textual criticism, making decisions on a word-by-word basis as to which of the variants they believe to be the original, and publishing their work in a form that shows not only the text but also the major variants. The text I'm referring to is the *Novum Testamentum Graece* by the Deutsche Bibelgesellschaft (current edition is the twenty-eighth revised), and it's often referred to as Nestle-Aland (or NA), named after two of its main authors. The same text is also published as *The Greek New Testament* by the United Bible Societies (currently in its fifth revised edition) and is often referred to as UBS. The only difference between these two is in the apparatus—the section of the Bible (sort of like the footnotes in a book) where they show variant readings and the manuscript evidence behind those readings. The Nestle-Aland lists some 30,000 variants, with only the major textual witness for each variant. The UBS shows 1,408 variants, with a much fuller list of manuscripts behind each of the variants. These are the texts that almost all modern scholars use when working with the Greek New Testament.

Categories

The standard way of discussing variants is to divide them into four categories. In the following discussion, I'm using the term *meaningful* to mean that the variant has a different meaning, and *viable* to mean that there is at least some chance of the reading being original. Of the four possible combinations, we don't need to discuss variants that are *not meaningful and not viable*.[3]

Viable and Not Meaningful

Variants are considered "viable and not meaningful" if they may be reflecting the original wording of the author ("viable") but don't affect the meaning of the passage ("not meaningful"). This is by far the largest category of the 400,000 variants.

In this category belong spelling differences, which make up about 70 percent of all the variants. "John" can be spelled with one *nu* (ν, the "n" sound) or two, with no difference in meaning—so the spelling can be Ἰωάνης (*Iōanēs*) or Ἰωάννης (*Iōannēs*). Daniel Wallace comments, "To be sure, whether John's name was spelled in Greek with one *nu* or two may remain a mystery. But the point is that John's name is not spelled *Mary*."[4]

Usually the definite article (ὁ, "the") precedes a proper name, but not always, again with no difference in meaning; Jesus can be referred to as ὁ Ἰησοῦς or Ἰησοῦς. The most common spelling difference is what is called a "movable *nu*." The *nu* can be added to the end of a word that ends with a vowel when the next word begins with a vowel, much like we say "a book" but "an apple." Whether the text says ἐστίν (*estin*) or ἐστι (*esti*) has no effect on meaning; both mean "he is" (or "she is" or "it is").

Wallace likes to talk about the sentence "Jesus loves John." His point is that because Greek is an inflected language, you can easily write, "Jesus loves John," sixteen different ways, and in fact you can write it hundreds of ways, without any change in meaning.[5] The different readings could be viable, but they're not meaningful. Such is the nature of Greek and any inflected language.

Unintentional changes also belong in this category. Perhaps the scribe transposed two letters or skipped a letter or word—or even skipped a line, which could happen when the last word of both lines was the same. Perhaps it was at the end of the day and the scribe was tired. These are easy variants to identify, and it's easy to determine what the original reading was. For example, if you saw "years" and "yaers," which would you deem to be the original reading (assuming the author's amanuensis could spell)? Obviously "years." If you read, "Four score and seven yards ago," it doesn't take much imagination to see that "yards" should be "years," especially if you know American history. If you read, "A bird, came the walk," and you know poetry, you could easily see that "down" had been skipped ("down the walk").[6]

The earlier manuscripts were written with either all capital letters ("majuscules") or a connected script ("cursive") but without spaces between words or punctuation between clauses and sentences. If you were copying "INTHEBEGINNINGWASTHEWORD" (ΕΝΑΡΧΗΗΝΟΛΟΓΟΣ, in lower case, εναρχηηνολογος), you can see how easily mistakes could be made. Consider Revelation 1:5. Has Jesus "washed" (λούσαντι, *lousanti*) us or "freed" (λύσαντι, *lusanti*) us? The evidence is strongly in favor of λύσαντι ("freed"), but you can see how easy it would have been to accidentally write λούσαντι.

The point is that these errors are easy to spot and the original reading is generally easy to determine. Well over 70 percent of all variants fit into this category, significantly reducing the number of variants.

Meaningful and Not Viable

There are other variants that change the meaning of the text ("meaningful"), but it's clear that they're not original ("not viable"). Some of these changes were unintentional mistakes made in the copying process; but most variants in this category were intentional, often made out of reverence and respect for the Bible and not for some nefarious reason.

Conflation is the blending of parallel passages (also called harmonizing, mentioned above). This happened when a scribe was aware of a slightly different wording in a parallel passage and wanted to combine the words from both verses.

The first beatitude in the Sermon on the Mount reads, "Blessed are the poor in spirit, for theirs is the kingdom of heaven" (Matt 5:3), but in the Sermon on the Plain we read, "Blessed are you who are poor" (Luke 6:20). However, there is a variant of Luke 6:20 that reads, "Blessed are you who are poor in spirit," conflating it with Matthew 5:3.

In the story I mention above of Jesus' healing of a demon-possessed boy, the response Jesus gives as to why the disciples could not drive out the demon is different in Mark and Matthew. In Mark, Jesus' reason is, "This kind can come out only by prayer" (9:29). In Matthew, his reason is, "Because you have so little faith" (17:20). There is nothing in Matthew similar to Mark. However, in the Greek manuscripts behind the KJV, the entire sentence from Mark 9:29 has been added at Matthew 17:21.

> [20]And Jesus said unto them, Because of your unbelief: for verily I say unto you, If ye have faith as a grain of mustard seed, ye shall say unto this mountain, Remove hence to yonder place; and it shall remove; and nothing shall be impossible unto you.
> [21]*Howbeit this kind goeth not out but by prayer and fasting.*

We also see **clarification**—information added to explain the text. In John 5, Jesus notices a group of people lying by the pool called

Bethesda. He sees a man who has been there for thirty-eight years and asks him, "Do you want to get well?" (v. 6).Why was this man lying there for so long? Decades after John wrote his gospel, we see two sentences added to the manuscripts after verse 3, which we now call verses 3b–4 (see the NIV footnote at verse 3):

> —and they waited for the moving of the waters. [4]From time to time an angel of the Lord would come down and stir up the waters. The first one into the pool after each such disturbance would be cured of whatever disease they had.

This addition explains why the man was lying there. Which is more likely—that this explanation would have been dropped out or would have been added? I'm grateful we know it was added; if it were original, it would have been an odd and unique practice for angels, almost magical in nature.

Clarification also occurs when the scribe replaces a pronoun with its antecedent. Daniel Wallace refers to eighty-six verses in Mark 6:31–8:26 in which the name of Jesus never occurs; rather, Mark just says "he."[7] Mark meant us to read the three chapters all together and did not feel the need to repeat the antecedent "Jesus." However, later scribes found the use of "he" without an expressed antecedent in the immediate context to be confusing. As a result, we find "he" replaced with "Jesus" in the Greek at 6:34; 7:27; 8:1; and 8:17.

We see the same thing in English translations. Consider how confusing the following translation would be, especially when we remember that the Greek doesn't punctuate sentences: "Then he again put his hands on his eyes, and he saw clearly, and his sight was restored, and he saw everything distinctly. And he sent him to his home" (Mark 8:25–26). Too many "he's." The ESV (as does the NIV) replaces the first "he" in verse 25 with "Jesus," and the ESV footnote reads, "Greek *he*." The NIV replaces the "he" with "Jesus" in verse 26: "Jesus sent him home." The same thing happens in the Greek manuscripts.

We also see **stylistic** changes. Most of the New Testament is written in common, everyday Greek. Mark and John are the most basic Greek; Luke, Hebrews, and 1 Peter have the highest literary style. Apparently some scribes were uncomfortable that the Bible was in the common vernacular and tried to "dress it up," much like using an Elizabethan style in English. A good example is the addition of the last line in the Lord's Prayer (Matt 6:13): "for yours is the kingdom and the power and the glory forever." This verse was clearly added centuries after Jesus,[8] probably by analogy to 1 Chronicles 29:11–13. Scribes were also uncomfortable with a simple name for Jesus, so there is a common expansion of "Jesus" to "Jesus Christ," "Lord Jesus," or "Lord Jesus Christ."[9]

Finally, we see **correction**. This happened when a scribe thought there was a mistake in the manuscript they were copying. Sometimes it was nothing more than a spelling change, but other times it could be more significant. The original text of Mark 1:2–3 reads:

as it is written in Isaiah the prophet:

"I will send my messenger ahead of you,
    who will prepare your way"—
"a voice of one calling in the wilderness,
'Prepare the way for the Lord,
    make straight paths for him.'"

The problem is that while the second citation is from Isaiah 40:3, the first is from Malachi 3:1. It's certainly possible that Mark wrote "Isaiah" in verse 2, since he is the dominant prophet in this citation. Some modern writers would call this an error, but certainly Mark and Peter knew their Old Testament well enough to see the issue and not be concerned. However, an anxious scribe decided to change "as it is written in *Isaiah the prophet*" to "as it is written in *the prophets*" (ESV footnote). It's easy to determine the later reading is not authentic.

Why would a scribe change "the prophets" to "Isaiah the prophet" and introduce what could be seen as an error?

These are meaningful variants because they change the meaning of the text, but they're not viable since they're clearly not original.

Meaningful and Viable

Variants that are "meaningful and viable" are the ones that deserve our full attention. I will mention a few here, and some of the more famous ones are described in the next chapter. This is the smallest category of variants—fewer than 1 percent of the 400,000. This still leaves many questionable texts, but drastically fewer than 400,000.

In Romans 1–4, Paul argues that all people are sinful and that salvation is possible only through faith. Romans 5:1 starts a new section of the epistle by summarizing the first four chapters in one phrase: "Therefore, *since we have been justified through faith*, we have peace with God" (italics added). "We have" is the indicative (ἔχομεν, *exomen*), but there is a variant that uses the subjunctive (ἔχωμεν, *exōmen*), "let us have." There is a difference of only one letter. Is Paul saying that we "are" (indicative) at peace or that we should "pursue" (subjunctive) peace? Almost all scholars think it's an indicative because of the flow of Paul's argument (internal evidence)—we are at peace because justification is by faith and not by the uncertainty of works—but the external evidence is strongly on the side of the subjunctive.

One of the more common variants is the difference between "we" (ὑμεῖς, *hymeis*) and "you" (ἡμεῖς, *hēmeis*). Paul writes in Ephesians 1:13, "*You* also are in him, having heard the word of truth, the good news of *your* salvation" (my translation, italics added). A variant reading shifts from second person to first. "*We* also are in him, having heard the word of truth, the good news of *our* salvation." Is there any significant difference in meaning between saying "you" and "we"? Is there any real difference between "Now *you*, brothers and sisters, like Isaac, are children of promise" and "Now *we*" (Gal 4:28)? There is a change is meaning, but not one that substantively affects the overall meaning of the verse (see also 1 John 1:4).

Some manuscripts says Jesus was "indignant" when faced with the disciples' inability to heal a man who had leprosy (Mark 1:41); other manuscripts say he was "filled with compassion." The external evidence supports "filled with compassion," but the internal evidence is on the side of "indignant." There is no good reason to change "filled with compassion" to "indignant," but you can easily see why a scribe might be confused with Jesus' indignation and change it to compassion. This makes "indignant" the harder and more likely original reading, but most English translations go with "filled with compassion." I'll discuss the meaning of this verse in greater detail in the next chapter.

The number of variants that fit into this category of "meaningful and viable" are a small fraction of the 400,000. The UBS text has a rating system for the variants it lists:

Rating	Description	Number of variants
A	"Text is certain."	502
B	"Text is almost certain."	533
C	"Committee had difficulty deciding."	366
D	"Committee had great difficulty deciding."	7

So the UBS text identifies 373 places out of 1,408 total where there was significant doubt about a meaningful variant, 0.09 percent of the 400,000.

Another way to visualize the number of variants is to count the number of footnotes in an English Bible that reflect textual variants. They say something like "Or" followed by an alternate reading, or they say something about another "ms" or other "mss," meaning "manuscript(s)." For example, in Mark 1:41 discussed above, the NIV translates, "Jesus was indignant," with the footnote, "Many manuscripts *Jesus was filled with compassion*." The NIV has 282 such footnotes; the ESV has 460. There are not many "meaningful and viable" variants.

Significance

One of the remarkable things about textual criticism is that theological liberals and conservatives basically agree that textual critics have done an excellent job, and we are comfortable with their conclusions in general. So what can we say in conclusion? Here are three points to summarize what we've learned:

1. We have more than 5,600 manuscripts of the Greek New Testament but none of the autographs.
2. Among the 400,000 textual variants, 99 percent make virtually no difference whatsoever. They are either not meaningful or not viable.
3. The fewer than 1 percent of the variants that are meaningful and viable do not affect or call into question a single biblical doctrine, cardinal or otherwise. Even Bart Ehrman, the most recent vocal critic of the biblical text, admits this in the appendix of the book *The Text of the New Testament*.[10] He says his doctoral supervisor and coauthor Bruce Metzger believed that "the essential Christian beliefs are not affected by textual variants in the manuscript tradition of the New Testament," and Ehrman adds, "For the most part, I think that's true."[11]

Conclusion

There are more than 400,000 differences among the 5,600 Greek manuscripts of the New Testament, and yet not even 1 percent of those variants are both meaningful and viable. Textual critics look at the external and internal evidence and have done excellent work in combing through all the manuscripts and making their decisions, and there is not a single viable variant that calls into question any point of biblical theology, major or minor.

Notes

1. See William D. Mounce, *Pastoral Epistles*, Word Biblical Commentary (Grand Rapids: Zondervan, 2000), lxiv.

2. For documentation, see Craig A. Evans, *Jesus and the Manuscripts* (Peabody, MA: Hendrickson, 2020), 89–91. He summarizes, "An 'autograph' was produced by a scribe, the author of the letter signed it in his own hand, usually along with a greeting, and then the scribe made a second copy, which was retained for the author's records. Sometimes it was the reverse: a draft was prepared, and then a polished autograph was written and dispatched. Autographic letters would be readily recognized, for the hand of the sender, who signed his name and perhaps added a line or two of personal greetings and well wishes, would be easily distinguished from the more practiced hand of the professional scribe who had penned the letter" (p. 90).

3. For an excellent (though detailed) discussion of the types of mistakes, see Bruce M. Metzger and Bart D. Ehrman, *The Text of the New Testament: Its Transmission, Corruption, and Restoration*, 4th ed. (Oxford: Oxford University Press, 2005), 250–71; see also J. Ed Komoszewski, M. James Sawyer, and Daniel B. Wallace, *Reinventing Jesus* (Grand Rapids: Kregel, 2006), 83–101.

4. Komoszewski, Sawyer, and Wallace, *Reinventing Jesus*, 60.

5. See Darrell L. Bock and Daniel B. Wallace, *Dethroning Jesus: Exposing Popular Culture's Quest to Unseat the Biblical Christ* (Nashville: Nelson, 2007), 56.

6. Emily Dickinson, "A Bird, came down the Walk (359)," in *The Poems of Emily Dickinson: Reading Edition*, ed. R. W. Franklin (Cambridge, MA: Harvard University Press, 1999).

7. Komoszewski, Sawyer, and Wallace, *Reinventing Jesus*, 59.

8. The line doesn't occur in our best manuscripts (Sinaiticus Vaticanus Bezae) or the Old Latin, nor is it in early patristic writings. The earliest manuscripts with the line are W (fourth or fifth century), L (eighth century), and K (ninth or tenth century).

9. See Romans 1:6; 16:20; 1 Corinthians 5:3–4; 12:3; Galatians 6:18; Colossians 3:17.

10. Bruce M. Metzger and Bart D. Ehrman, *The Text of the New Testament: Its Transmission, Corruption and Restoration*, 4th ed. (Oxford: Oxford University Press, 2005).

11. Bart D. Ehrman, *Misquoting Jesus: The Story behind Who Changed the Bible and Why* (San Francisco: HarperOne, 2005), 252.

Chapter 8

DIGGING DEEPER INTO TEXTUAL CRITICISM

In this chapter, we'll look at some of the better-known passages that are textually questionable, meaning they were probably added by scribes in later centuries and not written by the biblical authors. What you'll discover is that many of them have to do with differences between the Greek behind the King James Version (one of the older English translations) and the Greek behind the more recent translations.

Text-Types

I need to explain something called text-types.[1] The library in Alexandria, Egypt, was one of the great wonders of the ancient world. One of the characteristics of the manuscripts copied there was that they were faithfully and carefully copied. We don't find nearly as many errors, intentional or unintentional, as we find in manuscripts from other areas of the world. Because these manuscripts are from the same geographical area and they show the same characteristics of faithful preservation, today we group them together and call them the *Alexandrian* text-type. We find manuscripts of this text-type until the tenth century.

There are two outstanding manuscripts of the Alexandrian

text-type. Vaticanus is from the first half of the fourth century, and Sinaiticus is from the middle of the fourth century. Because they are Alexandrian manuscripts, are so old, and have been carefully copied, they have become two of the primary Greek manuscripts we use in textual criticism. When Vaticanus and Sinaiticus agree on a reading, it takes significant evidence from other manuscripts to prove they are in error.

We also have a group of manuscripts we call the *Western* text-type. Some scholars call these "missionary texts." Think of a Wycliffe translator working in Africa, learning a language, creating an alphabet, and then translating the Bible into that language. What kind of Bible will they create? Because they are missionaries, they will create a Bible that is, above all else, understandable, which means they will include interpretive information in the translation itself.

One of the more important manuscripts of the Western text-type is the fifth-century Codex D, and quite often the changes made in D had a goal of helping people better understand the biblical text. For example, in Acts 16:16–40 we read of Paul and Silas in prison and of God causing an earthquake to enable their release (v. 26). Eventually, the city magistrates sent word that Paul and Silas could be released. It's natural to ask what changed their minds. Codex D adds to verse 35, "because they remembered the earthquake and were afraid."

As the church expanded westward, the manuscripts needed to be understandable. That's why we find so many expansions and simplifications in these manuscripts. It's why the text of Acts is about 8.5 percent longer in the Western texts than in the Alexandrian texts. As a result, manuscripts from the Western text-type tend not to be as reliable as the Alexandrian, even though they're very old, dating back to the early centuries.

The church in the West turned to Latin, and today we have about ten thousand Latin manuscripts of the New Testament. The Latin Vulgate was the dominant Bible of the church for almost a millennium, and it was based on the Western text-type. As the use of the Greek language dropped off, so did the number of Greek manuscripts of this text-type, but they did continue to be used and copied until the ninth century.

Starting in the late fourth century, it appears that a new text-type was formed called the *Byzantine* text-type. These manuscripts were traditionally associated with Byzantium, the new name for Constantinople (modern Istanbul). When the emperor Constantine legalized Christianity in AD 313, he had fifty Bibles copied. These were probably of the Byzantine text-type.

Because of the role of Constantine in Christian history and a church father named John Chrysostom (d. 407) who aggressively favored this text-type, and because the church in this area continued to use Greek, the Byzantine texts are by far our most common Greek manuscripts. They appear to be a combination of the Alexandrian and Western text-types. We have no examples of a Byzantine text before the fourth century, but by the ninth century, 95 percent of all manuscripts are Byzantine. The Byzantine texts are more uniform than the Western and even the Alexandrian manuscripts, probably because they originated from a relatively small geographical area and would have been controlled by liturgical usage in the church.

When Byzantium fell to the Ottoman Empire in 1453, the Greek scribes fled to Europe with their precious manuscripts, and during the Renaissance, with its emphasis on Greek and Hebrew, this text-type flourished. These Byzantine manuscripts became known as the Majority Text (MT) because there were so many manuscripts. Three Byzantine texts were the primary texts used by Erasmus to edit the first Greek text published on Gutenberg's printing press, and manuscripts based on Erasmus's work became known as the Textus Receptus (TR), the "Received Text." It was a version of the TR that the KJV translators used. (See "The King James Version" later in this chapter for more information.)

For centuries, the Byzantine text-type was all we had. There are thousands of differences among these manuscripts, but in broad strokes, they agree with one another. They have the story of the woman caught in adultery (John 7:53–8:11). They have the longer ending of Mark in which believers handle snakes and drink poison (16:9–20). They have the last line ("for yours is the kingdom . . .") of the Lord's Prayer (Matt 6:13).

In the mid- to late-nineteenth century, archaeologists (and manuscript hunters) started finding more manuscripts that were older than and different from the Byzantine manuscripts. These finds include the Alexandrian manuscripts. The science of textual criticism was developed, especially through the work of Fenton John Anthony Hort (1828–1892) and Brooke Foss Westcott (1825–1901), in order to discover which of the variants most likely conveyed the original wording.

While this is a simplified description of the historical process, it should be enough to help you understand the following discussion.

Famous Variants

To read some skeptics today, you might get the impression that massive parts of the Bible are questionable. But we have already seen that only a relatively few of the 400,000 variants are meaningful and viable. In fact, we have in our Bibles today only two passages of paragraph length that the original authors never wrote: John 7:53–8:11 and Mark 16:9–20. Because of the impact of the KJV, most modern translations keep these two passages in the text, but they set them off typographically to indicate as clearly as possible that they were not part of the original biblical text but were added later.

John 7:53–8:11

The great majority of textual scholars don't regard this passage as authentic. Bruce Metzger says the evidence that these verses are later additions is "overwhelming."[2]

In order to set apart the story of the woman caught in adultery (John 7:53–8:11) from the rest of the gospel, the NIV includes dividing lines above and below the passage, uses a smaller font in italics, and includes this disclaimer: "The earliest manuscripts and many other ancient witnesses do not have John 7:53–8:11. A few manuscripts include these verses, wholly or in part, after John 7:36, John 21:25, Luke 21:38 or Luke 24:53." The ESV double brackets the text and says, "The earliest manuscripts do not include 7:53–8:11."

The following manuscript information for this passage and the next two are drawn primarily from Bruce Metzger and Bart Ehrman's *The Text of the New Testament*.[3] While there are untrained people (and a small handful of scholars) who discount the work of Metzger, they do so at their own peril. Scholars recognize Professor Metzger as one of the finest textual critics of all time, although his humility would probably chafe at my evaluation.

Incidentally, you have to keep references to "Metzger and Ehrman" separate from those to "Ehrman." Metzger was Ehrman's doctoral supervisor, and Ehrman was invited to help with the fourth edition of *The Text of the New Testament*. However, Metzger was not nearly as skeptical of the work of textual criticism as is Ehrman. Metzger said that "it has increased the basis of my personal faith to see the firmness with which these materials have come down to us, with the multiplicity of copies, some of which are very ancient." When asked about whether his scholarship had diluted his faith, Metzger responded, "It has built it. I've asked questions all my life, I've dug into the text, I've studied this thoroughly, and today I know with confidence that my trust in Jesus has been well placed."[4] In contrast, Ehrman abandoned his Christian faith and has serious objections to the accuracy of the Greek manuscripts.

Here are thirteen points that summarize why we should not treat John 7:53–8:11 as original to the text:

1. John 7:53–8:11 are missing from earliest manuscripts ($\mathfrak{P}^{66}$ $\mathfrak{P}^{75}$ Sinaiticus Vaticanus). Alexandrinus is defective at this point (pages are missing), but there doesn't appear to be enough room for 7:53–8:11 to have been included.

2. It's missing from the oldest (syr^c, s) and the best (syr^p) Syriac manuscripts.

3. It's absent in some of the Old Latin, Old Georgian, and Armenian manuscripts.

4. It's not in the best manuscripts of the Peshitta, the Syriac translation of the Bible made in the early third century.

5. It's not referenced in the Arabic version of Tatian's *Diatessaron*, which combined the four gospels but without our passage.

6. No church father writes a commentary on the passage until the twelfth century, and then Euthymius says it's not authentic. The earlier church fathers comment up to John 7:52 and then move directly to comment on John 8:12–20, and several church fathers (e.g., Origen, Chrysostom) commented verse by verse on the biblical book.

7. It's not found in most lectionaries.

8. The first manuscript to have it is D (fifth century), a Western text-type manuscript that was willing to repeat many added readings.

9. Many manuscripts mark it with scholia (critical or explanatory comments), indicating that it's not authentic.

10. Erasmus's number one manuscript omits it. He writes, "The story of the adulterous woman is not contained in the majority of Greek copies."[5]

11. One of the signs that a passage may not be original is that it appears in different locations in the New Testament. Our passage is located after John 7:36; 7:44; or 21:25; or Luke 21:38 or 24:53. If it were authentic, it would appear in only one location.

12. The style and vocabulary are different from the rest of the gospel.

13. It interrupts the flow of Jesus' discourse from chapter 7 of John to chapter 8.

Mark 16:9–20

The other long passage still included in most Bibles today is the longer ending of Mark 16:9–20. In the NIV, it too is set off with a dividing line, smaller italicized font, and this disclaimer: "The earliest manuscripts and some other ancient witnesses do not have verses 9–20." The ending was probably added because it felt inappropriate to some of the ancient scribes to end the gospel on this note of fear: "Trembling and bewildered, the women went out and fled from the tomb. They said nothing to anyone, because they were afraid" (16:8).[6]

Here are twelve points that summarize why we should not treat Mark 16:9–20 as original to the text:

1. Mark 16:9–20 is not found in the two most important manuscripts, Sinaiticus and Vaticanus (fourth century).
2. It's omitted in some manuscripts of the ancient translations (Old Latin, Syriac, Old Armenian, Old Georgian, Ethiopic).
3. Some church fathers knew of manuscripts that did not include it, and many early church fathers don't comment on it (e.g., Clement of Alexandria, Origen).
4. It's not accounted for in Eusebius's numbering system (fourth century).
5. Eusebius said that the accurate copies of Mark ended at 16:8 and the remaining verses were absent from almost all manuscripts.
6. Many manuscripts that include the passage indicate that the older manuscripts lack these verses. Other manuscripts include asterisks or obeli, which mark additions to the text.
7. Jerome included these verses in the Latin Vulgate but said, "Almost all the Greek copies do not have this concluding portion."[7]
8. Erasmus's number one manuscript said that the ending of Mark was uncertain.[8]
9. There are other alternate endings. If this ending were authentic, there would have been no reason to create alternatives.
10. The transition from verse 8 to verse 9 is awkward. The subject of verse 8 is the women, and the implied subject of verse 9 is Jesus but without clarification.
11. The style, grammar, and lexical choices are clearly non-Markan.[9]

The story is included in Alexandrinus and most of the Old Latin manuscripts. Irenaeus and possibly Justin Martyr (mid-second century) knew of it, and Justin Martyr's disciple Tatian included the ending in his second-century *Diatessaron*.

These two passages are the only variants of any substantial length, and all major Bible translations except the KJV make it clear that these passages are not authentic. So when Bart Ehrman says that "most of the changes are not of this magnitude"[10] (referring to both of the passages just mentioned), he is being slightly misleading. *Most*? He should more accurately say that *none* of the remaining textual changes are of this magnitude! In books and interviews, Ehrman complains that scholars object that he "leave[s] people with the impression that there are far more problems with the New Testament than there actually are. What most struck me about this objection was that it has to do with the *impression* left by the book [*Misquoting Jesus*] rather than about anything I actually *say* in the book."[11] But there are good reasons scholars have this objection, because Ehrman repeatedly overstates his case, failing to nuance his words appropriately, as is the case here.

Sentences and Phrases

Moving beyond the two major variants, we find a couple dozen variants that involve one or two verses. The most famous of these is the *Comma Johanneum*, 1 John 5:7b–8a ("Johannine Comma" in English). The words in italics below were added centuries after John wrote the epistle. These words are in the footnotes of most modern translations but are in the text of the KJV: "For there are three that bear record *in heaven, the Father, the Word, and the Holy Ghost: and these three are one. And there are three that bear witness in earth*, the Spirit, and the water, and the blood: and these three agree in one."

This passage proves to be perennially controversial with some people. I have lost count of how many times I have been accused of removing the Trinity from the Bible since I agree that these verses are not original. Thankfully, the doctrine of the Trinity doesn't depend on these verses! Even though modern translations put these verses in a footnote, there are many places in our Bible that do assert the doctrine of the Trinity. But these verses here are not original, and I believe it's better to base doctrine on words we know were written by the New Testament authors.

Here are seven points that summarize why we don't consider this verse to be original to the text:

1. The words occur in only eight late Greek manuscripts: in the text in four[12] and listed as variant readings in four.[13] This means every Greek manuscript until the fourteenth century lacks the words (except for a variant reading in a tenth-century manuscript).

2. They are not quoted by any of the early church fathers until the fifth century, who certainly would have used them in their defense of the Trinity if the words were authentic.

3. The words are absent from all ancient translations (Syriac, Coptic, Armenian, Ethiopic, Arabic, Slavonic) except Latin.

4. They are not present in the Old Latin used by Tertullian, Cyprian, or Augustine.

5. They are not in Jerome's original Latin Vulgate[14] but were added to the Vulgate in the ninth century.

6. The words first appear in a fourth-century Latin treatise, *Liber apologeticus*.

7. The *Comma Johanneum* was not in Erasmus's first or second edition.

How did these words get into the Bible? Erasmus states that they were not original, but due to church pressure, he added them from a suspected forged Greek manuscript[15] in his third edition of the Greek New Testament. And this edition was essentially the basis for the KJV.

In addition to this verse, there are several other verse-long variants that we know are not original. We have already seen that the ending of the Lord's Prayer—"For yours is the kingdom and the power and the glory forever. Amen"—was added centuries later, probably by analogy to 1 Chronicles 29:11–13, presumably because someone thought the real ending was too bland.[16]

The NIV (2011) includes Luke 22:43–44 in the text: "An angel from heaven appeared to him and strengthened him. And being in anguish, he prayed more earnestly, and his sweat was like drops of blood falling to the ground." The footnote at the end of verse 44 reads, "Many early manuscripts do not have verses 43 and 44" (ESV and CSB likewise). The NRSV brackets the text and includes a footnote. The verses are missing from many early manuscripts, but they are cited by the early church fathers, so even if the verses are an addition, it's a very old tradition. UBS gives the omission of the verses an A rating; they clearly are not viable.

John 5:3b–4 and Matthew 17:21, which we discussed earlier, fit in this category as well. Other sentence- or phrase-long variants include Matthew 18:11; 23:14; Mark 7:16; 9:44, 46; 11:26; 15:28; Luke 17:36; 23:17; Acts 8:37; 15:34; 24:6b–8a; 28:29; Romans 16:24; and 1 John 5:7. Kurt Aland and Barbara Aland cite only twenty-one other passages of significant variants, all but five being only a phrase in length.[17]

Words

The remaining variants are no more than a few words, short phrases (marked with italics below), or small portions of sentences. Many of these are obviously unintentional and easy to identify, and determining which variant is original is not difficult.

Daniel Wallace points out where Paul says he was "gentle" (νήπιοι, *nēpioi*), or like "young children" (ἤπιοι, *ēpioi*), among the Thessalonians (1 Thess 2:7); these are meaningful and viable variants (UBS gives νήπιοι a B rating). But an eighth-century manuscript has the variant "horses" (ἵπποι, *hippoi*), hardly a viable variant, and yet it counts as a variant.[18]

Wallace also likes to use the example of John 1:30. John the Baptist says, "A man [ἀνήρ, *anēr*] who comes after me has surpassed me because he was before me." The eighth-century Codex L has "air" (ἀήρ, *aēr*) instead of "man," which is hardly viable, and yet it too counts as a variant.[19]

Other variants appear to be intentional but are easy to explain. An example is found in one of Jesus' sayings in the Sermon on the Mount: "But I say to unto you, That whosoever is angry with a brother *without a cause* shall be in danger of the judgment" (Matt 5:22 KJV, italics added). "Without a cause" is an obvious addition, the kind of addition a scribe would make who thought the command was too extreme. Another example is found in Matthew 27:16 (italics added): "At that time they had a well-known prisoner whose name was *Jesus* Barabbas." You can see why some scribes would not like a prisoner to have the same name as Jesus, so "Jesus" was dropped in most manuscripts.[20]

Other variants are a little more difficult to determine, and some are quite important. Did Paul write his letter to the Ephesians or not? "Paul, an apostle of Christ Jesus by the will of God, to the saints who *are in Ephesus, and* are faithful in Christ Jesus" (Eph 1:1 ESV, italics added). Some manuscripts omit "are in Ephesus and." Does John explicitly call Jesus the only "Son" or the only "God" (John 1:18, discussed in the next chapter)? Thankfully, the doctrine of Jesus' divinity doesn't depend on this textually uncertain phrase.

Two Key Principles

It can be confusing, even discouraging, when someone points out textual variant after textual variant, until we understand two key principles:

1. In the vast majority of cases, and I mean *vast*, the science of textual criticism has given us the original reading, and there are very few cases where it cannot. Even Bart Ehrman agrees: "In a remarkable number of instances—most of them, actually—scholars by and large agree."[21]

2. It is misleading to emphasize how many variants we have while not talking about their significance. As we saw in the previous chapter, there are probably only 373 places where a variant is meaningful and viable.

So what are we to conclude? Are the manuscripts so riddled with variants that we can't confidently get back to the original? I don't think so. The larger variants are clearly not authentic, and none of the variants affect any basic biblical doctrine. They may be important, but they are not significant in terms of our understanding of Jesus and the Gospels.

The King James Version

You may have noticed that most of the famous variants are due to differences in the Greek texts used by the KJV and those used by all modern translations. Be aware that this is an emotional and highly charged topic. Just the other day, my ministry received an email that read, "Do you teach from the King James Bible or a perversion?" My answer: "Neither."

We hear the constant claim from a small but vocal minority of people that the Alexandrian manuscripts are defective, even evil, and that God has preserved his true text in the Majority Text (i.e., the Byzantine text-type). We hear claims that translators of modern translations are evil, dropping out verses for theological reasons.

Let's Look at the Facts

When Erasmus started to compile his Greek Testament in 1515, he relied primarily on three manuscripts. He had a twelfth-century manuscript for the Gospels, and another twelfth-century manuscript for Acts and the Epistles. He also had a third twelfth-century manuscript for Revelation, although it had lost the last six verses (the last leaf of the codex). In other words, the best manuscripts he had to work with had been copied a millennium after Jesus lived.

Erasmus compared the first two manuscripts with a few others (the oldest being a tenth-century minuscule that he rarely used) for his text from Matthew through Jude. He used the third manuscript for Revelation, but for the last six verses he translated from Latin back into Greek. This was the first edition of his Greek text, published in 1516.[22] Erasmus did a second edition in 1519 to clean up hundreds of typographical errors, and this edition was used by Martin Luther and William Tyndale in their German and English translations, respectively. This edition did not include the *Comma Johanneum* (1 John 5:7b–8a). Erasmus published a third edition in 1522 that did include the *Comma Johanneum*, and this edition was, in all reality, the basis for the KJV. Erasmus also did a fourth (1527) and fifth (1535) edition.

Stephanus (the Latin version of his Parisian name, Estienne) published four editions of the Greek text. His first two (1546, 1549) were basically corrections of Erasmus's work based on the Complutensian Polyglot.[23] His third edition (1550) depended more on Erasmus's fourth and fifth editions and was the first to list variants. This was the Greek text used for the Geneva Bible, and for all practical purposes it became the standard Greek text. Stephanus's fourth edition (1551) added verse references.

Theodore Beza published at least nine editions, all quite similar to Stephanus's fourth edition. The 1588–1589 and the 1598 editions were heavily used by the KJV translators, but in reality, the Greek goes through Stephanus back to Erasmus's third edition.

The Elzevirs (uncle and nephew, 1624) used Beza's 1565 edition, and in their second edition (1633), they included an advertising blurb: "Textum *ergo habes, nunc ab omnibus* receptor."—"The text you have is now received by all," hence the name Textus Receptus, the TR. They meant that this text is now viewed as the standard Greek text.

Erasmus		
1.	1516	
2.	1519	Used by Luther and Tyndale
3.	1522	
4.	1527	
5.	1535	

(continued)

Stephanus		
1.	1546	Uses Erasmus 1522
2.	1549	Uses Erasmus 1522
3.	1550	Uses Erasmus 1527 and 1535 Includes variants Used by the Geneva Bible Standard Greek text
4.	1551	Uses verse references
Beza		Basically uses Stephanus 1551
	1588–1589, 1598	Used by KJV
	1565	
Elzevir		Uses Beza 1565
	1624	
	1633	Textus Receptus

Almost no true textual critic uses the TR today. Some people continue to argue that God has preserved his words in the TR, but among the many problems, the insurmountable one they face is, "Which TR?" There are about twenty editions of the TR that are based on the work of Erasmus, and each one of them is different from the others. Bruce Metzger and Bart Ehrman comment, "So superstitious has been the reverence accorded the Textus Receptus that in some cases attempts to criticize or emend it have been regarded as akin to sacrilege. Yet, its textual basis is essentially a handful of late and haphazardly collected minuscule manuscripts, and in a dozen passages its rendering is supported by no known Greek witnesses."[24]

While there are no true textual critics who regard the TR as reflecting the original wording, there are a few who argue that the MT, the Byzantine text, is the purest text-type and goes back to the original.[25] But here we face a similar problem. No two of the Byzantine manuscripts are identical, and the arguments for the superiority of the MT have not swayed many scholars.

To bring this to a practical and personal level, one of the most common questions I'm asked is why the NIV (on whose Bible translation committee I currently serve) drops out seventeen verses.[26] First of all, I explain that they are not "dropped out"; they are still there, just in the footnotes. Second, this is not unique to the NIV; it is true of all modern translations. (I don't consider the NKJV a modern translation, as it was a stylistic update of the KJV.) I understand how disconcerting it can be to be to read your English Bible and suddenly notice missing verse numbers. John, chapter 5, verses 1, 2, 3 . . . and then 5. Where did verse 4 go? A little history can help us understand why verse four and other verses are "missing."

Stephen Langton (d. 1228) added chapter divisions to his Latin Vulgate. Robertus Stephanus added verses to his Greek and Latin text (1551). Theodore Beza's Latin Bible had verses for the Old and New Testaments (1555), and the Geneva Bible (1557) was the first English Bible with verse numbers. However, all these verses were assigned based on the Latin Vulgate and on Erasmus's Greek text, both of which included the seventeen verses. None of the major English translations include the verses, and the references to the verses may or may not be included in the text, depending on the publisher's decision. Hence, John 5:4 is not in the text, not because we dropped it out of the Bible, but because someone other than John added it in.[27]

So are modern translations "perversions" for relying on the Alexandrian and not the Byzantine texts? Of course not. As we have seen, no major biblical doctrine is taught only in these verses (unless you want to handle snakes and drink poison), and Alexandrian texts are closer in time to the lives of Jesus, Paul, and the other biblical writers, and show substantially fewer alterations. I would never call either the Byzantine or Alexandrian manuscripts "perverse" as they both contain a clear presentation of the gospel and do not lead people into error.

On a final note, it's unfortunate that so much attention is spent on where the Alexandrian and Byzantine texts are different, when in fact they are basically the same in the vast majority of passages. For example, Peter Williams compares five different Greek texts on John 1:1–14 and finds that all five are identical.[28]

Conclusion

Text-types are a theoretical construct for grouping together manuscripts that show similar tendencies. Textual critics are confident that the Alexandrian manuscripts are the best manuscripts for determining what was originally written. Most of the famous variants have to do with the differences between the manuscripts behind the King James Version and all modern translations. Even some of the passages that often evoke the greatest emotional response, such as the *Comma Johanneum* with its explicit reference to the Trinity, are not original, and we should base our theology on words we know the biblical writers actually wrote.

Notes

1. The term has gone out of technical use today, but for our purposes it is sufficiently descriptive.
2. Bruce Metzger, *A Textual Commentary on the Greek New Testament*, 2nd ed. (Stuttgart: Deutsche Bibelgesellschaft/German Bible Society, 1994), 187.
3. Bruce M. Metzger and Bart D. Ehrman, *The Text of the New Testament: Its Transmission, Corruption, and Restoration*, 4th ed. (Oxford: Oxford University Press, 2005), 319–21.
4. Quoted in Lee Strobel, *The Case for the Real Jesus: A Journalist Investigates Current Attacks on the Identity of Christ* (Grand Rapids: Zondervan, 2007), 99.
5. Quoted in Peter J. Williams, *Can We Trust the Gospels?* (Wheaton, IL: Crossway, 2018), 114.
6. For an academic discussion of this passage, see R. T. France, *The Gospel of Mark*, New International Greek Testament Commentary (Grand

Rapids: Eerdmans, 2002), 685–88; Paul L. Danove, *The End of Mark's Story: A Methodological Study* (Leiden: Brill, 1993).

7. Quoted in Metzger and Ehrman, *Text of the New Testament*, 322.

8. Cited in Williams, *Can We Trust the Gospels?*, 114.

9. See Metzger, *Textual Commentary*, 104.

10. Bart D. Ehrman, *Misquoting Jesus: The Story behind Who Changed the Bible and Why* (San Francisco: HarperOne, 2005), 69.

11. Ehrman, *Misquoting Jesus*, 259.

12. 629 (Codex Ottobonianus) is fourteenth century; 918 is sixteenth century; 2318 is eighteenth century. On 61 (Codex Montfortianus), see the note below.

13. 88[v.r] (sixteenth-century addition to the fourteenth-century Codex Regius); 221[v.r] (tenth century); 429[v.r] (sixteenth century); 636[v.r] (sixteenth century).

14. The Latin codices are Fuldensis (AD 541–46) and Amiatinus (AD 76).

15. The manuscript was minuscule 61, Codex Montfortianus. Bruce Metzger recounts the story behind the forgery. Erasmus did not include the words because he could find no Greek manuscript with the words, but he felt the pressure to insert the *Comma Johanneum* "in future editions if a single Greek manuscript could be found that contained the passage. At length, such a copy was found— or was made to order. As it now appears, the Greek manuscript had probably been written in Oxford about 1520 by a Franciscan friar named Froy (or Roy), who took the disputed words from the Latin Vulgate. Erasmus inserted the passage in his third edition (1522), but in a lengthy footnote that was included in his volume of annotations, he intimated his suspicion that the manuscript had been prepared expressly in order to confute him" (*Text of the New Testament*, 146–47).

16. These words do not occur in any of the earliest manuscripts, and the manuscript tradition has alternate forms, a sure sign of inauthenticity; see Metzger for documentation (*Textual Commentary*, 13–14).

17. Kurt Aland and Barbara Aland, *The Text of the New Testament: An Introduction to the Critical Editions and to the Theory and Practice of Modern Textual Criticism*, trans. Erroll F. Rhodes (Grand Rapids: Eerdmans, 1987), 300–307. The five longer variants are at Matthew 16:2b–3; Luke 9:56; 11:2; 22:43–44; and Acts 28:16. See my website www.MissingBibleVerses.com for more information.

18. See Darrell L. Bock and Daniel B. Wallace, *Dethroning Jesus: Exposing Popular Culture's Quest to Unseat the Biblical Christ* (Nashville: Nelson,

2007), 54; see also Metzger and Ehrman, *Text of the New Testament*, 328–30.

19. See Daniel B. Wallace, ed., *Revisiting the Corruption of the New Testament: Manuscript, Patristic, and Apocryphal Evidence* (Grand Rapids: Kregel Academic, 2011), 41.

20. For a discussion of other variants, see Craig L. Blomberg, *The Historical Reliability of the New Testament* (Nashville: B&H Academic, 2016), 633–39; Ehrman, *Misquoting Jesus*, 90–99.

21. Ehrman, *Misquoting Jesus*, 94.

22. For a fuller description of the process, see Metzger and Ehrman, *Text of the New Testament*, 143–45; Daniel B. Wallace, "Erasmus and the Book That Changed the World Five Hundred Years Ago," *Unio cum Christo* 2, no. 2 (October 2016): 29–48.

23. A polyglot is a book that has the text in different languages in parallel columns. The Complutensian Polyglot contains the Old and New Testaments, the latter having the Greek and the Latin Vulgate side by side. The New Testament was completed before the work of Erasmus, but its publication was delayed until the Old Testament (Hebrew, Latin Vulgate, Septuagint) was complete and the book would be sanctioned by Pope Leo X. It was published in 1520.

24. Metzger and Ehrman, *Text of the New Testament*, 152.

25. See Maurice A. Robinson and William G. Pierpont, *The New Testament in the Original Greek: Byzantine Textform*, 2nd ed. (Southborough, MA: Chilton, 2005).

26. Matthew 17:21; 18:11; 23:14; Mark 7:16; 9:44; 9:46; 11:26; 15:28; Luke 17:36; 23:17; John 5:4; Acts 8:37; 15:34; 24:7; 28:29; Romans 16:24; 1 John 5:7; also John 7:53–8:11 and Mark 16:9–20.

27. For more on "the King James Debate," see D. A. Carson, *The King James Version: A Plea for Realism* (Grand Rapids: Baker, 1979).

28. Williams uses Erasmus's 1516 edition; the 1979, 1993, and 2012 editions of the German Bible Society; the 2005 edition by Robinson; the 2010 edition by Michael Holmes under the auspices of the Society of Biblical Literature (SBL); and the 2017 edition made at Tyndale House, Cambridge, England (*Can We Trust the Gospels?*, 119).

Chapter 9

DIGGING MUCH DEEPER INTO TEXTUAL CRITICISM

I will warn you in advance. The discussion in this chapter may get a little complicated in places, but because textual criticism and questions about the manuscripts of the Greek Testament are the focus of much of the discussion today, especially from Bart Ehrman, many questions need to be answered. I encourage you to push through to the end. It's worth the investment! We'll first talk about variants and then manuscripts.

Who Is Bart Ehrman?

Much of this chapter is in debate with Dr. Bart Ehrman, and it is helpful to know a little about him. He uses his own spiritual pilgrimage as a persuasive tool in debates.

Ehrman was a Christian who attended the conservative Moody Bible Institute and then Wheaton College. His struggles began there with what he saw as contradictions in the Bible, which led to a growing skepticism about the integrity of the entire Greek Testament. He then earned an MDiv and PhD at Princeton Seminary under the tutelage of one of the world's leading textual critics, Dr. Bruce Metzger (who disagrees with Ehrman's skepticism). Ehrman has continued his journey, and today he calls himself a "happy agnostic." His books have made it to the *New York Times* and Amazon bestseller lists, especially *Misquoting Jesus*,[1] and he has appeared on many radio and television shows. He is a world-class textual scholar and debater.

Variants

Let's focus first on the issue of variants, asking how many there are and, more importantly, why they are, or are not, significant.

How Do We Count Variants?

First, how many variants are there? Numbers vary widely from much lower to much higher than 400,000, even 1.5 million if you include spelling and nonsense variants.[2] But how do textual critics actually count variants?

Let's say we have a passage of ten words in which one word is in question. One hundred manuscripts read "John" (Ἰωάνης, *iōanēs*, spelled with one *nu*), ten have "John" (Ἰωάννης, *iōannēs*, spelled with two *nus*), three read "Peter," and one has no name. Textual critics say there are four variants. In other words, it doesn't matter how many manuscripts have the same variant; for a variant to be counted, it only has to be unique.

This gets interesting when we realize we have more than 5,600 Greek manuscripts of the New Testament. Some are fragmentary, and some are complete. The average Greek manuscripts are four hundred pages long, although most of the longer manuscripts are from later centuries. One of the reasons we have so many variants is that we have so many manuscripts. We are thankful to have so many, since they give us confidence that we can get back to the original text in 99 percent of the variants.

You may think that with so many manuscripts, we can simply "count noses" to decide on the original reading—whichever variant occurs in the most manuscripts must be original. But it's not that simple. Let's say Paul writes a letter to the church in Rome, and in Romans 5:1 he uses the indicative ἔχομεν (*exomen*), "we have peace with God." Tertius makes a copy. One manuscript is sent to Ephesus, where ten copies are made (total: eleven). The other is sent to Rome. The manuscript with the indicative is copied ten times (total: eleven), but the eleventh copy mistakenly shifts to the subjunctive ἔχωμεν (*exōmen*), and 500 more copies are made of that manuscript (total: 501). Twenty-two manuscripts have one reading, and 501 have another. Which variant is original? See the diagram below. If you think this is confusing, you ought to try actually practicing textual criticism!

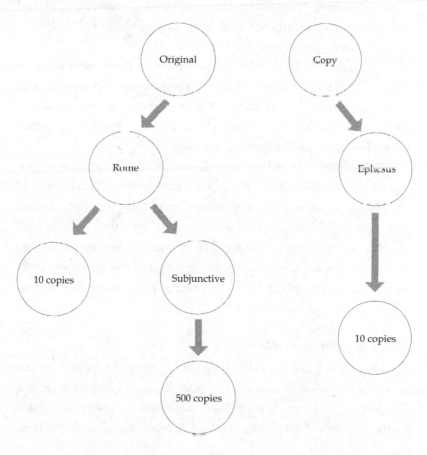

The point is that you can't simply count the number of manuscripts; you have to "weigh" them. The 501 manuscripts that have the subjunctive are no more significant than the twenty-two that have the indicative. A textual critic weighs the evidence by looking at the internal evidence ("we have" versus "let us have") and the external evidence (manuscript text-type, versions, and patristic quotations) and makes a judgment call.

How Many Words Have Variants?

It's a different question to ask how many words have variant readings. Saying that we have more variants (400,000) than words (137,801)[3] gives the mistaken impression that every word is suspect. As a random sample, I picked the salutation to the Ephesians in 1:1–2, and the longest sentence in the Greek Testament, Ephesians 1:3–14. I'm using the 28th edition of Nestle-Aland.

Ephesians 1:1–2 has thirty words with only three variants listed; *twenty-five of the words have no variants listed in the NA text.* I'm sure other manuscripts do have variants for these two verses, but they're not among the 30,000 variants listed by NA. The only one of consequence is whether the words "in Ephesus" are original.

In Ephesians 1:3–14, there are 202 words with only fourteen variants listed in NA28; *187 of the words have no listed variants.* The only one of any real consequence is whether verse 11 should read "we were chosen" (ἐκληρώθημεν, *eklērōthēmen*) or "we were called" (ἐκλήθημεν, *eklēthēmen*).

The vast majority of the words in these fourteen verses have no variants among the manuscripts, and only two variants have any effect on the meaning of the passage. So how helpful is it to say that we have more variants than we have words?[4]

The Significance of Variants

Darrel Bock and Daniel Wallace cite the Bart Ehrman interview with the *Charlotte Observer* (December 17, 2005) in which he says, "We have copies that were made hundreds of years later—in most cases, many hundreds of years later. And these copies are all different from one another."[5] Elsewhere Ehrman states that "we have only error-ridden copies, and the vast majority of these are centuries removed from the originals and different from them, evidently, in thousands of ways."[6]

The lack of precision in Ehrman's statements is significant. It's true that most of our manuscripts are from hundreds of years later, but that fact is irrelevant. Very few textual critics use late manuscripts to determine the original text. And they are not "all different." It's true that there are many differences among them, but there are more that are the same than are different. Saying "all different" gives the impression that there are more differences than similarities—a statement that simply is not true. Ehrman seems to admit this himself.

> It is probably safe to say that the copying process of early Christian texts was by and large a "conservative" process. The scribes ... were intent on "conserving" the textual tradition they were passing on. Their ultimate concern was not to modify the tradition, but to preserve it for themselves and for those who would follow them. Most scribes, no doubt, tried to do a faithful job in making sure that the text they reproduced was the same text they inherited.[7]

It is hard to reconcile this statement with his frequent rhetorically powerful statements about the "error-ridden" copies that are "all different."

In his debate with Wallace, Ehrman says if you compare second or third-century manuscripts with those from the eleventh century, "there will be enormous differences, tons of differences."[8] But this fact is hardly relevant. Textual critics don't use eleventh-century Byzantine manuscripts to discover the original wording, except in rare cases. But even if they did, *enormous* is an overstatement. Fourth-century Alexandrian and eleventh-century Byzantine manuscripts have more similarities than differences.[9] Besides, we have only twelve manuscripts from the second century and sixty-four from the third, and most of these are fragmentary. On what basis can Bart Ehrman say there are "enormous differences, tons of differences" when we are dealing with fragments of seventy-six manuscripts?

The facts can also be argued in reverse. If there were no variants, we would be safe to assume someone artificially destroyed the manuscripts with alternate readings. This is what happened with the Qur'an when the caliph Uthman produced a single text and destroyed all other copies in ca. AD 650.[10] There are very few variants because there are very few manuscripts. The fact of variants in the New Testament manuscripts gives us a more historically reliable basis on which to talk about the original text.

In *Misquoting Jesus*, Ehrman says, "We can't interpret the words of the New Testament if we don't know what the words were," and "We don't have the original words."[11] This type of rhetorical flourish is misleading, giving the impression that we don't know what *any* of the words are. But in the vast majority of the variants, we *can* tell what the original is, and thousands of the words in the New Testament have no viable variant readings at all.

The point is this: we should not talk about variants without at the same time speaking about the significance of the variants. We should not point out the thousands of variants without at the same time clarifying that most of the variants are neither meaningful nor viable. Even though Ehrman repeatedly emphasizes the enormous number of variants, elsewhere he says, "To be sure, of all the hundreds of thousands of textual changes found among our manuscripts, most of them are completely insignificant, immaterial, of no real importance."[12]

Manuscripts

Now let's shift focus from variants to manuscripts.

Copies of Copies

Bart Ehrman is famous for his line that we don't even have "copies of the copies of the copies of the original"[13] New Testament documents, giving the impression that the copies we do have are so far removed from the originals that they can't be trusted. He bases his claim partially on his belief that the materials of the manuscripts would survive only a few decades.

The facts are considerably different. George Houston did an exhaustive study showing that library books would often last 150 to 200 years.[14] Craig Evans cites Houston's summation:

> The evidence from our collections indicates that a usable lifetime of about 100 to 125 years was common and can reasonably be considered the norm; a small but significant number of manuscripts were still usable some 300 years after they were first created; and on rare occasions a manuscript might last, it seems, for half a millennium.[15]

Evans adds, "Late fourth- or early fifth-century Codex Bezae (D) was repaired 'between 830 and 850,'[16] some four centuries after it had been produced. Many other biblical codices show signs of re-inking, correcting, and annotations hundreds of years after they were produced, which again testifies to their great longevity."[17]

Even if the characters were fading, they could be reinked, each character being carefully traced. Vaticanus was reinked six hundred years after being written.[18] Even in the fourth edition of *The Text of the New Testament*, Bart Ehrman and Bruce Metzger admit that a manuscript could have been copied directly from a manuscript that was hundreds of years old.[19]

Daniel Wallace cites Tertullian's comment (early third century) that the "authentic" writings of the apostles were still present (*Prescription against Heretics* 36).[20] Even if "authentic" doesn't mean "original," it does indicate that Tertullian believed there were *reliable* copies of the New Testament manuscripts still present one hundred years after the events they report. The problem is that *authenticae* could refer to the "authentic" (i.e., original) autographs or else "unmutilated" copies of the autographs. Craig Evans prefers the latter interpretation. In *Prescription against Heretics* 36.1–2, Tertullian writes:

Come now, you who would indulge a better curiosity, if you would apply it to the business of your salvation, run over to the apostolic churches, in which the very thrones of the apostles are still pre-eminent in their places, in which their own authentic writings [*ipsae authenticae litterae eorum*] are read, uttering the voice and representing the face of each of them severally. Achaia is very near you, (in which) you find Corinth. Since you are not far from Macedonia, you have Philippi; (and there too) you have the Thessalonians. Since you are able to cross to Asia, you get Ephesus. Since, moreover, you are close upon Italy, you have Rome, from which there comes even into our own hands the very authority (of apostles themselves).[21]

Daniel Wallace also points out an interesting truth about two Greek manuscripts.[22] 𝔓[75] (third century) and Vaticanus (fourth century) show a strong agreement. 𝔓[75] is about 125 years older than Vaticanus, but we believe Vaticanus was not copied from 𝔓[75] but from a document predating 𝔓[75]. He concludes, "The combination of these two manuscripts in a particular reading must surely go back to the *very beginning of the second century*."[23] "Copies of the copies of the copies of the original" could now become "copies of the original."

It is true that many of our later manuscripts could be copies of copies of copies, but that's irrelevant for our purposes. Scholars rely on the manuscripts from the early centuries, which could in fact be copies, or copies of copies, of the original.

But another point should be emphasized. In his debate with Wallace, Ehrman says about a manuscript of Mark, "It's a copy probably of a copy made a few years later, which is a copy of a copy made a few years earlier, which is a copy of a copy made a few years earlier, and so on and so on. There have been innumerable stages between the original and our first copy."[24]

But how does he know this? How does he know how many generations of manuscripts existed between the autograph and the manuscript in question? He can't, because as he admits, he doesn't have the intervening manuscripts. Maybe there were ten, maybe five, perhaps one. He has no way of knowing. Again, this type of rhetorical flourish may dazzle and amaze a university audience, but fact-checking scholars know it is an argument without merit.

How Many Early Manuscripts?

How many early manuscripts do we currently have?[25]

- We have one fragment of a manuscript possibly from the end of the first century, but more likely it is from the first half of the second century. It's called $\mathfrak{P}^{52}$. John 18:31–33 is on one side, and 18:37–38 on the other.
- We have as many as twelve manuscripts from the second century, containing fragments of three of the gospels, nine of Paul's letters, Acts, Hebrews, and Revelation.
- We have sixty-four manuscripts from the third century, mostly fragments.
- We have forty-eight manuscripts from the fourth century.

This totals 124 manuscripts within three hundred years, and "the whole NT text is found in this collection multiple times."[26] Since the emperor Diocletian ordered all Christian texts destroyed in AD 303, and since manuscripts written on papyrus are biodegradable, the fact that we have this many manuscripts is remarkable.

Looking at the data from a different direction, Wallace points out that we have parts of 43 percent of all New Testament verses within 150 years of the autographs.[27] This should not surprise us. As the church exploded throughout the Roman Empire, and explode it did, believers brought their manuscripts and read them faithfully. Both the Roman governor Pliny (in *Epistles* 10.96) and the early church father Justin Martyr tell us that the Christians were faithful to meet once a week and among other things read "the memoirs of the apostles or the writings of the prophets" (*First Apology* 67). For this to happen, numerous manuscripts had to be transcribed.

Along with the Greek, we also have many early translations of the New Testament. While there are difficulties in moving from a translation of Latin, Coptic, Syriac, and other languages back into Greek, these thousands of manuscripts do help us determine what the Greek originally said. In addition, we have about one million citations of the New Testament in the early church fathers. Bruce Metzger and Bart Ehrman comment that if we had no Greek manuscripts, the writings of the church fathers would be sufficient to reconstruct "practically the entire New Testament."[28]

What this means is that the textual critic has a significant amount of data to work with in determining the original reading of the autographs.

Sloppy Scribes

Bart Ehrman has a strong distrust of the earliest scribes who copied the earliest manuscripts. By "earliest," I assume he means the ones from the second and third centuries. In a debate with Daniel Wallace, he said, "Scribes just couldn't spell, nor did they care. Scribes were often incompetent or they were sleepy or they were inattentive, and so they made mistakes."[29] A bit later in the debate, he said, "Earliest scribes were much worse than the later scribes. They certainly made a lot more accidental changes. They may have made a lot more intentional changes. And there is no way for us to know."[30] As a result, he discounts the quality of their work:

> Because they [the scribes] were not highly trained to perform this kind of work, they were more prone to make more mistakes than professional scribes would have been. This explains why our *earliest* copies of the early Christian writings tend to vary more frequently from one another and from later copies than do the later copies (say, of the Middle Ages) from one another.[31]

It is true that the scribes of the second and third centuries don't appear for the most part to be literary scribes, people intent on producing works of art. But that doesn't mean they were all unlearned and sloppy or inaccurate. While this description may be a little more applicable to the manuscripts of the Western text-type and to a few of our papyri (e.g., $\mathfrak{P}^{47}$ $\mathfrak{P}^{72}$), it certainly does not describe the bulk of our early papyri or the great uncials of the fourth century.[32]

An important distinction needs to be made between what is called the "documentary" hand and the "literary" hand." The distinction had to do with the style of the writing and not the accuracy of the scribe's work. The literary hand was concerned with beauty and style, much like calligraphy today. The documentary hand tended to be more basic with less flourish, and it was used when writing on more practical topics such as letters and shopping lists, but also for contracts and tax receipts. The classical scholar Colin Roberts shows that Christian manuscripts have certain characteristics shared with other writings of the "documentary hand" type. They tend to be in the codex form, use abbreviations, have "unpretentious" scripts, and use punctuation and paragraphing.[33]

But it is a mistake to assume that because the scribes wrote with less flourish, somehow they were less careful. It's safe to assume that a business owner would expect contracts and tax receipts to be accurate. Zachary Cole remarks, "In reality, there is no evidence to assume a necessary connection between *calligraphy* and *care* in transcription . . . [Roberts] simply makes the point that early Christian copyists appear to have been trained to copy documents rather than works of literature—yet *trained* they were!"[34]

Cole cites further studies by Kim Haines-Eitzen and Alan Mugridge,[35] who argue that the earliest scribes were very much trained and competent, showing characteristics of being skilled in both documentary and literary styles (citing $\mathfrak{P}^{45}$ $\mathfrak{P}^{46}$ and $\mathfrak{P}^{75}$).[36]

Starting with Constantine (AD 331) and his request to Eusebius to produce fifty Bibles, we see scribal work being done in a smaller area (around Byzantium), with more controls, and in better conditions, such as in a scriptorium, so we should expect that the number of scribal changes would lessen and the literary style of the manuscripts would heighten. It is from this time period on that thousands of manuscripts have survived into the present, but these later manuscripts, especially the medieval manuscripts, are of lesser value for determining the original text than the earlier manuscripts.

In summary, Cole comments, "When we look at the early manuscripts themselves, what we find is that they clearly are not the work of incompetent fanatics. Rather, most of them bear the marks of trained and capable scribes who blended techniques of documentary and literary writing styles. So much for 'amateurs.'"[37] Daniel Wallace argues that the early scribes don't appear to have been messy transcribers; rather, they give the impression that they were accountants and "bean counters," people who by nature would have been careful and accurate.[38] Craig Evans says "he has personally examined originals or facsimiles of all the pre-Constantinian manuscripts (pre–AD 325), and not one is written in an informal scrawl that might indicate sloppy copying by barely literate scribes."[39]

Beyond this, there is an argument for the accuracy of the early scribes. When papyri from the second, third, and fourth centuries began to be discovered, we learned that the papyri included no new variant that scholars believe is an authentic reading.[40] In other words, we already had the original text somewhere in our existing variants. All the papyri do is give us an earlier date for readings we already knew from later manuscripts. Jacob Peterson agrees: "If the bulk of the papyri discovered at the beginning of the twentieth century and all other manuscripts since then have not resulted in major revisions of our critical editions, then this attests to a remarkably stable text that can reliably be reconstructed even without them."[41] This is a tribute to the scribes who, while making mistakes, were quite careful and faithful in the copying process.

Craig Evans also cites the work of Lonnie Bell,[42] who investigated "thirteen second- and third-century papyri and one parchment . . . He finds that as a rule these papyri do not exhibit 'laxity, carelessness, or willingness/openness to change the text.' Bell's findings are consistent with the observations others have made, to the effect that the early papyri do not contain any surprising readings."[43]

Bart Ehrman has not proven his point, and this is a pivotal part of his argument.

Early Changes

Bart Ehrman and others also make the charge that the early scribes made more mistakes and intentional changes than later scribes, but there are once again serious objections to this claim.

The first is the scarcity of early papyri. According to the Institut für neutestamentliche Textforschung, the official body that maintains the formal list of manuscripts, there are eighty-seven papyri from the first four centuries (not including papyri marked as from the fourth to fifth century). However, all but five are fragments ($\mathfrak{P}^{45}$ $\mathfrak{P}^{46}$ $\mathfrak{P}^{66}$ $\mathfrak{P}^{72}$ $\mathfrak{P}^{75}$), and there is little overlap in content among these five papyri.[44]

- $\mathfrak{P}^{45}$ covers the Gospels and Acts (mostly fragments).
- $\mathfrak{P}^{46}$ includes Paul (mostly fragments).
- $\mathfrak{P}^{66}$ has John.
- $\mathfrak{P}^{72}$ includes 1 and 2 Peter and Jude.
- $\mathfrak{P}^{75}$ has Luke and John (half are fragments).[45]

As far as I can tell, Ehrman never gives the evidence for his claim, and I don't see how he can reach this conclusion based on so little evidence. His conclusion certainly cannot be reached by comparing the papyri; there is insufficient overlap of content. You can download my list of papyri from my website,[46] and I encourage you to go to the website of the Center for the Study of New Testament Manuscripts and see their wonderful images of many of the papyri.[47] You will start to appreciate how difficult this work is and how the evidence urges caution.

A second objection is that recent work has shown to be false this claim that the early scribes made more mistakes and intentional changes than later scribes. The earliest manuscripts do not show a freewheeling attitude toward changing the manuscripts. In fact, it can be argued that we have a relatively stable text, especially in its macro structure, despite the minor variants. Zachary Cole cites the similarities of the uncials Sinaiticus (01) and Vaticanus (03), and the papyri $\mathfrak{P}^{75}$, $\mathfrak{P}^1$, $\mathfrak{P}^4$, $\mathfrak{P}^{64}$ and $\mathfrak{P}^{77}$, which show a strong similarity with the uncials as proof of a stable text.

It is also important to note that there were controls in place in the early centuries:

- The autograph (and perhaps its initial copy) would have been available for consultation and control.
- The writings would have been respected as authoritative, and there is little evidence that the scribes were trying to change the message of the text wholesale.
- The fact that scribes made corrections suggests, at least in some situations, that their desire was to be accurate, correcting what they felt was an incorrect reading.[48]
- As was true in their early Jewish heritage, Christians read their documents outloud (1 Tim 4:13),[49] and people would have memorized what they heard. This certainly would have helped standardize the text.
- Some of the earliest scribes would have been Jewish, inheriting the Jewish near obsession for accuracy.
- If there had been serious changes to the text in the first century and the beginning of the second century, it is nearly impossible to explain the relative uniformity of the text in the third and fourth century.[50]
- Appeal to how Matthew and Luke were willing to modify Mark is irrelevant. Matthew and Luke were not creating a new recension of Mark; they were writing their own gospel.
- While minor changes were certainly made in the early manuscripts, there is no evidence that major changes were made that

have since gone unnoticed. Once copies started to be distributed, they would provide checks and balances to one another, maybe not so much in the incidentals but certainly in preventing whole-sale change. The two largest variants, the story of the woman caught in adultery in John 8 and the longer ending of Mark 16, have left significant evidence they were later insertions (see the next chapter). Not only are they not present in the best manu-scripts, but many manuscripts include scholia (marginal notes), indicating that the scribe knew the passages were inauthentic. The existence of multiple manuscripts provides the checks and balances they needed.

Finally, comparing the earliest manuscripts with medieval man-uscripts is not really relevant. Yes, there are fewer variants among the Majority Text manuscripts than among the earlier manuscripts, which is to be expected, considering the historical realities of the Enlightenment and the Reformation. But the real issue is a comparison between the earliest manuscripts and what we now believe is the origi-nal text (or close to it).

I should also point out that the charge that the early scribes were fanatical Christians bent on manipulating the text for their theologi-cal purposes fails at another point. There is no indication that all the scribes were Christians. If I had been a wealthy first-century Christian or a leader of my church and wanted a copy of a biblical writing, why wouldn't I want to go to a scribe who would do a faithful job, regardless of their beliefs?

Earliest (Missing) Changes

In an interesting twist, but one that is central to his public pre-sentations, Bart Ehrman argues that we have no way of knowing how many errors crept into the manuscripts *before* the manuscripts we do have. In his debate with Daniel Wallace, he says: "How many mistakes have crept into the text before we start getting copies? There is no way to know, because we don't have earlier copies."[51] Later he says, "There probably were even more accidental changes in the years *before* we have surviving manuscripts ... Who was copying the manuscripts to begin with? Most people couldn't read; most people couldn't write. Who copied the manuscripts? ... Probably whoever the guy was in the church who could read something copied the manuscripts."[52] In Ehrman's thinking, this includes the adding of stories wholesale, comparable to the story of the woman caught in adultery (John 7:53–8:11) and the longer ending of Mark (16:9–20). And a little later, Ehrman asks, "How many stories were added before our earliest manuscripts? We have no way of knowing. They may have been some of our favorites.[53]

But how can he legitimately suggest that stories *might* have been added before there was any evidence? How can he say "probably" when there is zero evidence; we don't have the manuscripts. The burden of proof is surely on Ehrman to bring forth some evidence, any evidence, that significant alterations and additions were made prior to the manuscripts we do possess. I assume he would argue that there were changes to the earliest manuscripts we *do* have, and this suggests more changes were made *before* our earliest manuscripts. But as we've seen, there were no wholesale changes in our earliest manuscripts—just minor ones.

The reason we know that the story of the adulterous woman and the longer ending of Mark were added is that we have manuscript evidence, but they were added not in the first hundred years but a century or two later, when we do have manuscript evidence. (The longer ending was probably added in the mid-second century, and the adulterous woman in the third century.) Ehrman's statement strikes me as rhetorical manipulation. Craig Blomberg rightly says that Ehrman's claim is "sheer hypothesis unsubstantiated by any actual data."[54]

In fact, the issue of burden of proof is central to the debate. Ehrman repeatedly insists that people such as myself prove that the earliest scribes did not change or add to the manuscripts as they were copying. However, I think the burden of proof lies on whomever makes an assertion. Ehrman's entire reconstruction is based on the unprovable assumption of significant scribal corruption, not just scribal variations but wholesale corruption, significantly changing the text and even adding whole stories. But his only "proof" is his insistence that his critics prove their position. That's not proof.

Competing Theologies

The idea that there were different sets of beliefs in the early church that conflicted with each other was originally argued by a German scholar named F. C. Baur 150 years ago, and it has resurfaced in the work of Bart Ehrman.[55]

Obviously, some differences in the early church existed relative to the relationship between Judaism and Christianity, but the council at Jerusalem (Acts 15) made a formal decision that a Gentile did not have to be circumcised in order to become a Christian, and that ended the conflict. Some of the Corinthians denied the reality of a physical resurrection (1 Cor 15), and the Thessalonian church was confused or misled about Christ's return, but these were local beliefs never shared by mainstream Christianity.

The second century saw the rise of three heresies, with fingers going back into the first century, which Ehrman sees as competing theologies, with some scribes changing the biblical text to confront what they felt were false teachings. *Adoptionism* denied the full divinity of Jesus, believing him to be only human. According to this view, God adopted him at his baptism (Matt 3:17) and left him before his death (Matt 27:46). So Ehrman makes his challenge that scribes changed the biblical text to claim that Jesus was fully God (Luke 2:33; 3:22; John 1:18; 1 Tim 3:16) in order to confront this false teaching. He uses the phrase "orthodox scribes" to describe the scribes who made these changes; their beliefs eventually won (hence "orthodox"), and their beliefs were formalized in the Nicene Creed.

The second heresy was *docetism*, a denial of the full humanity of Christ, so Ehrman's challenge here is that orthodox scribes changed the original text of Luke 22:19, 43–44; 24:12; and 22:51–52 to affirm Christ's divinity. *Gnosticism*, the third heresy, split Jesus into two parts, the material and the divine, so the supposed orthodox scribes changed Hebrews 2:9 to emphasize the unity of Christ's being (also Mark 15:34 and 1 John 4:2–3). I will discuss some of these verses later.

The basic answer is straightforward. Adoptionism, Docetism, and Gnosticism were never accepted by mainstream Christianity. It is not as if Baur was right and there were all kinds of different ideas about who Jesus was floating around and no one knew the truth for sure. The apostles guarded the teaching of the true gospel. While some local groups taught aberrant theology, they were judged to be heretical based on what the core of the church had always believed. This topic has already surfaced in our discussion of canon, where I argued that the (ontological) canon was established as soon as the authoritative books were written, and this core was always present to define orthodoxy and heresy.

When Variants Affect the Meaning of the Passage

Since time does not permit a detailed discussion of all the verses Bart Ehrman uses, I want to recite his conclusion and deal with the seven passages he references:

> Was Jesus an angry man? Was he completely distraught in the face of death? Did he tell his disciples that they could drink poison without being harmed? Did he let an adulteress off the hook with nothing but a mild warning? Is the doctrine of the Trinity explicitly taught in the New Testament? Is Jesus actually called the "unique God" there? Does the New Testament indicate that even the Son of God himself does not know when the end will come? The questions go on and on.[56]

No one debates the point that textual-critical issues can affect the meaning of a passage, even if the variant doesn't affect a core theological topic. The real question is whether we can determine which of the variants reflect the original text, and what these variants mean.

Was Jesus an Angry Man? (Mark 1:41)

> Jesus was *indignant* [i.e., angry]. He reached out his hand and touched the man. "I am willing," he said. "Be clean!" (NIV, italics added)

> *Moved with pity*, he stretched out his hand and touched him and said to him, "I will; be clean." (ESV, italics added)

Ehrman believes the original reading was that Jesus "became angry" at the leper and an orthodox scribe changed it to "moved with compassion." This, he concludes, would mean Jesus was an angry person and would affect how we read the book of Mark as a whole.[57]

I agree that Mark could have used the Greek word for "angry," although the external evidence for the reading "angry" is quite poor, being found in only one fifth-century Western text-type Greek manuscript (Bezae) and three Latin manuscripts. However, the internal evidence for "indignant" is strong; there is no reason for a scribe to have changed "compassion" to "indignant."

But the issue of the variants has no impact here on how we view Jesus. We already know that Jesus can respond in anger, so this is not a major change that significantly alters our view of Jesus. Mention of Jesus' anger directed at the religious leaders in Mark 3:5 has no variant, so apparently the scribes did not have an issue with Jesus being irate. If they changed 1:41, you would expect them to have done the same at 3:5. While the text does not say Jesus was angry when he was clearing the temple, it is certainly possible. He did become exasperated from time to time (Mark 9:19). Why would Jesus have responded with anger? Perhaps it was because he had already made it clear that he wanted to heal (Mark 1:32–34), and the man's comment "if you are willing" was inappropriate. In today's vernacular, perhaps Jesus was saying, "Are you kidding me? *If* I am willing?" Perhaps Jesus was angry with the effects of sin on his good creation (and not at the man with leprosy himself).

Ehrman weakens his case by misrepresenting a similar passage in Mark 9. The father says in verse 22, "If you can do anything, take pity on us and help us." Ehrman writes, "Jesus fires back an angry response, 'If you are able? Everything is possible to the one who believes.'"[58] "An angry response"? The text doesn't say Jesus is angry. To me, that's not a natural reading of the text.

Jesus Was Completely Distraught (Heb 2:9)

> But we do see Jesus, who was made lower than the angels for a little while, now crowned with glory and honor because he suffered death, so that *by the grace of God* he might taste death for everyone. (italics added)

According to Ehrman, Hebrews 2:9 originally said that Jesus died "apart from God" (χωρὶς θεοῦ, *xōris theou*), meaning Jesus was "terrified in the face of death and died with no divine succor or support."[59] This was changed, he claims, to "by the grace of God" (χάριτι θεοῦ, *xariti theou*).

The external evidence for "apart from God" is weak. The phrase occurs in only two Greek manuscripts from the tenth century and later. To be fair, one of them may reflect an older tradition (MS 1739), and the phrase is discussed by some of the early church fathers.[60] UBS gives "by God's grace" an A rating, meaning it is convinced it is the original reading.

In terms of internal evidence, it's easy to see how a scribe could have inadvertently changed "grace of God" (χάριτι θεοῦ, *xariti theou*) to "apart from God" (χωρὶς θεοῦ, *xōris theou*). It also could have been a deliberate change. When verse 8 says that God put everything under submission to Jesus, a scribe could have wanted to qualify the statement by making it clear that the submission to Jesus does not apply to God the Father (cf. 1 Cor 15:27). This type of scribal emendation is common, and yet the variant "apart from God" seems unlikely, and most scholars reject it.

In addition, if "apart from God" was in fact original, it does not follow that Jesus was "terrified in the face of death and died with no divine succor or support." It could simply mean that God the Father was not present when Jesus was paying the penalty for human sin. More importantly, Jesus' citation of Psalm 22:1, "My God, my God, why have you forsaken me?" (Matt 27:46) is properly seen as a reference to the entire psalm, which ends on a note of faith (vv. 9–11, 19–31). It is typical especially of Paul to reference one part of an Old Testament passage and expect his audience to know the whole of it. Apparently Jesus did so as well.

> But you, LORD, do not be far from me.
>   You are my strength; come quickly to help me . . .
> I will declare your name to my people;
>   in the assembly I will praise you . . .
> For he has not despised or scorned
>   the suffering of the afflicted one;
> he has not hidden his face from him
>   but has listened to his cry for help.
>
> *Psalm 22:19, 22, 24*

Jesus was anything but "terrified in the face of death." It was for this very reason that he came (John 12:27); he could have asked his Father for twelve legions of angels to save him (Matt 26:53), and his wish would have been granted. Jesus was not expressing fear and despair; he was expressing pain within the context of faith, just as the psalmist did.

Snakes and Poison (Mark 16:9–20)

The longer ending of Mark teaches that disciples can drink poison and handle snakes and not be harmed. But this longer ending was added centuries after Mark wrote his gospel, and no one (except the "King James only" crowd) thinks it's original, including Bart Ehrman.[61]

He is right that this would change our understanding of what we would do with poison and snakes, but that's irrelevant, since the passage is so clearly inauthentic and late in origin. Frankly, I'm glad this verse is not original. My father's family is from the hills of Gravelswitch, Kentucky. Those are my distant cousins drinking poison and handling what I would never touch. This passage is totally irrelevant within the discussion of the changes that affect how we read the book.

An Adulterous Woman Is Let Off the Hook (John 7:53–8:11)

As is the case above, Bart Ehrman acknowledges that this passage is not original.[62] Even if it were authentic, it doesn't support his thesis that the variant would change what we thought of Jesus or adultery. This is not necessarily how Jesus treated all adultery, and he was more than willing to befriend the tax collectors and sinners. I'm not sure why this passage made its way into Ehrman's summary.

The Trinity (1 John 5:7b–8a)

For there are three that bear record in heaven, the Father, the Word, and the Holy Ghost: and these three are one.

And there are three that bear witness in earth, the Spirit, and the water, and the blood: and these three agree in one. (KJV)

For there are three that testify: the Spirit, the water and the blood; and the three are in agreement. (NIV)

This is the only biblical passage that *explicitly* teaches the Trinity. The important word is "explicitly." Ehrman agrees that there is absolutely no question that this passage was added centuries after Constantine, and it proves nothing about the habits of the early scribes, so once again I'm not sure why Ehrman includes it in his summary. Even without 1 John 5:7b–8a, the seeds that developed into the doctrine of the Trinity are elsewhere in the Bible (Matt 28:19–20; Eph 1:3–14), beginning with the teaching of the divinity of Christ.

Jesus Is the "Unique God" (John 1:18)

No one has ever seen God; the *only [unique]* God, who is at the Father's side, he has made him known. (ESV, italics added)

Ehrman claims that originally the text declared Jesus to be the "unique Son" (μονογενὴς υἱός, *monogenēs huios*), which was later changed to "unique God" (μονογενὴς θεός, *monogenēs theos*) by the orthodox scribes who wanted to assert the divinity of Christ in contrast to the adoptionists.[63] He argues that the phrase "unique God" logically can refer only to God the Father, or else God is not unique, and the change to "unique God" was to increase the exalted view of Christ in contrast to adoptionism.

"Only God" does have strong external support, but so does "only Son." UBS gives "only God" a B rating. Ehrman argues that the phrase "unique Son" occurs elsewhere in John (3:16, 14) but never the phrase "unique God." But scholars acknowledge that the language of John's prologue is different from the rest of his gospel, so Ehrman's point is not significant.[64]

However, a good argument can be made that "unique God" is in fact the original reading of the verse. It certainly is the harder reading; there is no reason that a scribe would change "only God" to "only Son," as it lessens the Christology of Jesus. But this does not change the picture of Jesus as a whole in a book that repeatedly affirms the deity of Christ.

Jesus Doesn't Know (Matt 24:36)

"But about that day or hour no one knows, not even the angels in heaven, *nor the Son*, but only the Father." (italics added)

Bart Ehrman argues that "nor the Son" was original and was later dropped by scribes who thought it detracted from Jesus' divinity. This would support his theory that the scribes changed the text to enforce their own particular theology.

But even without the phrase, the uncontested part of the verse still reads "only," so it's a moot point whether "nor the Son" was originally present or absent. For the hypothesis to work, the scribes would have had to remove both "nor the Son" and "only." Besides, the same truth is affirmed in Mark 13:32, where there is no textual issue.

Jesus' ignorance of the time could also be the limitation of the incarnation, and Jesus is speaking as the Messiah. More likely, this is a look into the mystery of the Trinity, and the decision to send Jesus back is the prerogative of God the Father alone. It does not have to mean that a scribe was protecting the deity of Christ in opposition to the adoptionists.

It should be asked which viable variants in these passages would actually change our understanding of the biblical book they are in or any biblical teaching from other passages. We know Jesus could respond in anger (Mark 3:5). We know that God the Father was in some way not present when God the Son was dying on the cross (Matt 27:46). We know that Paul was not affected by snakebites (Acts 28:4–5), although this cannot be generalized to all Christians. We know Jesus was accepting of people whom others would classify as "sinners" and replaced an "eye for eye" mentality with love (Matt 5:38). We know that forgiveness and hypocrisy are covered in places outside of John 7:53–8:11. We know that the seeds of the doctrine of the Trinity are firmly planted in the Bible—expressed in the Great Commission (Matt 28:18–20) and required by the biblical doctrine of the divinity of Christ. We know that there is mystery in the relationship among the members of the Godhead. So what teachings and doctrines are truly in question?

Conclusion

The issue is not the number of variants but the significance of the variants. Yes, it would be nice to know how to spell the name of the pool in John 5:2—"Bethesda" (Βηθεσδα), "Bethzatha" (Βηθζαθά), or "Bethsaida" (Βηδσαιδαν). But does not knowing the correct spelling really call into question the reliability of the textual tradition and our Bibles?

The earliest manuscripts may not have been made by literary scribes attempting to create a work of art, but they are carefully and precisely copied. Papyrus manuscripts can last much longer than a decade, and we have no idea how many iterations of manuscripts lie behind any extant manuscript. The seventy-six manuscripts we have from the second and third centuries do not show a sloppiness or willingness to change that would call into question the accuracy of the manuscript tradition. We know nothing of the earliest manuscripts that we do not have, so we cannot know if they changed the message of the gospel. Truth is not determined by rhetorical flourish; it is determined by facts.

For Further Reading

Blomberg, Craig L. *The Historical Reliability of the New Testament: Countering the Challenges to Evangelical Christian Beliefs*. Nashville: B&H Academic, 2016, 612–45.

———. "Aren't the Copies of the Bible Hopelessly Corrupt?" in *Can We Still Believe the Bible? An Evangelical Engagement with Contemporary Questions*. Grand Rapids: Brazos, 2014, 13–41.

Bock, Darrell L. *The Missing Gospels: Unearthing the Truth behind Alternative Christianities*. Nashville: Nelson, 2006.

Bock, Darrell L., and Daniel B. Wallace. "The Original New Testament Has Been Corrupted by Copyists So Badly That It Can't Be Recovered." In *Dethroning Jesus: Exposing Popular Culture's Quest to Unseat the Biblical Christ*. Nashville: Nelson, 2007, 35–76.

Bruce, F. F. *The New Testament Documents: Are They Reliable?* Grand Rapids: Eerdmans, 2003.

Carson, D. A. *The King James Version Debate: A Plea for Realism*. Grand Rapids: Baker, 1979.

Evans, Craig A. *Fragments of Truth: Can We Trust the Bible?* Video. Bellingham, WA: Faithlife Films, 2018.

———. *Jesus and the Manuscripts: What We Can Learn from the Oldest Texts*. Peabody, MA: Hendrickson, 2020.

Hixson, Elijah, and Peter J. Gurry, eds. *Myths and Mistakes in New Testament Textual Criticism*. Downers Grove, IL: IVP Academic, 2019.

Jones, Timothy Paul. *Misquoting Truth: A Guide to the Fallacies of Bart Ehrman's* Misquoting Jesus. Downers Grove, IL: InterVarsity, 2007.

Komoszewski, J. Ed, M. James Sawyer, and Daniel B. Wallace, *Reinventing Jesus: How Contemporary Skeptics Miss the Real Jesus and Mislead Popular Culture*. Grand Rapids: Kregel, 2006, 53–117.

Osborne, Grant. *Three Crucial Questions about the Bible*. Grand Rapids: Baker, 1995.

Sailhamer, John H. *How We Got the Bible*. Grand Rapids: Zondervan, 1998.

Strobel, Lee, *The Case for the Real Jesus: A Journalist Investigates Current Attacks on the Identity of Christ*. Grand Rapids: Zondervan, 2007, 65–100.

Wallace, Daniel B., ed. *Revisiting the Corruption of the New Testament: Manuscript, Patristic, and Apocryphal Evidence*. Grand Rapids: Kregel Academic, 2011.

———. "Textual Criticism: The History of the Greek Text behind Modern Translations." Biblical Training Institute, https://gk2.me/textual-criticism.

———. "Why We Trust Our Bible." Lectures 22–27. Biblical Training Institute, https://gk2.me/we-trust.

Advanced

Comfort, Philip Wesley. *Early Manuscripts and Modern Translations of the New Testament*. Grand Rapids: Baker, 1990. Repr. Eugene, OR: Wipf & Stock, 2001.

Metzger, Bruce M., and Bart D. Ehrman, *The Text of the New Testament: Its Transmission, Corruption, and Restoration*. 4th ed. Oxford: Oxford University Press, 2005.

Notes

1. Bart D. Ehrman, *Misquoting Jesus: The Story behind Who Changed the Bible and Why* (San Francisco: HarperOne, 2005).
2. See Peter J. Gurry, "The Number of Variants in the Greek New Testament: A Proposed Estimate," *New Testament Studies* 62, no. 1 (2016): 113. Truth be told, we don't know how many variants there are; no one has yet tabulated all the variants in all the manuscripts.

3. Ehrman, *Misquoting Jesus*, 89.

4. We look forward to the completion of the *Editio Critica Maior*, which will show us a much greater number of variants.

5. Quoted in Darrell L. Bock and Daniel B. Wallace, *Dethroning Jesus: Exposing Popular Culture's Quest to Unseat the Biblical Christ* (Nashville: Nelson, 2007), 74.

6. Ehrman, *Misquoting Jesus*, 7.

7. Ehrman, *Misquoting Jesus*, 177.

8. "Can We Trust the Text of the New Testament? A Debate between Bart D. Ehrman and Daniel B. Wallace," Southern Methodist University, October 1, 2011, https://gk2.me/ehrman-wallace, at 1:33.17.

9. Daniel Wallace compared the MT (using Zane C. Hodges and Arthur L. Farstad, eds., *The Greek New Testament according to the Majority Text*) with the NA27 and discovered only 6,577 variants between the two, most of which are of no consequence. Confirmed by personal correspondence (November 2020).

10. See Keith E. Small, *Holy Books Have a History: Textual Histories of the New Testament and the Qur'an* (Lafayette, CA: Avant, 2010).

11. Ehrman, *Misquoting Jesus*, 69, 211.

12. Ehrman, *Misquoting Jesus*, 207, also 10.

13. Ehrman, *Misquoting Jesus*, 10.

14. See George W. Houston, "Papyrological Evidence for Book Collections and Libraries in the Roman Empire," in *Ancient Literacies: The Culture of Reading in Greece and Rome*, ed. William A. Johnson and Holt N. Parker (Oxford: Oxford University Press, 2009), 233–67; see also Timothy N. Mitchell, "Myths about Autographs: What They Were and How Long They May Have Survived," in *Myths and Mistakes in New Testament Textual Criticism*, ed. Elijah Hixson and Peter J. Gurry (Downers Grove, IL: IVP Academic, 2019).

15. Cited in Craig A. Evans, *Jesus and the Manuscripts* (Peabody, MA: Hendrickson, 2020). 79; see his full discussion of this issue (pp. 75–97).

16. Citing D. C. Parker, *Codex Bezae: An Early Christian Manuscript and Its Text* (Cambridge: Cambridge University Press, 1992), 282.

17. Evans, *Jesus and the Manuscripts*, 82.

18. Cited in Craig A. Evans, *Jesus and His Word: The Archaeological Evidence* (Louisville, KY: Westminster John Knox, 2012), 75; Evans, *Jesus and the Manuscripts*, 82.

19. Bruce M. Metzger and Bart D. Ehrman, *The Text of the New Testament: Its Transmission, Corruption, and Restoration*, 4th ed. (Oxford: Oxford University Press, 2005), 91.

20. Cited in Bock and Wallace, *Dethroning Jesus*, 45.

21. Quoted in Evans, *Jesus and the Manuscripts*, 85.

22. "Can We Trust the Text of the New Testament? A Debate between Bart D. Ehrman and Daniel B. Wallace," Southern Methodist University, October 1, 2011, https://gk2.me/ehrman-wallace, at 1:12.04.

23. Bock and Wallace, *Dethroning Jesus*, 47, italics added; see "Can We Trust the Text of the New Testament?" https://gk2.me/ehrman-wallace at 1:12.04.

24. "Can We Trust the Text of the New Testament?" https://gk2.me/ehrman -wallace at 17:25.

25. The following numbers are from Daniel B. Wallace, ed., *Revisiting the Corruption of the New Testament: Manuscript, Patristic, and Apocryphal Evidence* (Grand Rapids: Kregel Academic, 2011), 28–29. The numbers from the online database of the Institut für neutestamentliche Textforschung (http://ntvmr.uni-muenster.de/liste) are somewhat different: second century: four; second to third century: six; third century: forty-six; third to fourth century: fifteen; fourth century (not including papyri marked fourth to fifth century): eighteen.

26. Wallace, *Revisiting the Corruption*, 29.

27. Wallace, *Revisiting the Corruption*, 30 n. 28.

28. Metzger and Ehrman, *Text of the New Testament*, 126.

29. "Can We Trust the Text of the New Testament?" https://gk2.me/ehrman -wallace at 26:30.

30. "Can We Trust the Text of the New Testament?" https://gk2.me/ehrman -wallace at 31:22.

31. Metzger and Ehrman, *Misquoting Jesus*, 71. He is leveling two charges: (1) The early scribes were *not trained* and therefore made many mistakes. (2) The early scribes made *more* mistakes and intentional changes than later scribes.

32. Origen's frustration with scribes is well known, although it is not necessarily anything more than a sidenote made in frustration and not necessarily indicative of all scribes. He says, "The differences among the manuscripts have become great, either through the negligence of some copyists or through the perverse audacity of others; they either neglect to check over what they have transcribed, or, in the process of checking,

they make additions or deletions as they please" (*Commentary on Matthew* 15.14, quoted in Ehrman, *Misquoting Jesus*, 52.

33. Cited in Zachary J. Cole, "Myths about Copyists: The Scribes Who Copied Our Earliest Manuscripts," in *Myths and Mistakes in New Testament Textual Criticism*, ed. Elijah Hixson and Peter J. Gurry (Downers Grove, IL: IVP Academic, 2019), 135.

34. Cole, "Myths about Copyists," 136, italics in original.

35. See Kim Haines-Eitzen, *Guardians of Letters: Literacy, Power, and the Transmitters of Early Christian Literature* (Oxford: Oxford University Press, 2000); Alan Mugridge, *Copying Early Christian Texts: A Study of Scribal Practice* (Tübingen: Mohr Siebeck, 2016), 291).

36. See Cole, "Myths about Copyists," 137–40.

37. Cole, "Myths about Copyists," 141; see Cole's takeaways on p. 151.

38. See Daniel Wallace, "A Brief History of the Transmission of the Text," Biblical Training Institute, https://gk2.me/early-scribes at 20:10; see also "Can We Trust the Text of the New Testament?" https://gk2.me/ehrman-wallace at 1:28.

39. Quoted in Craig L. Blomberg, *Can We Still Believe the Bible?* (Grand Rapids: Brazos, 2014), 233 n. 38; cf. Blomberg, *The Historical Reliability of the New Testament* (Nashville: B&H Academic, 2016), 619 n. 24.

40. Confirmed with Daniel Wallace through personal correspondence (November 2020).

41. Jacob W. Peterson, "Math Myths: How Many Manuscripts We Have and Why More Isn't Always Better," in *Myths and Mistakes in New Testament Textual Criticism*, Hixson and Gurry, eds., 67.

42. See Lonnie D. Bell, *The Early Textual Transmissions of John: Stability and Fluidity in Its Second and Third Century Manuscripts* (Leiden: Brill, 2018).

43. Quoted in Craig A. Evans, *Jesus and the Manuscripts: What We can Learn from the Oldest Texts* (Peabody, MA: Hendrickson Academic, 2020), 92.

44. Kurt Aland and Barbara Aland provide a wonderful chart of all the papyri and references to which chapters of biblical books they include, indicating which chapters are fragmentary (*The Text of the New Testament*, trans. Erroll F. Rhodes [Grand Rapids: Eerdmans, 1987]).

45. The other significant papyri is the seventh-century P[74], which contains Acts and fragments of other books (Acts 1:2–28:31†; Jas 1:1–5:20†; 1 Pet 1:1–2, 7–8, 13, 19–20, 25; 2:6–7, 11–12, 18, 24; 3:4–5; 2 Pet 2:21;

3:4, 11, 16; 1 John 1:1, 6; 2:1–2, 7, 13–14, 18–19, 25–26; 3:1–2, 8, 14, 19–20; 4:1, 6–7, 12, 16–17; 5:3–4, 9–10, 17; 2 John 1, 6–7, 13; 3 John 6, 12; Jude 3, 7, 11–12, 16, 24).

46. See "Digging Much Deeper," Bill Mounce: Why I Trust the Bible, www .billmounce.com/trust/9.

47. "Manuscript Search," Center for the Study of New Testament Manuscripts, www.csntm.org/Manuscript. You can also buy fascimiles from Hendrickson Publishers (*New Testament Papyri P45, P46, P47: Facsimiles*; *New Testament Papyrus P47: A Transcription*, both done in conjunction with the Center for the Study of New Testament Manuscripts [Daniel B. Wallace, director], www.hendrickson.com/html /product/708440.trade.html; www.hendrickson.com/html/product /073147.trade.html).

48. See Peter Malik, "Myths about Copying: The Mistakes and Corrections Scribes Made," in *Myths and Mistakes in New Testament Textual Criticism*, Hixson and Gurry, eds., 152–70.

49. I have yet to be able to convince my translation colleagues to translate all three definite articles in 1 Timothy 4:13. Paul is telling Timothy to devote himself to *the* public reading of Scripture, to *the* preaching, and to *the* teaching. Reading, exhortation, and theological instruction were distinct parts of the early church service. Christians read their book, and read it out loud. See my commentary, *Pastoral Epistles*, vol. 46 (Word Biblical Commentary; Grand Rapids: Zondervan, 2000), 260–61.

50. Craig Evans (*Jesus and the Manuscripts*, 96) cites Frederik Wisse: "If indeed the text of the Gospels had been subject to extensive redactional change and adaptation during the second century, the unanimous attestation of a relatively stable and uniform text during the following centuries in both Greek and the versions would have to be considered nothing short of a miracle" (F. Wisse, "The Nature and Purpose of Redactional Changes in Early Christian Texts: The Canonical Gospels," in *Gospel Traditions in the Second Century: Origins, Recensions, Text, and Transmission*, William L Petersen, ed. (University of Notre Dame Press, 1989), 52–53).

51. "Can We Trust the Text of the New Testament?" https://gk2.me /ehrman-wallace at 17:35 and 19:35.

52. "Can We Trust the Text of the New Testament?" https://gk2.me /ehrman-wallace at 28:12.

53. "Can We Trust the Text of the New Testament?" https://gk2.me /ehrman-wallace at 37:36–43.

54. Blomberg, *Can We Still Believe the Bible?*, 27.

55. See Bart Ehrman, *The Orthodox Corruption of Scripture: The Effect of Early Christological Controversies on the Text of the New Testament* (Oxford: Oxford University Press, 2011); see also the critique by Darrell L. Bock, *The Missing Gospels* (Nashville: Nelson, 2006).

56. Ehrman, *Misquoting Jesus*, 208.

57. See Ehrman, *Misquoting Jesus*, 127.

58. Ehrman, *Misquoting Jesus*, 138.

59. Ehrman, *Misquoting Jesus*, 144.

60. Origen, Ambrose, Jerome, and a few others (see UBS notes); see William L. Lane, *Hebrews 1–8*, Word Biblical Commentary (Grand Rapids: Zondervan, 1991), 43 note g.

61. See Ehrman, *Misquoting Jesus*, 65–68.

62. See Ehrman, *Misquoting Jesus*, 63–65.

63. See Ehrman, *Misquoting Jesus*, 161–62.

64. The expansive translation of "one and only Son, who is himself God" (CSB; cf. NIV, NET, NLT), which attempts to remove the logical conundrum, views "only" as a substantival adjective and the noun "God" in opposition to the adjective. See the expanded note in the NET Bible. Daniel Wallace made the text-critical decisions for the NET, so presumably this note is his work.

TRANSLATIONS

Can We Trust Our
Translations?

Challenge

Bible translations are so different that they can't be trusted. If you compare the same passage in two translations, you'll see that they're so different and sometimes contradictory that they can't both be correct. Besides, publishers just want to have their own translation so they can drive up profits, and translators have their own theological agendas. The only way to know what the Bible actually says is to read it in its original languages—Hebrew, Aramaic, and Greek. Islam is certainly right to insist that if you don't read the Qur'an in Arabic, you aren't reading the Qur'an. The same is true of the Bible.

Author's Note: Before we jump into this topic, I need to make a full disclosure of my background, if you don't already know this. I have been a member of the translation committees of two popular English translations of the Bible—the English Standard Version (ESV) and the New International Version (NIV). I was the New Testament chair of the ESV translation committee for ten years, and for the past ten years I've been a member of the Committee for Bible Translation that is responsible for overseeing the NIV.

One popular writer characterizes translations as "more or less clumsy renderings of these [Greek and Hebrew] words into a language, such as English, that has nothing to do with the original words."[1] *Nothing?* I'm not sure what English translation he is reading, but it certainly isn't one that I worked on.

Notes

1. Bart D. Ehrman, *Misquoting Jesus: The Story behind Who Changed the Bible and Why* (San Francisco: HarperOne, 2009), 7.

Chapter 10

TRANSLATION THEORY

In this chapter, we will look at the translation process of transferring meaning, not words, from one language to another, as well as the five different types of translations.

It can be frustrating to attend a Bible study where different translations are being used. At times they seem to contradict each other. One translation reads "brother," and another reads "brother and sister"—which is correct? If one translation reads "he" and the other translation reads "they," which is correct? Why does one translation speak of Christian "saints," and another of "holy people"? Why does the Bible's most famous verse get translated with "so" in some translations and not in others?

"For God so loved the world, that he gave his only Son." (ESV)

"For this is how God loved the world: He gave his one and only Son." (NLT)

Which one is right? And why are they different?

These are real concerns that can lead us to lose trust in our Bible. Thankfully, there are answers that can clear up the confusion, but we first need to understand some of the basics of Bible translation and especially its two stages. I'll introduce them with two questions.

1. What does the Greek or Hebrew word mean in its biblical context? Words have what are called a "semantic range." Few (if any) words have just one meaning; they have several meanings. The Greek word δοῦλος (*doulos*) can mean "servant," "slave," or "bondservant." What does it mean in Philippians 1:1? Are Paul and Timothy "servants" or "slaves" of Christ Jesus? This is an interpretive stage, and different translators will interpret the meaning of the words differently. Even a sentence as simple as John 11:35 can mean either "Jesus wept" or "Jesus burst into tears," depending on your interpretation of the verb δακύω (*dakuō*).

2. How do I say the same thing in English? Languages are not codes; a word in one language has no exact equivalent in another language. Therefore, we have a second interpretive stage, but now we are interpreting English.

When Paul was shipwrecked on Malta, the indigenous people were kind to him (Acts 28:2). Do we call them "islanders" (NIV), "natives" (NASB, NRSV), "native people" (ESV), "local people" (CSB), "local inhabitants" (NET), "people of the island" (NLT), or "barbarous people" (KJV)? What do you see in your mind when you hear words like *natives* and *islanders*? Are these words accurate reflections of the people on Malta? Probably not. Every translation has its own translation philosophy to guide it at this stage of the process, and issues such as English style are subjective and varied.

However, neither of these issues prevent you from understanding the basic message of the Bible and trusting your translation. As a friend of mine says about the major translations available today, none will lead you to heresy—and all will lead you to the cross.

Languages Are Not Codes

When I started learning Greek forty years ago, I was naive in my approach to languages. I thought of languages as different codes. In Morse code, my name "Bill" is "–... .. .–.. .–.." I assumed that Greek would simply be a different set of dots and dashes—that Greek and English were nearly identical at their core, and the differences were just at the surface level. Once I learned the Greek word for "flesh" (σάρξ, *sarx*), I assumed that σάρξ would have the same meaning in Greek as "flesh" has in English. I thought that once I learned the present tense in Greek, it would function the same way as in English.

I could not have been more wrong.

Vocabulary

To understand why I was wrong, let's start with vocabulary. What does the Greek word δοῦλος (*doulos*) mean? As I said earlier, its meaning overlaps with the English words *servant, slave,* and *bondservant,* but not one of these three English words corresponds exactly to δοῦλος.

Does Paul tell a *slave* or a *servant* to obey his master (Eph 6:5)? Does Jesus say that "whoever wants to be great among you must be your" *servant* or *slave* (Matt 20:27)? Was Paul a *servant* or *slave* of Christ (Titus 1:1)? Because there is no exact equivalence for δοῦλος in English, it must be translated in context, allowing the overall meaning of the passage to determine which of the different meanings of δοῦλος applies in a particular verse. Some translations will use "slave" and others will use "servant" or "bondservant," depending on the translators' interpretation of what the word means.

Or consider another example. How would you translate σάρξ (*sarx*)? Sometimes it means "flesh," the stuff that hangs on your bones. "The Word became *flesh* and made his dwelling among us" (John 1:14, italics added). At other times the context makes it clear that σάρξ is being used to describe our "sinful human nature." "I know that good itself does not dwell in me, that is, in my *sinful nature*" (Rom 7:18, italics added). The ESV uses sixteen different English words or phrases to translate the one Greek word σάρξ.[1]

What I'm saying applies to Hebrew as well. The traditional translation of Psalm 23:4 is, "Yea, though I walk through the valley of the shadow of death, I will fear no evil" (KJV, also ESV, NASB). Here's the problem. The two Hebrew words that lie behind "valley of the shadow of death" are "valley of gloom," which the KJV interprets to mean "death." Other translations properly understand the Hebrew to refer to a dark, lonely, desolate, and hence dangerous valley. So we find translations such as, "Even when I go through the darkest valley" (CSB; see NIV, NRSV, NET, NLT). People may not like translators changing one of their favorite verses, but the fact of the matter is that the Hebrew does not mean "death," and it's always best to translate what the text actually means.

Further complicating things is the reality that it's impossible to bring all the nuances of any Greek or Hebrew word into English. Words are much too rich in meaning to be encapsulated by a single word in another language. Jesus is our ἱλασμός (hilasmos, 1 John 2:2). But how do you say the same thing in English? The NASB uses "propitiation," and the RSV reads "expiation"; the difference theologically is significant. The NIV translators felt that both of these terms were too difficult for the average reader to understand, and so they helped the reader by providing a little more explanation, using the phrase "atoning sacrifice." Similarly, the NLT reads "sacrifice that atones for our sins."

This brings up an interesting point. Sometimes, albeit rarely, a difference in translation is due to the translators' theological interpretation. "Propitiation" means that Jesus' death on the cross was primarily focused on appeasing God's wrath against our sin, paying the penalty for what we have done wrong. "Expiation" means Jesus' death was focused on our guilt, enabling us to receive forgiveness. The Greek word ἱλασμός can also refer to the "mercy seat" on the top of the ark of the covenant where the blood of the yearly offering for the nation's sin was sprinkled (see Heb 9:5 ESV). For Jesus, the place of atonement was the cross. But your choice between "propitiation" and "expiation" involves two issues: (1) theologically, what happened on the cross, and (2) stylistically, what words your audience can understand.

Another example of a theologically motivated translation is the evangelical belief that Jesus was born of a virgin, and so we translate the Hebrew word עַלְמָה ('almah) in Isaiah 7:14 as "virgin." We believe Jesus is God, so we put the comma in the right place in Romans 9:5: "the Messiah, who is God over all." But by and large, my experience is that personal theologies have very little impact on translation.

So one reason translations are different is that languages are not codes, and it's not possible to bring one word directly from one language into another. Translation involves two interpretive stages where we look at the Greek word, determine what the Greek word means in its biblical context, and then determine which English word or words will express the same meaning. Because we interpret the Bible differently, and we all hear English words a little differently, we use different words in translation, and hence there are differences in our Bibles.

Phrases and Grammar

What is true of individual words is also true of phrases. You can't simply transpose word for word. You have to see what the phrase meant in Greek and then ask how to say the same thing in English. Languages can say the same thing, but they say it differently.

Idioms illustrate this point beautifully. Idioms are phrases that have a meaning when the words are put together that is not conveyed by the words individually. Consider the story of the prodigal son. When the father saw his wayward son returning, he ran and "fell on his neck" (Luke 15:20 KJV). Word for word, ἐπέπεσεν ἐπὶ τὸν τράχηλον αὐτοῦ is "he fell on the neck of him." While this is word for word, it certainly does not convey to English listeners what Jesus means. Even the NASB, the most word-for-word translation in English, says that the father "embraced" him (also ESV, NLT), adding the footnote, "Lit[erally] *fell on his neck*." The NET says the father "hugged" his son. The NIV is clever in preserving the idiom in an understandable way: "threw his arms around him" (CSB: "threw his arms around his neck").

Or consider Romans 6:15, where Paul asks, "What then? shall we sin, because we are not under the law, but under grace?" and then responds, "God forbid" (μὴ γένοιτο, *mē genoito*) (Rom 6:15 KJV). The words *God* and *forbid* don't occur in the Greek, but "God forbid" is an excellent translation of μὴ γένοιτο. Why? Because μὴ γένοιτο expresses the strongest prohibition possible in Greek. If Paul were to do an audible Bible, he would be practically screaming at this point. So the question is, what expresses a similarly strong prohibition in English? "By no means!" (NIV, ESV, NRSV)? "May it never be!" (NASB)? "Absolutely not!" (NET, CSB)? The translation "Of course not!" (NLT) is surprisingly weak, but you can see why there are differences. The phrase μὴ γένοιτο means something like "it should not even be a wish," and translators will vary in how to say that.

A few years ago, I was speaking to a Chinese audience and used the expression "to straddle the fence." If my translator had simply translated the words, the sentence would have had no meaning to my audience. Instead, she didn't translate the words but rather used a Chinese metaphor that has different words but has roughly the same meaning: "a foot in two boat." (That's not a typo. Chinese, basically, doesn't have plurals, and they let context show that there are two "boats" since there are two feet.) English and Greek grammar may say the same thing, but they say it differently, and you can't simply substitute an English word for a Greek word.

When I was learning German, I went to the Goethe-Institut in Schwäbisch Hall, Germany. There's nothing like learning a language in an immersive experience. Some of my friends knew a lot more German than I did, and they forced me to speak in German rather than rescuing me with English. One day it was cold outside, so I thought I would say I was cold. "I" is "Ich"; "am" is "bin"; "cold" is "kalt." So I proudly announced, "Ich bin kalt." If you know German, you can imagine what happened. My friends hit the ground, rolling and laughing hysterically.

I reviewed my words, wondering what was so funny. Yes, "Ich bin kalt" are the right words. I had conveyed my meaning accurately, or so I thought. Yet my friends' laughter clearly conveyed their disagreement. When they managed to regain their composure, they told me that if I wanted to say I was cold, I should have said, "To me it is cold"—"Mir ist kalt." I asked what I had "said," and they replied, "You said you were sexually frigid." Later that spring, I still had not learned my lesson and announced, "Ich bin warm" (instead of "Mir ist warm"). I will let you figure out what "Ich bin warm" means.

My German friends taught me that it's naive to think that a word-for-word substitution from one language to another is even possible. If you disagree with me, I suggest you avoid traveling through Germany and practicing your German there in the late fall.

The Italian proverb "*traduttore, traditore*" is roughly translated as "translators are traitors." I'm told that even this translation loses some of the force of the Italian original. We are all traitors to the full meaning of the original, so something will always be lost in translation. Translations can certainly convey the basic meaning of the speaker from one language to another, but bits and pieces will be lost. You can't just transpose words from Greek to English and have the English mean the same thing as does the Greek.

Just remember that all translation involves interpretation. I sometimes encounter people who think their translation is not interpretive. That's impossible. All translations involve interpretation, albeit some are willing to be more interpretive than others (a topic we'll discuss next). But it's impossible to go from one language to another without some interpretation, and there will be a variety of differences in interpretation and English style as well.

Translation Philosophy

When we translate, we interpret by looking at what the Greek words mean and at what the Greek grammar means and then asking how to say the same thing in English. We have seen how this process contains a subjective element, because we all interpret meaning differently and speak differently. But a translation must be consistent. It must try to transfer meaning in a consistent way. This is where a translation *philosophy* comes in. The translation team will agree as to the type of translation it wants to produce and how they will be consistent in applying that philosophy.

Issues such as the audience's age, geographical location, and religious background, as well as the committee's view on the nature of language, all play a role in determining a translation philosophy. If you are translating for a younger audience that has no Christian background, you probably won't use terms like "propitiation" or "expiation" to describe what Jesus accomplished on the cross. Instead you'll talk about the way Jesus made an "atoning sacrifice" (1 John 4:10 NIV) or a "sacrifice to take away sins" (NLT). If you are writing for an international audience that has English as a second language, you will break up long Greek sentences into shorter English sentences. Ephesians 1:3–14 is one sentence in Greek; the English translations divide it into five (ESV), eight (NIV), or fifteen (NLT) sentences in order to help their respective audiences understand Paul's teaching. These and many other issues go into determining a translation's philosophy, and those decisions generally account for many of the differences among Bibles.

Most people wrongly say there are two basic approaches to translation. They will say that, on the one side, the "formal equivalence" approach says that the purpose of translation is to adhere as closely as possible to the grammatical structures of the original language, altering the translation only when necessary to convey meaning. On the other side, the "functional" or "dynamic" view of translation tries to discover the original meaning—the "authorial intent"—and then convey the same meaning in the target language, regardless of the grammar used by the original language.

Part of the problem with this twofold approach is that translations don't fit neatly into one or the other of these two approaches; rather, they fit along a continuum, with significant overlap. Also, the same translation can be formal in one verse and functional in the next. While the ESV is generally considered a "formal equivalent" translation and the NIV a "dynamic equivalent" translation, we find significant overlap between the two. They are not different points on a line but overlapping circles.

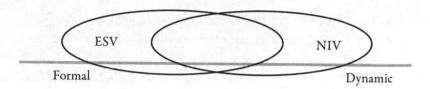

The other challenge is that there are at least *five* categories of translation theory. As you get to know the different categories, you'll see why translations are different—and yet still trustworthy.

1. Interlinear

An interlinear will list the Greek words in Greek word order, and under each Greek word you'll see a gloss for its meaning. (A "gloss" is an approximation of the main meaning of a word.) My favorite example is John 3:16. Here is a "literal" translation laid out as an interlinear.

In this way	for	he loved	the God	the world
οὕτως	γὰρ	ἠγάπησεν	ὁ θεὸς	τὸν κόσμον,

with the result that	the son	the only	he gave	
ὥστε	τὸν υἱὸν	τὸν μονογενῆ	ἔδωκεν,	

in order that	each	the believing	into	him	not
ἵνα	πᾶς	ὁ πιστεύων	εἰς	αὐτὸν	μὴ

he might perish	but	he might have	life	eternal.
ἀπόληται	ἀλλ'	ἔχῃ	ζωὴν	αἰώνιον.

Not only is this an impossible English style, but it's only an approximation of the Greek.

- You have to drop the "the" (ὁ) before "God" because we do not speak of our God as "the God." He is simply "God."

- "Each the believing" is a way to express an indefinite idea in Greek and therefore can be more properly translated as "whoever believes."
- You also need to use punctuation. Despite the traditional rendering of the verse, "so" (οὕτως, *houtos*) can't mean "so much" but rather means "in this way," and you may need to find punctuation that properly conveys this meaning. "How do we know that God loved the world? He gave his Son." This is why the NLT has, "For this is how God loved the world: He gave his one and only Son." Note the use of the colon.
- Even the translation "for" (γάρ) has its difficulties. Verse 16 is not introducing a reason for verse 15, which is the standard meaning of the English word "for." Rather, verse 16 is pulling out implications of what was just said, an idea for which English has no equivalent; we use punctuation, which is in this case a new paragraph.

In the next chapter, I will share why I dislike the word *literal*, but for now, let me say that if someone wants a "literal" Bible, the closest you'll get is an interlinear. None of our standard modern English Bibles can be categorized as a "literal" Bible. *There is not a single sentence in which the translators merely translate the words.* Each word must be analyzed for meaning, an interpretive decision made, and then the meaning expressed in English, which involves another interpretive decision. This is not being "literal" as most people understand the word.

2. Formal Equivalence

Formal equivalent translations often try to reflect the grammatical structures of the original text, making the translation more "transparent" to the original. This means translating indicative verbs as indicative, participles as participles, and trying to use the same English word for the same Greek word if possible ("concordance"). When it makes no sense to translate word for word, the translators ask what the verse means and then how they can convey the same meaning while adhering as closely as possible to the formal Greek structures. The ESV, NASB, and KJV all fall into this camp.

A good example of this is how the ESV keeps the pun in 1 Timothy 1:8, which is lost in the NIV because the translators presumably felt "lawfully" was too difficult to understand:

> Now we know that the *law* [νόμος, *nomos*] is good, if one uses it *lawfully* [νομίμως, *nomimōs*]. (ESV, italics added)

> We know that the *law* is good if one uses it *properly*. (NIV, italics added)

However, as I have been saying, not a single verse translated in the Bible is word for word. The differences in vocabulary and grammar simply don't allow for such a translation, so formal equivalent translations must also be quite dynamic at times. No one translates Philippians 2:4—to pick a verse at random—word for word and without interpretation: "Not the things of yourselves each looking out for but also the things of others each [μὴ τὰ ἑαυτῶν ἕκαστος σκοποῦντες ἀλλὰ καὶ τὰ ἑτέρων ἕκαστοι]." We see what the Greek means and try to say the same thing in English. "Each person should look out not only for his own interests, but also for the interests of others" (my translation).

The value of a functional equivalent translation is that the translators try to adhere as closely as possible to the Greek and Hebrew words and be minimally interpretive. The disadvantage is that in many cases their English style is so awkward and often antiquated that it is difficult to understand. Also, the fact of the matter is that the translators make changes to every single Greek sentence, so it's questionable to say its approach is significantly less interpretive than other translation approaches.

3. Functional (or Dynamic) Equivalence

These translations argue that the purpose of translation is to convey the meaning of the original text in the target language. This may mean a Greek participle is translated as an English indicative verb, or that a few Greek words are skipped over (such as conjunctions) or translated with punctuation marks in order to produce proper English style. On the one hand, this approach introduces an additional amount of interpretation, which can be problematic. On the other hand, it tends to produce a more understandable translation, which is the purpose of translation. The downside is that these versions can be somewhat idiomatic, not speaking a fully natural English but adhering somewhat to the underlying Greek and Hebrew structures. The NIV and CSB fit into this camp (although some place the CSB in the formal equivalent camp).

If you compare, for example, the ESV and the NIV, you start to see the differences in translation philosophy and *why* they're different. The ESV wants to stick closer to the actual Greek words, even if it results in the meaning of the passage being less clear and its English style clunkier. The NIV wants to more clearly convey the meaning of the Greek, even if it means it has to be more interpretive.

Consider Matthew 10:29: "Are not two sparrows sold for a penny? Yet not one of them will fall to the ground apart from your Father" (NRSV; see also NASB, ESV, KJV). "Apart from your Father" what? While this translation is more word for word, it doesn't mean anything, and so some translations add words based on the context of the verse: "your Father's care" (NIV); "your Father's consent" (CSB); "your Father's will" (NET); "your Father knowing it" (NLT). A translation should at least make sense, regardless of what type of translation it is.

4. Natural Language

This category tries to repeat the meaning of the Greek in the most natural English style possible. Eugene Nida and Charles Taber say that the purpose of a translation is to transport "the message of the original text . . . into the receptor language [such] that the response of the receptor is essentially like that of the original receptors."[2] In other words, English readers should hear and understand the passage in the same way as did the original Greek reader. The best example of a natural language translation is the NLT. Most people categorize the NLT as a dynamic translation, but it is significantly different from the NIV and deserves its own category. The NIV and especially the CSB often stick closer to the Greek and Hebrew than fully natural speech allows.

The beauty of a natural language translation is that it's easy to understand. You generally don't need an English dictionary and don't have to contemplate the meaning of a verse. Here is the salutation of 1 Peter in a formal equivalent and a natural language translation:

> To those who are elect exiles of the Dispersion in Pontus, Galatia, Cappadocia, Asia, and Bithynia, according to the fore-knowledge of God the Father, in the sanctification of the Spirit, for obedience to Jesus Christ and for sprinkling with his blood. (ESV)

> I am writing to God's chosen people who are living as foreigners in the provinces of Pontus, Galatia, Cappadocia, Asia, and Bithynia. God the Father knew you and chose you long ago, and his Spirit has made you holy. As a result, you have obeyed him and have been cleansed by the blood of Jesus Christ. (NLT)

The disadvantage of a natural language translation is that it will often introduce ideas that are not in the Greek. It does this in an effort to achieve natural English style and to convey the meaning of the Greek as clearly as possible. But if you compare the NLT with any other translation, you'll see a great number of differences. For example, Luke tells us that the sailors feared they would run aground on the Syrtis and thus lowered the sea anchor (see Acts 27:17 ESV). The capitalization of the word *Syrtis* and mention of the ship running aground may be enough for certain audiences to understand that Syrtis is a place in the ocean where the water is shallow. The NIV isn't willing to assume people will understand this, and so they write that the sailors "were afraid they would run aground on *the sandbars of* Syrtis" (italics added). The NLT adds even more words: "They were afraid of being driven across to *the sandbars of Syrtis off the African coast*" (italics added). The NLT does achieve its goal of conveying the full meaning of the original, but to do so it had to add quite a few words not actually in the Greek.

Jesus tells us, "If anyone forces you to go one mile, go with them two miles" (Matt 5:41). Culturally, he is probably thinking of the Roman law that specifically granted a soldier the right to have a person carry his pack for a mile, and so the NLT reads, "If a soldier demands that you carry his gear for a mile, carry it two miles." While this is clear, the problem is that the NLT limits the application of the verse to a situation in which there are soldiers who can force you to carry their pack. If Jesus had meant that, I suspect he would have said so. While I personally enjoy the NLT, you have to be careful as you study from it, since many of the words do not reflect the Greek behind it.

5. Transculturations

There is no widely accepted term for this final category of translations that change or distort the historical meaning of the text to make the meaning more apparent. Some people call them "paraphrases," but linguists use the term *paraphrase* for a rewording for the purpose of simplification in the *same* language, not in a different language. So *The Living Bible* is a true paraphrase, since it's a simplification of the (English) ASV, but viewing a translation from the Hebrew and Greek as a paraphrase is an incorrect use of the term. Others use the phrase "thought for thought" (as opposed to "word for word") for this category; however, every competent linguist knows that all translation is thought for thought and therefore this is not a helpful designation.

Better terms for this category might be "contemporary relevance versions" or "transculturations,"[3] but I doubt these terms will catch on. Whatever we call them, I don't believe these should be called "Bibles" because at any point it's hard to tell what is the Bible and what is the author's attempt to make the message of the Bible relevant to their own culture. In this category are J. B. Phillips's wonderful *The New Testament in Modern English*, Eugene Peterson's *The Message*, and Kenneth Taylor's original *The Living Bible*.

These publications sacrifice historical precision for contemporary relevance. So Peterson will say that the Pharisees are "manicured grave plots" instead of "whitewashed tombs" (Matt 23:27 MSG). He has the Pharisees living as "perpetual fashion shows, embroidered prayer shawls one day and flowery prayers the next" instead of saying the Pharisees "make their phylacteries wide and the tassels on their garments long" (Matt 23:5 MSG). Peterson is making the text relevant for the twenty-first century at the expense of historical accuracy.

Conclusion

While we have five distinct theories of translation, we must remember that there is much overlap. I would guess that despite following different translation philosophies, we have about an 80 percent overlap between the ESV and NIV. They are not two distinct, unrelated translations; they are overlapping circles. In addition, at times the ESV is quite formal, but at times it is quite functional. The same can be said of all translations. Even the NLT periodically displays some of the underlying language structures, and at times the NASB is quite dynamic.

We have five clearly defined schools of translation, and all but the interlinear are committed, in varying degrees, to conveying meaning and not just the words. My purpose in this chapter is not to critique any one translation, but rather to show that different translations follow different philosophies. In the next chapter, we'll see what this means in practice.

Notes

1. Flesh, body (bodily), human being, physical, earthly, natural, fellow Jews, worldly standards, troubles, anyone (flesh and blood), one (no one justified), condition, face to face (in the flesh), sensuous, lust, (unnatural) desire, and it is not translated in 1 Corinthians 15:39.
2. Eugene A. Nida and Charles R. Taber, *The Theory and Practice of Translation* (Leiden: Brill, 1982), 200.
3. See Gordon D. Fee and Mark L. Strauss, *How to Choose a Translation for All Its Worth: A Guide to Understanding and Using Bible Versions* (Grand Rapids: Zondervan, 2007), 32–34.

Chapter 11

DIGGING DEEPER INTO TRANSLATION

In the previous chapter, I discussed the fact that there is not a one-to-one correspondence in both vocabulary and grammar between languages, which means that all translations require interpretation. Because different translation committees have different translation philosophies and different varieties of English style, we find differences among the translations. In this chapter, we'll look into the specific types of decisions we make on translation committees, and you'll see why translations are different yet still trustworthy.

"Literal"

I want to start by talking about the idea of a "literal" translation. I laid the groundwork for this discussion in the previous chapter, but I'll now go into more detail to drive the point home.

If you ask most people what kind of a Bible they want, many will say they want a "literal" Bible. What complicates matters is their assumption that "literal" means as close to word for word as possible, and they equate word for word with "accurate." But this mistaken belief about "literal" is inaccurate on many levels.

The fact of the matter is that there is only one literal Bible. The literal Old Testament is written in Hebrew and Aramaic, and the literal New Testament is written in Greek. However, if you want to read the Bible in English, there is no such thing as a literal translation, nor is one even possible. The first meaning of the word *literal* listed in the *Oxford Dictionary of English* is "taking words in their usual or most basic sense without metaphor or allegory." In other words, *literal* primarily refers to the *meaning* of a word or passage, not its *form*. So a literal translation is one that conveys the meaning of the original faithfully, but it doesn't mean the translation must convey the meaning of the original in the same form. Just because a Greek sentence uses eight words doesn't mean that the English translation also must use eight. Just because the Greek uses a participle doesn't mean English must do likewise. What we want is a translation that accurately conveys the *meaning* of the Greek words, not their *form*.

The latest edition of the *Oxford Dictionary of English* has a new, second definition for the word *literal*: "(of a translation) representing the exact words of the original text." Again, however, we should ask if this is even possible and whether any translation actually does this. In the following discussion, I'm using *literal* in this second sense.

Let's start with words. Does a single word have a "literal" meaning? What does the word *key* literally mean? The answer is that it has no literal meaning. "Did you lose your key?" "What's the key to the puzzle?" "What's the key point?" "What key is that song in?" "Press the A key." "He shoots best from the key." "I ate my first key lime pie in Key West in the Florida Keys."

I like to refer to words as having a bundle of sticks, with each stick representing a different (and sometimes related) meaning. One of the sticks may certainly be larger than the rest, representing the most used idea of the word, or what we teach in first-year Greek as "the gloss," but it's only one among many. So if you are producing a "literal" translation, how will you decide on the literal meaning of a word? *Key* has no core meaning; there is no big stick in its bundle.

One of the most difficult interpretive decisions in the Pastoral Epistles is the word γυνή (*gunē*). In 1 Timothy 3, Paul has been laying out the qualities of a church elder (vv. 1–7) and then a church deacon (vv. 8–13). When we come to verse 11, we find "γυνή [plural] likewise must be dignified, not slanderers, clear-minded, faithful in all things" (my translation). Who is Paul talking about? The Greek word γυνή can be translated either "woman" or "wife." Both usages are common, and in this passage both meanings are possible. If γυνή in verse 11 means "women," then Paul has shifted to female deacons before going back to discussing male deacons in verse 12. If γυνή means "wives," then Paul is saying that part of the deacon's qualifications are related to his family— both his wife (v. 11) and his children (v. 12). The point is that γυνή does not have a literal meaning; it has a range of meanings, and a specific meaning in a specific context.

What about a literal translation not of a word but of a phrase? When I'm speaking on this topic, I often write the common phrase τοῦ θεοῦ (*tou theou*) on the whiteboard and ask someone to translate it literally. (It occurs 501 times in the New Testament.) Some brave soul will suggest "of God," which is how we teach first-year Greek students to translate the phrase. Their smile generally disappears from their face when I ask these follow-up questions:

1. Where is the Greek preposition corresponding to "of"? There is none. Are you adding to God's Word?
2. Why did you not translate the definite article τοῦ? You left out half of the words in the phrase.
3. Did you translate θεοῦ as lowercase "god" or uppercase "God"?

The phrase τοῦ θεοῦ is in the Greek genitive case, which English doesn't have. The word for "God" in the Greek is generally preceded with the article, as is the case with proper names (e.g., ὁ Ἰησοῦς, *ho Iēsous*), but we don't say "the God" or "the Jesus" in translation; it isn't standard English. We would never say, "For *the God* so loved the world."

It's impossible to translate even the simple τοῦ θεοῦ literally. If you can't translate words or phrases literally into English, a literal translation of the Bible is a hypothetical impossibility.

What about a literal translation of an entire sentence? To the best of my knowledge, not a single sentence in the New or Old Testament can be translated word for word in an understandable fashion, except for perhaps John 11:35: "Jesus wept." But even this is an approximation of the Greek ἐδάκρυσεν ὁ Ἰησοῦς (*edrakrusen ho Iēsous*). Word for word it reads, "he wept the Jesus." But even this is not a fully accurate translation because the verbal tense of ἐδάκρυσεν probably conveys the idea of bursting into tears. If there were such a thing as a literal translation, I suspect there would be fewer English Bibles. But since there is no such thing as a literal translation of a word, of a phrase, or of a sentence, then the myth of a literal translation of the Bible needs to be abandoned.

In the following section, we'll consider six factors that require interpretive decisions as one seeks to translate the Bible.

1. Words or Meaning?

If a literal translation is an impossibility, how do translation committees make their decisions? I like to think of the translation process as moving down the cutting edge of a knife blade. We start with the Greek sentence and translate the words, and as long as the translation makes sense and is using proper English, we stay balanced on the knife blade. Very quickly, however, we hit a Greek word that interrupts the flow of the English sentence. If we simply translate that word, the resulting sentence will be awkward English or, worse yet, not make any sense at all. What side of the knife's blade do you fall off on? One side of the blade is "Words," and the other side is "Meaning." The most fundamental decision every translation committee must make is whether it is going to err on the side of words or on the side of meaning.

If the translators err on the side of words, they will just translate the words. And as a result, the translation will be less interpretive but more difficult to understand and most likely will reflect poor English style. If they err on the side of meaning, the committee will have to be a little more interpretive, but they will be able to accurately convey the biblical author's meaning to the modern reader.

For example, Hebrews 1:3 says of Jesus, "He is the radiance of the glory of God and the exact imprint of his nature, and he upholds the universe by the word of his power" (ESV). But what does "by the word of his power" even mean? I have no idea. Most translations understand that transposing the words from Greek to English doesn't convey the meaning accurately, and so they translate this phrase as "by his powerful word" (NIV, CSB, NRSV, NET; cf. NLT).[1]

The Greek text says that Joseph went to the πόλις (*polis*) of Nazareth (Matt 2:23), and that the devil took Jesus to Jerusalem, the holy πόλις (Matt 4:5). Will you translate πόλις both times as "city," even though in the first example Nazareth had only about six hundred inhabitants and could scarcely be called a "city"? Translation demands interpretation, and we should probably translate πόλις as "town" when referring to Nazareth.

The Greek of Romans 12:16 reads in English (keeping the word order), "The same toward one another think [τὸ αὐτὸ εἰς ἀλλήλους φρονοῦντες]." The same what? The NASB errs on the side of words and reads, "Be of the same mind toward one another"—keeping the word *same* (τὸ αὐτό) and adding the word *mind* (without italicizing it; italics in the NASB is used for words not found in the original text but implied by it). To me this sounds a bit cultish—that the group has to agree with everything the leader says. The NIV falls more on the meaning side, choosing not to use the word *same* in its translation so as to avoid potential misunderstanding: "Live in harmony with one another" (so also most translations).

Let me again stress that all translations are interpretive. Every single translation has to look at what the Greek words say, interpret what those words mean in context, and then try to convey the same meaning in English. Some translations try to reduce the amount of interpretation, but all translations are interpretive.

2. Who Is Your Audience?

Every translation has an intended audience, which necessitates taking into account readers' ages, church backgrounds, and geographic locations. For example, the NIrV is specifically intended for people who have learned English as a second language; it also works great for children. But this meant the words had to be simplified, sentences shortened, and certain cultural issues explained. Translations like the ESV are comfortable with longer, more complicated sentences and larger words. Their audience is expected to study the Bible, which may involve using resources like a Bible dictionary. The letters *NIV* stand for the New *International* Version, which means we think about how people on every continent will hear the words. The NASB wants to be as word for word as possible, which means issues of word meanings and sentence length take a back seat to this central concern.

Consider an example from Romans 16:1. Is Phoebe a "servant" or a "deacon" (διάκονος, *diakonos*) of the church in Cenchreae? In the northern part of the United States, the translation choice doesn't raise the issue of church leadership for the most part, because a deacon is someone who serves the church, but not with institutional authority. In the southern part of the United States, because of the history of how the church was administered, the deacon tends to have institutional authority. So διάκονος has a significantly different meaning based on geography. This accounts for the lengthy footnote in the NIV, which uses *deacon* in the text of Romans 16:1: "The word *deacon* refers here to a Christian designated to serve with the overseers/elders of the church in a variety of ways; similarly in Phil. 1:1 and 1 Tim. 3:8, 12."

Paul tells the Roman church, "Greet one another with a holy kiss" (Rom 16:16 CSB, ESV, NASB, NET, NIV, NRSV). What's a "holy kiss"? Most translations are content to make the reader struggle with the meaning, but some translate it differently (italics added in all examples):

- "Greet each other with a *sacred kiss*" (NLT).
- "Greet one another with the *kiss of peace*" (GNT).
- "*Shake hands warmly* with each other" (TLB).
- "Give each other *a hearty handshake* all round" (Phillips).

One of the ways this sensitivity to the audience manifests itself is in the translation of metaphors. Everyone would agree that a dead metaphor must be interpreted. (A dead metaphor is one that used to mean something in English but no longer does.) The question is whether or not the metaphor is alive for the audience you're translating for. Paul says we are to "walk in love" (Eph 5:2 ESV). The NIV (1984) thought the metaphor of "walk" was dead, so they wrote, "live a life of love." In the 2011 update, we chose a mediating position and wrote, "walk in the way of love." But no one thinks that the Hebrew metaphors based on God's nose are still alive; therefore they must be interpreted. A long nose depicts patience (Exod 34:6, "longsuffering" in the KJV), a short nose impatience or quick-temperedness (Prov 14:17), and a hot nose anger (Exod 4:14).

3. The Role of Style

All translations want to use understandable English, but they disagree on how important this goal is compared to their other concerns. By now you should see that in almost every case, multiple factors are in play when deciding on a specific translation. For example, are you willing to add an English word to make your translation understandable, or does the policy of trying not to add words override the issue of English style?

Or consider that an aorist adverbial participle followed by an indicative verb is a common Greek construction. This is one way the Greeks indicate sequence. To show they understand it's an aorist adverbial participle, a first-year Greek student would most likely distinguish the participle from the indicative verb, as well as include the word *after*.

Using this technique, Matthew 2:3 would read, "King Herod, *after hearing*, was troubled" (my translation). This translation distinguishes the aorist participle "hearing" from the indicative "was troubled," but at the expense of English style. In English, we handle sequence differently. If we hear A and B, we default to understanding "A and *then* B," which means we would use two indicative verbs in translation. "King Herod *heard* and *was troubled*." Which is more important, using the smoothest English style or clearly indicating that "hearing" is a participle?

The Greek language prefers to start every sentence with a conjunction, explicitly indicating its connection to the previous sentence. However, many people today feel it's poor English style to start a sentence with a conjunction, so initial conjunctions are dropped hundreds of times in most translations. Just check the footnotes of the New English Translation (NET) for mention of not translating δέ (*de*), a word that can mean "and" or "but" and provides a weak connection to the previous sentence. We don't need this word (most of the time) because we use periods and paragraphs to link sentences together, which is the very function of a Greek word like δέ.

In Greek, you can ask a question in a way that indicates whether you think the answer is going to be yes or no. In 1 Corinthians 12:30, we would say, "All do not have gifts of healings, do they?" (NASB; see NET); the expected answer is no. But English translations often omit this piece of information since it makes for somewhat awkward English. "Do all possess gifts of healing?" (ESV; see NIV, CSB, NRSV, KJV). The NLT cleverly adds a sentence to the end of the list to make the expected answer clear: "Do we all have the gift of healing? . . . Of course not!"

This is the biggest difference between formal, dynamic, and natural language translations. A formal equivalent translation has as its goal that the translation will be *understandable*, a dynamic translation that it will be *clear*, and a natural language translation that it will sound *natural*. These different goals account for many of the differences among the translations.

4. Is There Ambiguity in the Original?

How do you handle a verse whose Greek is ambiguous yet whose meaning is clear? Of course, to say a verse's meaning is clear is an interpretive decision, but let's say for the sake of argument that we all agree on the meaning of a verse. How interpretive are you willing to be to make the meaning of an ambiguous expression clear?

"The anger of man does not achieve the righteousness of God" (Jas 1:20 NASB). What does "righteousness of God" mean? I would think it's clear that James is talking about the righteousness that God requires of us. There is nothing we can do to achieve the righteousness that God himself possesses, which makes the NRSV's translation strange: "Your anger does not produce God's righteousness." The NIV reads, "Human anger does not produce the righteousness that God desires."

In the Greek, Paul asks in Romans 8:35, "Who shall separate us from the love of Christ [τῆς ἀγάπης τοῦ Χριστοῦ, *tēs agapēs tou Xristou*]?" Is Paul speaking of my love for Christ or of Christ's love for me? The Greek allows for both. Thankfully, context and theology make it clear that it's Christ's love for me that binds us together. Most translations fall on the side of words here and leave the expression ambiguous—namely, "the love of Christ." The NLT almost always falls on the side of meaning and clarifies what Paul means: "Can anything ever separate us from Christ's love?"

Translation is more difficult when the meaning of an ambiguous statement is *not* clear. When I teach on the Pastoral Epistles, I will often ask if a divorced person can be an elder. When someone says no, I ask them for the biblical basis, and they'll often point to 1 Timothy 3:2. When I ask them to show me the word *divorced*, obviously it's not there. Paul writes, "It is necessary for an overseer to be above reproach: a man of one woman [μιᾶς γυναικὸς ἄνδρα, *mias gynaikos andra*]" (my translation). Word for word, μιᾶς γυναικὸς ἄνδρα reads "one of woman man." The meaning of the Greek is not clear. It's a strange expression not found in any Greek literature, Christian or secular. To make the translation even more challenging, the Greek could also mean "one of wife husband." And to make it even harder, there is an emphasis on the word μιᾶς (*mias*). When Greek wants to emphasize a word, it pushes it forward in the word order of the sentence. How would you convey that emphasis?

So what's a translator to do? You can't translate word for word because to do so would be meaningless. What translators do is spend time researching the words, the verse, and the biblical and theological backgrounds of the passage, and then they make a decision. If it's a truly difficult and important decision, you'll sometimes find a second interpretation in the footnote. But translators tend not to like footnotes (except the NET), so when a footnote is present, it signals an important issue. You can see how the translations struggle with 1 Timothy 3:2:

- "the husband of one wife" (ESV, CSB, NASB)
- "married only once" (NRSV, the "only" giving force to the placement of μιᾶς)
- "the husband of but one wife" (NIV 1984, the "but" also giving force to the placement of μιᾶς)
- "faithful to his wife" (NIV, NLT)

Fortunately, not many passages in the New Testament are this difficult to interpret. Many more fit that category in the Old Testament.

5. Avoiding Misunderstanding

All translators are especially sensitive to translating in such a way that people might misunderstand. We may disagree on an interpretation, but no one wants people to misunderstand the original author's meaning.

An interesting example is John 20:13. Mary is weeping at Jesus' tomb, and the angels say, "Woman [γύναι, *gynai*], why are you weeping?" (most translations). There is only one way to understand the English word "woman" in this translation, and it's in a pejorative sense. The problem is that while the angels do use the word γύναι and translations want to translate every word, there is no sense of cruelty or misogyny in the angels' statement in the Greek, so what's a translator to do? The NLT adds "dear" to soften the statement: "Dear woman, why are you crying?" But to simply translate this question as "Woman, why are you weeping?" carries the risk of miscommunicating.

Before I joined the NIV translation committee, I interpreted the NIV's decision to use a different term than *saints* as an example of the translators not wanting to use technical terms. When I joined the committee in 2010, one of my first questions was about this word. Take Romans 1:7 in the CSB, for example: "To all who are in Rome, loved by God, called as saints [ἁγίοις, *hagios*]." The NIV reads, "To all . . . called to be his holy people." I was told that the issue was not an aversion to technical terms like *saints*; they simply did not want people to misunderstand what the Greek was meaning. Today there is a common and unbiblical distinction between the "regular" people in the church and those who want to fully follow the commands of Christ. The normal terms are *lay* and *clergy*, which is a dreadful distinction, since we are all called to be fully devoted followers of Jesus Christ all the time. By referring to "the saints," the NIV committee feared that it would give tacit permission for people to sit in the back pews at church and let the pastor (the "saint") do the work. Whether or not you agree with their decision, it does show how careful translation committees are when trying to avoid miscommunication.

6. Gender Questions

Translations also must deal with the issue of gender language. For some people, "man" and "he" are still understood generically, referring to men and women alike. But for many others, "man" and "he" only mean "male." Some people may not like this and may want our language to go back in time. But it's a fact that many people don't hear "man" and "he" generically, and that using these masculine terms will make it difficult for them to hear the message of the Bible accurately. It's not an issue of a theological or cultural agenda; it's an issue of the meaning of the words.

I will never forget the day I walked into my daughter's bedroom when she was eight years old. Kiersten had photocopied a verse out of the Bible and pinned it to her bulletin board; in the verse she had crossed out "he" and replaced it with "she." After I complimented her on her desire to read and memorize the Bible, I asked her why she had made the alteration. I'll never forget her innocent response: "The Bible is for me too and not just Tyler, isn't it?" (Tyler is her big brother.)

We are in the middle of a sea change in our language as the pronoun "they" is becoming detached from number and can therefore refer to one or to more than one. Many people decry this shift, but it's becoming a reality in the English language. "They" was not marked for number in Elizabethan English (check out Shakespeare), and the "indefinite they" is coming back in vogue, whether we like it or not.

Since the issue of gender language accounts for many differences among translations, let's be sure we're using the terminology correctly. Like the five translation camps above, people often use these phrases with different meanings.[2]

Gender Neutrality

This kind of translation seeks to neutralize or eliminate gender-specific references as much as possible. "Parent" would be used instead of "father," "ancestor" for "forefather," "child" for "son," and "person" for "man" without regard to the actual referent. When my daughter writes a bio about herself for a PhD symposium, the academy requires her to refer to herself as "they." My daughter is a female, but she can't refer to herself as "she." Instead, she has to write, "Kiersten Mounce... They is pursuing a PhD in Art History." This is being gender-neutral. I'm not aware of any translation that intentionally does this; at a minimum, all translations still refer to God as "Father."

My son Hayden came home from university the other day and asked why the NIV was gender-neutral. I asked him why *he* thought it was, and he said his teacher reads from the ESV. Time after time, the teacher reads "he ... he ... he ... ," but the NIV has "they ... they ... they ..." I assured him the NIV was not gender-neutral, but that the issue was one of meaning. If a person hears "he" and understands it to mean "male" and not "male and female," then using "he" is (for that person) a mistranslation.

Gender Inclusivity

"Gender-inclusive" is the more commonly used term when referring to gender language in translation, yet it too can be used differently. A gender-inclusive translation tries to make everything inclusive, including both male and female, whether the source text makes gender-specific statements or not. So biblical statements about men would consistently be translated as if they were referring to both men and women.

The only translation that does this is the NRSV when, for example, it changes "man" to "child" and "father" to "parent."

> A *man* who loves wisdom brings joy to his *father*. (Prov 29:3 NIV, italics added)

> A *child* who loves wisdom makes a *parent* glad. (Prov 29:3 NRSV, italics added)

The NRSV will also change third person singular to second person, or drop out the pronoun altogether.

> If any of you lacks wisdom, let *him* ask God, who gives generously to all without reproach, and it will be given *him*. (Jas 1:5 ESV, italics added)

> If any of you is lacking in wisdom, ask God, who gives to all generously and ungrudgingly, and it will be given *you*. (NRSV, italics added)

Gender Accuracy

Gender-accurate translations intentionally clarify gender. They refer to "men" using male language and to "women" using female language, and they use inclusive terms when referring to both men and women. Their goal is to be accurate and specific with reference to gender. Most modern translations do this, but they often do it differently. This can be seen in four different scenarios.

1. Indefinite referent. Translations can differ in the use of the pronoun that refers back to an indefinite noun or pronoun. Consider Psalm 1:1:

> Blessed is the one
>> who does not walk in step with the wicked
> or stand in the way that sinners take
>> or sit in the company of mockers.

"One" is an indefinite referent. When you get to verse 3, how do you refer back to the indefinite word? "_____ is like a tree planted by streams of water" (v. 3). The ESV and CSB will refer back to an indefinite with the anaphoric "he."

> *He* is like a tree planted by streams of water.

The NIV often uses a singular "they," although in this case, we wanted to be emphatically singular:

> *That person* is like a tree planted by streams of water,
>> which yields its fruit in season
> and whose leaf does not wither—
>> whatever they do prospers. (italics added)

The NRSV often employs other ways, such as using plurals or second person, but in this verse, it uses "they."

They are like trees planted by streams of water.

2. Representative male. Another decision has to do with how to handle references to a male when the male stands as a representative for men and women. Proverbs 3:11–12 is the classic passage:

> My *son*, do not despise the LORD's discipline,
>> and do not resent his rebuke,
> because the LORD disciplines those he loves,
>> as a father the *son* he delights in. (NIV, italics added)

This technique preserves a classic form of wisdom literature, and the expectation is that the reader will understand that what is true of the son is also true of the daughter. Compare this to the NLT's rendering:

> My *child*, don't reject the LORD's discipline,
>> and don't be upset when he corrects you.
> For the LORD corrects those he loves,
>> just as a father corrects a *child* in whom he delights.
>> (italics added)

Note that the NLT uses "father" and not "parent." It's not gender-inclusive in this verse.

3. "Brother." The third situation affected by gender issues is the translation of ἀδελφός (*adelfos*), traditionally translated as "brother." The CSB translates Matthew 18:15 as, "If your *brother* sins against you, go tell him his fault, between you and him alone" (italics added). With whom do we have to reconcile—only our male Christian friends or all our Christian friends? It depends (at one level) on whether you hear "brother" as "male" or as "fellow believer." The NIV reads, "If your *brother or sister* sins, go and point out their fault, just between the two of you" (italics added). When referring to a member of your faith community, what term or phrase do you use?

4. "Man." A related word is ἄνθρωπος (*anthrōpos*). Should we translate it as "man" (or "men" in the plural) or with words that mean "men and women"? One of the most difficult biblical passages to translate is 1 Timothy 2:1–7. Paul's basic argument is that the Ephesians should pray on behalf of all "men" (v. 2) because God wishes all "men" to be saved (v. 4), and there is only one mediator between God and "men," the "man" Christ Jesus (v. 5). Only the NASB (1995) keeps the concordance (translating the same Greek word with the same English word), but to do so suggests to some modern readers that verse 2 declares that the Ephesians should pray on behalf of all *males*. Even the ESV, which has a strong commitment to concordance, translates πάντων ἀνθρώπων (*pantōn anthrōpōn*) as "all people" in verse 2, with a footnote on verse 5: "*men* and *man* render the same Greek word that is translated *people* in verses 1 and 4." But God wants all people to be saved, not just all men, and the point is not that Christ Jesus is a male but that he is part of humanity.

Let me stress that this is not an issue of theology or an expression of a cultural agenda, at least not in my experience. All the translators I know and have worked with see this as an issue of meaning. What does "he" or "man" or "brother" mean to our intended audience?

Conclusion

I hope you can see now why translations are different. Languages are not codes, and the process of moving meaning from one language to another requires interpretation and a consistent translation philosophy. There is no such thing as a literal translation, and all translations are interpretive, committing to look at what the Greek says and means and then to try to convey the same meaning faithfully into English. Hopefully you can also see how complicated the process can become and why translations are different but still trustworthy.

If you enjoy comparing translations, as I do, you'll discover that the translations rarely disagree with each other in terms of meaning.

Typically one is more vague ("love of Christ") and the other is more specific ("Christ's love"). The next time you're in a group Bible study where the translations seem to be different, ask yourself if you can find a way to view all of the translations as accurate and recognize that they are simply using different words to make the full meaning clear.

For Further Reading

Blomberg, Craig L. "Can We Trust Any of Our Translations of the Bible?" In *Can We Still Believe the Bible? An Evangelical Engagement with Contemporary Questions*. Grand Rapids: Brazos, 2014, 83–118.

Carson, D. A. *The Inclusive Language Debate: A Plea for Realism*. Grand Rapids: Baker, 1998.

———. *The King James Version Debate: A Plea for Realism*. Grand Rapids: Baker, 1979.

Köstenberger, Andreas J., and David A. Croteau, eds. *Which Bible Translation Should I Use?: A Comparison of Four Major Versions*. Nashville: B & H Academic, 2012.

Mounce, William D. "Translation Philosophy." Lecture 28 in "Why We Trust Our Bible." Biblical Training Institute, https://mybt.us/translations. See also lectures 29–32.

Strauss, Mark L. *Distorting Scripture? The Challenge of Bible Translation and Gender Accuracy*. Eugene, OR: Wipf & Stock, 2010.

Advanced

Metzger, Bruce M. *The Bible in Translation: Ancient and English Versions*. Grand Rapids: Baker, 2001.

Notes

1. For you Bible nerds, τῷ ῥήματι τῆς δυνάμεως is a Hebraic attributive genitive. It uses the noun δύναμις ("power") as an adjective ("powerful").
2. For further discussion, see Mark L. Strauss, *Distorting Scripture? The Challenge of Bible Translation and Gender Accuracy* (1998; repr., Eugene, OR: Wipf & Stock, 2010); D. A. Carson, *The Inclusive Language Debate: A Plea for Realism* (Grand Rapids: Baker, 1998).

THE OLD TESTAMENT

Is the Old Testament Believable?

Challenge

The challenges against the reliability of the Old Testament are of a somewhat different nature than those against the reliability of the New Testament, and the answers are often more complex. To do them justice would require hundreds of pages. These two chapters, therefore, seek to offer an overview of the basic issues and provide some of the basic answers.

Chapter 12

THE CHARACTER OF GOD

In this chapter, we will look at attacks on the character of God and the inability of many people to understand his love (which moves him to forgive) and his holiness (which moves him to judge), and how these two qualities are perfectly balanced in his character and actions, including such actions as the flood and the extermination of the Canaanites.

This is an immense topic that takes entire books to explain. The best I can do is share what has been meaningful to me in the hope that it will encourage you. My wife, Robin, and I have lost two children, Rose in a miscarriage and Rachel four hours after birth. As difficult as that was, it pales in comparison to the pain of a tragic ministry experience. What follows is what helped Robin and me (and our children) work through the pain.

Challenges

Many of the challenges against the Old Testament begin with an attack on the character of God. One of the most ferocious is from Richard Dawkins:

> The God of the Old Testament is arguably the most unpleasant character in all fiction: jealous and proud of it; a petty, unjust, unforgiving

control-freak; a vindictive, bloodthirsty ethnic cleanser; a misogynistic, homophobic, racist, infanticidal, genocidal, filicidal, pestilential, megalomaniacal, sadomasochistic, capriciously malevolent bully.[1]

Biblical Interpretation

Assessments like those of Richard Dawkins are understandable when coming from someone outside the Judeo-Christian faith community who has not committed himself to the entire revelation of the character of God in the Old and New Testaments. He doesn't have a balanced view of God and all his attributes, especially the perfect balance of God's love and holiness as demonstrated in both the Old and New Testaments. But for those who accept the entire Bible, nothing could be further from the truth. Let's look more closely at a few of the charges Dawkins levels against God.

"God of the Old Testament." We first need to note that Christians believe only one God is revealed in both Testaments. It's common to hear, even in the conservative church, that the God of the Old Testament is different from the God of the New Testament, but people are rarely thinking through what they mean when they say this. Do they worship two Gods? Did God change between the Old and New Testaments? The Bible is clear that there is only one God (Deut 6:4–5; Isa 45:6; Mark 12:29), and he never changes (Jas 1:17; Heb 13:8). If you are to understand him, you need to read the whole Bible.

"Fiction." In attacking the character of God, Dawkins clearly indicates he doesn't believe that the Bible is true. The problem is that much of the Bible is spiritual and understandable only by those possessed by God's Spirit (see 1 Cor 2:12–14). As brilliant as Dawkins may be in his area of expertise, as brilliant as many of the antagonists of Christianity may be, their opinions are of relative worth since they are not able to fully understand the Bible. But their responses are valuable to us so we can see how the world views the Bible.

"Jealous and proud of it." I'm thankful that God is a jealous God. I'm thankful that he doesn't want to share us with the evil of this world.

I'm thankful that my wife is jealous of me. We are both free to have relationships and share life with many people, but when it comes right down to it, I belong to my wife, Robin, and she belongs to me. I would never share my wife intimately with another man; to do so would be a disgusting violation of our marriage vows. I understand that jealousy can have an ugly dimension to it, but God's jealousy is a perfect jealousy, controlled by his love and his knowledge of what is best for us (Song 8:6; 2 Cor 11:2). Yes, God is a jealous God, and perfect jealousy is an expression of love.

"Unjust." This particular charge is especially important if we are to understand the character of God. Let me ask you a question. Who defines what is just? If Richard Dawkins were to say that we human beings define what is just, then there is no valid definition of justice, since most people would define justice differently.[2] Was Stalin just to exterminate twenty million of his people and to rob the Ukrainians of their harvest in order to build his empire and leave them to starve? Stalin would have said yes, because in Marxism the ends justify the means.

Biblical theology does not teach there is a universal code of justice under which God submits himself, because that would mean there is something greater than God. Rather, God determines what is just. When I was teaching in graduate school, I remember Dr. Greg Beale discussing this topic in the cafeteria, pounding the table and declaring, "Justice is what God does." He could not have been more right. Only God determines what is just, and whatever he does is just, because what he does is an expression of his just character. This is obviously a faith position, but it's a position that makes sense and is internally consistent, even if we don't always understand all of the specific implementations of that principle in time. Is it just to punish people for their sin? Yes, because God punishes people. Is it just for God to forgive sins? Yes, because he does forgive sins. Is it just for someone to die as a substitute for another? Yes, because that's what Jesus did on the cross. From a human standpoint, there was no greater act of evil than for God to allow his own Son to be killed because of human sin, but doing so was just because God did it. So when I go through a painful experience, I remind myself that nothing happens that isn't filtered through God's fingers, that what happens is ultimately just, and I will more fully understand that conviction when I see my life through God's eyes.

These are just a few points extracted from Dawkins's charges, but I think you get the idea. Dawkins's assessment, like so many others, is based on an *incomplete* reading of the Bible that fails to take into account the full revelation of God and especially the balance of his love and holiness—the topics to which we now turn.

Love and Holiness

Of all the divine characteristics of God that are commonly misunderstood, God's love and holiness are at the head of the pack. Each of these qualities is often misunderstood, and how they work together is especially misunderstood. God declares to Moses in Exodus 34:6–7:

> "The LORD, the LORD, the compassionate and gracious God, slow to anger, abounding in love and faithfulness, maintaining love to thousands, and forgiving wickedness, rebellion and sin. Yet he does not leave the guilty unpunished; he punishes the children and their children for the sin of the parents to the third and fourth generation."

God is compassionate, gracious, loving, and faithful. God's love leads him to act. He does not have to forgive, but his love leads him to forgive. His love led him to send his Son to earth to die so that through his death all his children could live forever with him.

But God is also a holy God. He is as holy as he is loving. He is not more loving than holy, and not more holy than loving. Because he is holy, he cannot tolerate sin. Anything contrary to his character is sin, and his holiness, often expressed as "righteousness," requires punishment of sin. God doesn't punish because he enjoys it; he punishes because to do otherwise would render him unjust. This is why Jesus had to die. If God had simply ignored sin, he too would have been unrighteous (see Rom 3:25–26).

God is loving, which leads to forgiveness. God is holy, which leads to punishment of sin. Both of these divine attributes of love and holiness are true, but it's in the balance of both that we gain the clearest picture of who God is. As we think about God's allowing of evil and pain, we must always keep this balance in mind. God forgives repentant sinners and does not ask them to experience all the pain their sin deserves. But there is an end to God's patience with sin, and people do experience the painful consequence of their own decisions and sometimes the decisions of others. In everything that happens to me, I have to remind myself that my experiences are the result of a mix of both God's love and God's justice.

The Presence of Evil

How can God be all powerful, all knowing, and all loving and yet allow pain and suffering? This is one of the most common objections raised in reference to the character of the biblical God, which in turn discourages people from trusting the Bible. This is a question not just for the Old Testament but for the entire Bible.

It is one thing to accept at a theoretical level these thoughts I will share, but it's another thing altogether to accept it when it is your child who is hurting or dying. Faith in the midst of personal pain is a real challenge. I trust that what I say will not sound callous or indifferent. It is certainly not my intention. As I said at the beginning of this chapter, Robin and I have lost two children—Rose and Rachel. As painful as their deaths were, the pain of losing a ministry we had helped found and had deeply loved was significantly greater. The following truths are part of who I have become, albeit imperfectly.

Faith

First, we must admit that part of this question of evil simply cannot be answered. We are called, by faith, to hold the presence of evil and the character of God in tension. We are called to believe that, along with the martyred saints, we will someday confess, "Just and true are your ways, King of the nations" (Rev 15:3). This is the message of the Old Testament books of Habakkuk (see 2:4; 3:17–18) and Job.

To Job, the world had become chaotic, out of control, and he cries out to God for an answer. God's answer is that, despite the seemingly chaotic nature of reality, God is in control, and Job (and we) must by faith accept the words of the prophet Isaiah: "As the heavens are higher than the earth, so are my ways higher than your ways and my thoughts than your thoughts" (Isa 55:9). Job responds in repentance and faith (Job 42:2–6).

One of the reasons faith is required is because there is so much we don't understand about evil, and this ignorance is by God's design. We don't ultimately know why there is evil in this world. Couldn't God have made the world in such a way that evil was not an option and yet allow us to make our own choices? We don't know where Satan came from. God must have created him, since God created all things (Col 1:16), but why did God create Satan? I'm sure most of us have said at one time or another that evil doesn't make sense, and we are right to say so. Ultimately, evil does *not* make sense,[3] and apparently we don't need to know where it came from and ultimately why God allows it to happen.

However, even if pain and suffering don't ultimately make sense in a world created by an all-good, all-powerful, all-loving God, we *do* know how to respond to evil. We know to call evil "evil." We know to resist it (1 Pet 5:8). We know to call on God to keep us from the power of the evil one (Matt 6:13). We know to lament it (see the Old Testament book of Lamentations). And most importantly, we know that one day all evil will be vanquished (Rev 21–22).We who love and trust God have the privilege of walking into our Father's throne room and crying out to him in pain; this is the privilege we have because we are the children of a loving heavenly Father, and this truth has been illustrated time and time again in the book of Psalms. As Christopher Wright says, "Lament is the voice of faith struggling to live with unanswered questions and unexplained suffering."[4] These are all things we *do* know.

Whenever we talk about pain and suffering, it must be held up against the backdrop of heaven. Pain often forces our heads down, looking only to ourselves, only to the present, focusing on the reality of the pain. Faith lifts our heads up, acknowledging the pain of the present but seeing it in light of eternity. This is what Paul means when he tells the church in Rome, "I consider that our present sufferings are not worth comparing with the glory that will be revealed in us" (Rom 8:18). He tells the church in Corinth, "For our light and momentary troubles are achieving for us an eternal glory that far outweighs them all. So we fix our eyes not on what is seen, but on what is unseen, since what is seen is temporary, but what is unseen is eternal" (2 Cor 4:17–18). I know that one day pain and evil will be gone and someday it will make sense, but until then we live by faith.

Of course, when God does prevent pain, we often don't know that he did. One of the things I'm looking forward to in heaven is to discover all the pain and suffering that God saved me from. My guess is that the pain and suffering from which I was protected far outweigh the pain I experienced.

To the non-Christian, I understand that this whole discussion about faith appears to sidestep the issue. But for the Christian, it is central. We are content to live by faith, acknowledging that someday this world will all make sense, as difficult as it is to accept when there is so much pain and suffering everywhere in the world—and in our own homes—right now. The Bible teaches that "without faith it is impossible to please God, because anyone who comes to him must believe that he exists and that he rewards those who earnestly seek him" (Heb 11:6). Part of our heavenly reward will certainly be an understanding of the character of God and the world as we now see it. For me, personally, this is enough.

Besides, knowing the full story now would not bring my girls back or restore my ministry, and frankly, Rose and Rachel are really happy right now where they are.

Human Sin

Other parts of the question of evil, pain, suffering, and the character of God can be answered, or at least explained to some degree. The Bible tells us that much of the evil in this world is the result of human sin. Adam and Eve sinned, and therefore sin entered the world and we suffer the consequences. We personally sin, and we suffer the consequences (Rom 5:12). Mankind sins, and creation suffers the consequences (Rom 8:19–21). The soil produces weeds; childbirth is painful; and marriage relationships are damaged (Gen 3:16–19). I suspect that the great majority of pain in this world is caused by human sin, directly or indirectly. I often say that life is made up of choices, some that we make and some that others make for us. It is in these human choices and our responses that much of the pain in this world should be understood.

Clay Jones makes this point forcefully as he documents the millions and millions of people who have died at the hands of other people.[5] Reading his description of how all this happened may not be for the faint of heart, but this account truly should be read by all people. But he adds a sobering reality check to these numbers. These atrocities were carried out not by sociopathic madmen but by ordinary people.[6] We now know that the German people knew the Holocaust was happening, as did the majority of Europeans. I remember talking with a European friend who watched as Jews were herded onto boxcars, and he told me that most of Europe knew exactly what was happening—and frankly, he added, they were glad someone was "getting rid of the Jews." Jones asks, "Is this inhuman?" and concludes, "No this is what humans do." People may do "nice" things, but that does not make them "good" (Jones's distinction).[7] Humans are responsible for so much of the pain in this world.

Christopher Wright also speaks of the *indirect* ways that humans cause evil and suffering in the world:

> So it seems to me ... that the vast bulk of all the suffering and pain in our world is the result, direct or indirect, of human

wickedness. Even where it is not caused directly by human sin, suffering can be greatly increased by it. What Hurricane Katrina did to New Orleans was bad enough, but how much additional suffering was caused by everything from looters to bureaucratic incompetence? HIV-AIDS is bad enough, but how many millions suffer preventable illness and premature death because corporate and political greed and callousness put medicines that are affordance and available in the West totally out of their reach? What the cyclone did to Myanmar was horrendous, but its effects were multiplied by the characteristically brutal refusal of the government to allow international aid organizations into the country until weeks later. Human callousness undoubtedly precipitated the death of thousands and prolonged the misery of the survivors.[8]

To use a personal example, my daughter's PhD thesis is on the "Chaise Sandows," a chair made by René Herbst during the interwar period (1919–1939) in France. One of its innovations was the use of bungee cords. The rubber for the cords was manufactured by the Michelin company in the country's largest rubber plantation—in what can only be called concentration camps—in Vietnam (at that time called Indochina). As I drive down the highway on my Michelin tires, does my support of that company in some way tie me to their historical evil?

I want to be very clear on this point. When we hear people complain that God allows evil, it is wholly disingenuous if we do not first address the evil *we* have caused, directly or indirectly, and the evil *we* have turned a blind eye to because it occurs on the other side of the planet or because it's just inconvenient to care about it or do something about it. After all, I enjoy how Michelin tires drive.

On a different but related point, people often treat God as if he were their personal nanny. They live their lives in relative independence from God, and when something bad happens, they cry out to God—and then they are angry when he doesn't do their bidding. I remember a scene in a movie where a mother was screaming accusations against God after her child died. As horrid as the death of a child is, she had no right to blame God. The God of the Bible isn't a nanny to all people, making sure nothing bad happens to them and then receding into the background and waiting for the next time pain heads their way.

God in fact makes few promises to people who are not his children. If a person lives their life outside of a relationship with God, as someone who is not God's child, they should not expect the privileges of sonship. I don't mean to sound harsh, but God doesn't owe them anything. If they have not made a commitment to Jesus as Lord and Savior, he has not made commitments to them, other than to let the rain fall on the righteous and unrighteous alike (Matt 5:45).

But why does pain and suffering come on those of us who are his children? After years of struggle, I have become content with the answer of Romans 8:28–30.[9] God's good for me is not the cessation of pain and the presence of pleasure. God's good for me is that I be "conformed to the image of his Son" (v. 29). Because this is God's best, he is at work in all situations to accomplish his goals for me and for you (v. 28). This was his decision before the creation of all things, and in time he accomplishes his purposes by calling us to himself, justifying us, and fully glorifying us (v. 30). Having experienced the pain of the death of two children and the loss of a beloved ministry, I can say with conviction that it's better for me to be conformed to the image of his Son, for me to look more like Jesus, than to be kept safe from all pain, despite the fact that the pain was very real.

To put this in perspective, I'll share a story. I reconnected a while back with an old friend, a medical doctor who now runs a rehab center for alcohol and drug addiction. Over the course of the past twelve years, he had gone through a divorce, lost connection with his children, become an alcoholic, and almost pulled the trigger of a loaded gun in his mouth. He told me that someone the other day had commented about all the *bad* things that have happened to him. "What bad things?" he responded. "All those events are *good* things because they have made me into who I am today. When men come into the rehab center, I know what they're going through." That's Romans 8:28–30 in action.

Satan

Another source of evil is the person of Satan. We do not know for sure who he is—the assumption is that he was a powerful angel who revolted against God. He and his followers ("demons") were cast out of heaven, and they now torment the earth until their time of punishment (Isa 14:4–21; Ezek 28:1–17; 2 Pet 2:4; Jude 6; Rev 12:7–9). Satan is also responsible for much of the evil and pain and suffering in the world (e.g., Job 1:9–11; Luke 13:16; 22:31; Acts 5:3; 26:18; 1 Cor 7:5; 2 Cor 2:11; 2 Thess 2:9; Rev 2:13). He is not all-powerful or all-knowing, but he is extremely powerful and has a "wisdom" born out of years of causing pain.

Once again the book of Job helps us understand. Duane Garrett summarizes the theme of Satan in the book as follows.

> Job 41 speaks of Leviathan as the great enemy, a representation of Satan and the source of all evil. All the troubles in this world that Job laments over (see especially Job 24) have their source in Satan. God, in his speech to Job (chaps. 38–41) essentially tells Job that he (God) knows what he is doing, and that he will take care of evil in his own time and in his own way. God does not tell Job *how* he will deal with Satan, only *that* he will do it, and Job must trust God to resolve the problem of evil in his own time in his own way.
>
> This takes us back to the hidden wisdom of God described in Job 28. This chapter makes the point that there is a divine wisdom we cannot grasp, and that the best we can do (what constitutes wisdom for us) is trust God and turn from evil while we wait on the ultimate salvation from God (28:28). This, in turn, leads to 1 Corinthians 1:18–25 in which Christ is shown to be the hidden wisdom of God, a wisdom that seems like folly to humans. It turns out that the secret wisdom of God, the means by which he defeats Satan, is the cross.[10]

To be able to understand the wiles of Satan is important, as is understanding his limitations. Paul says that "our struggle is not against flesh and blood, but against the rulers, against the authorities, against the powers of this dark world and against the spiritual forces of evil in the heavenly realms" (Eph 6:12). When I was pastoring, month after month, every Sunday morning at exactly 3:00 a.m., I was awakened by demonic forces—speaking, screaming, rattling chains, and even pulling the covers off my bed and pushing Robin. The demonic world did not want me preaching, but thankfully they are not all-powerful (see Dan 10) and had to submit to my divine protection.

Ultimately, goodness is greater than evil, and nowhere is this more visible than on the cross.[11] God takes human sin upon himself, pays the punishment for it, and makes our freedom from pain ultimately possible.[12] Goodness won on the cross, and Christ will return to make all things new, destroying all that is evil and causes pain, including Satan (Rev 20:10). Then there will be no more tears or death (Rev 21:4). We will never again experience pain. Until then, we live by faith.

Natural Evil

While we've been noting several considerations that help us understand some aspects of moral evil—evil caused by human sin, directly or indirectly—natural evil is much more difficult to understand. Natural evil is the pain and suffering caused by events that are not directly related to human sin. Whether they be hurricanes, tsunamis, or earthquakes, how can we believe in an all-powerful, all-loving, all-knowing God who allows these things to happen?

In 2014, the people in Oso, a small town in northwest Washington state, awakened to a sound they had never heard before. The mountain behind the town had turned into a giant mudslide. Thousands of tons of mud slipped down the mountain, burying buildings and killing forty-three people in its path. Why did God allow this to happen?

Part of the answer may lie with the human deforestation of the mountain, removing the God-given controls that held the topsoil in place, but most of it lies in the mystery of natural evil. And part of the answer for natural evil lies in God's curse on the ground *because of human sin*.

When Adam and Eve sinned, God not only cursed the serpent and Eve, but he also cursed the ground (see Gen 3:17–19).

Whereas mankind was put on earth to subdue the earth, the earth would now fight back. How much of the "ground" did God curse? Certainly "ground" stands for all the created order, and I suspect that "thorns and thistles" include more than weeds. When God curses something, it is truly cursed.

I am not a geologist, nor the son of a geologist, so this is mostly a mystery to me. I understand that the movement of the tectonic plates floating on the magma will surely someday cause the San Andreas Fault to shift, and perhaps my son Tyler and his family, my sister and her family, and my good friend Scott Kinnes, who all live in Southern California, will suffer the consequences. Did they "deserve" to be inflicted with pain? Of course not, and yet the earthquake could perhaps be directly connected to God's curse on the ground as a consequence of Adam and Eve's sin. There is so much more that could be said on this point, but this will have to suffice for now.

God's View

I love the throne room scene in Revelation 4–5. It gives me the perspective from which to view my world. God is the center of it all, sitting on his throne. In front of him are seven blazing lamps—"the seven spirits of God"—and the four living creatures, and around him are the twenty-four elders on their thrones, and around them are angels, thousands upon thousands of angels, ten thousand times ten thousand.

In God's hand is the scroll that only the slain lamb is able to open, the scroll that prophecies all that is to come in history. As the seals are removed, history is revealed and explained. We learn that God is sovereign; it is he who sends out the white horse whose rider was bent on conquest, the red rider who has power to take peace from the earth and make people kill each other, the black rider who brings famine, and the pale rider who is death. These riders are sent out into the world at God's command and wreak the havoc for which they were created. God is sovereign and in control. Under the altar are the martyred saints, crying out "How long, Sovereign Lord, holy and true, until you judge the inhabitants of the earth and avenge our blood?" Eventually the great day of God's wrath comes, and the saints are able to cry out, "Salvation belongs to our God, who sits on the throne, and to the Lamb" (Rev 7:10).

All of history is at God's bidding. He is sovereign over all. He is in control of all, even though it looks like chaos to us. But eventually God will make all things right, and we too will see things from God's perspective. We will understand; it will all make sense. Until then, like Habakkuk and Paul, we live by faith.

The Flood

The flood and its ensuing destruction of almost all life on earth is sometimes viewed as the act of a cruel God. But this is a misreading of the biblical text.

When Adam and Eve's son Cain killed his brother Abel, God responded by forgiving him, but the ongoing decisions of human beings in the generations that followed moved things from bad to worse. Just six generations from Adam, the earth was filled with wickedness (Gen 6:5–8). Noah was the sole righteous person (7:1):

Why, then, did God send a flood?

The flood performed two functions. First, it punished the rampant sin in the world—an act of justice. God is a holy and righteous God, and while he is patient with sin, there is an end to his patience. For one hundred years, Noah and his family built the ark (Gen 5:32; 7:6). For one hundred years, people were given the opportunity to repent, but they did not, and so judgment came. The church does a disservice to people when it paints a picture of the ark in only positive terms; it was also a dark and ugly act of judgment.

Second, the flood protected Noah and as such was an act of grace, limiting the increasingly destructive effects of human sin. Eventually, it is all too likely that the evil of the world would have infected Noah and his family as well, and the flood saved him from that possibility. Human beings were on a path toward annihilation and self-destruction. The flood—and the salvation of Noah and his family—was also an act of grace.

Despite what someone may think after reading the account of the flood, life *is* precious to God. He created it. He made human beings in his own image as the apex of creation by breathing "the breath of life" into Adam (Gen 2:7). He provided vegetation for food for everything that has "the breath of life" in it (1:30). He created an idyllic garden and allowed his creation to live in his presence. When sin entered the world in Genesis 3, you can feel his pain as that fellowship is broken. When Cain killed his brother (4:8), it too feels fundamentally wrong, like something that was not supposed to happen. But even the murderer Cain was protected with a "mark" (4:15) so that he wouldn't be killed. Life is precious to God.

In order to save life, God called on Noah to build an ark so that "pairs of all creatures that have the breath of life in them came to Noah and entered the ark" (7:15). The value of human life is again asserted after the flood, when God promises never again to destroy all life on his earth, and lays down this rule: "Whoever sheds human blood, by humans shall their blood be shed; for in the image of God has God made mankind" (9:6).

The account of the flood and the coming accounts of Sodom and Gomorrah must not overshadow these central biblical truths: God created life; all that has his breath of life is precious to him. *For God to destroy something as precious as life meant that the sin must have been severe and demanded punishment.* Thousands of years later, God will do the same thing again. His Son will die on the cross, punished for human sin, and by doing so will graciously give us access back into the Garden of Eden and the full presence of our God (Rev 21–22). One act is both judgment and grace.

Again, I don't mean to sound harsh, but the Creator's rights over his creation is a fundamental biblical truth. For those of us who recognize that we are lumps of clay on *his* potter's wheel, it's still a difficult doctrine to grasp. It takes a strong and mature faith to accept the pain that comes our way in life, to say with Job, "Naked I came from my mother's womb, and naked I will depart. The Lord gave and the Lord has taken away; may the name of the Lord be praised" (Job 1:21). It requires a strong and mature faith to accept the fact that there is an end to God's patience and sin will be punished on a massive scale. Even though we understand that nothing happens that is not filtered through God's fingers, pain is real, and it hurts.

Genocide

People often see God's demand that Joshua destroy all Canaanite life as another example of his cruelty. When the Israelites were to enter the Promised Land, Moses told them that God had declared that they must destroy the inhabitants totally (Deut 7:1–6). But is this truly genocide? Let's consider a few alternative ways to understand what is happening here.

Punishment for sin. God had told Abraham that his descendants would be enslaved in another country for four hundred years, but eventually his descendants "will come back here, for *the sin of the Amorites has not yet reached its full measure*" (Gen 15:16, italics added). In his patience, God gave the Canaanites (also called "the Amorites") four hundred years to repent of their sin. When they didn't, God brought back Abraham's descendants and punished the Canaanites for their sin. First and foremost, the destruction of the Canaanites was punishment for their unrepentant sin. This is not consistent with the definition of genocide.

Purity. God's desire was not simply to destroy people. The nation of Israel was his special nation, "his treasured possession" (Deut 7:6). His people were to be holy, dedicated completely to him. The call to destroy the people of the Canaanite nations and the relics of their religion was so that God's nation would not intermarry with the Canaanites and thus be drawn away from true worship and become a blessing to the entire world. This is not genocide.

Rahab. The account of Rahab, who assisted the Israelite spies, can give us insight into the historical situation (Josh 2:1–21; 6:17, 22–23). She told the two spies that her people had heard what the Israelite army had done to Sihon and Og, two Amorite kings. Rahab said, "When we heard of it, our hearts melted in fear and everyone's courage failed because of you, for the LORD your God is God in heaven above and on the earth below. Now then, please swear to me by the LORD that you will show kindness to my family, because I have shown kindness to you" (2:11–12).

Rahab and her family were saved while the rest of Jericho was destroyed. The point is that the spies and Joshua did not see a contradiction between obeying God's command to destroy everyone and showing kindness to Rahab. Judgment can be averted in light of repentance. God is compassionate and gracious, forgiving those who align themselves with him, even in the face of imminent destruction.

Ḥērem. Part of the answer to the charge of genocide may be to recognize the specific nature of the warfare. The Hebrew word *ḥērem* means "to devote to the ban." It occurs in Joshua 2:10, translated as "completely destroyed" (NIV), "utterly destroyed" (NRSV), or "devoted to destruction" (ESV; see also, e.g., Num 21:2–3; Deut 2:34; 3:6; 7:2; 13:15; 20:17). The idea is that the land has always belonged to God, and the war will return to God everything that was his. Because *ḥērem* warfare resulted in a total (or near total) destruction of the enemy, *ḥērem* can be translated "completely destroyed."

It may be helpful to note that this was a common idea in the ancient world. It's not as if God told the Israelites to do something that no king ever told his armies.[13] While the total destruction of a neighboring country sounds barbaric to a modern person, it was not uncommon to the ancient. But never forget that wars waged in our lifetime are far more destructive than anything that could happen in the ancient world. To them, *we* would be barbaric.

The Old Testament scholar Meredith Kline spoke of an "intrusion ethic."[14] It's what happens when God suspends common grace (Gen 9:1–7) and a form of his eschatological judgment intrudes into reality. In Canaan, as well as in Sodom and Gomorrah (Gen 19), we catch a glimpse of what the final judgment will be like. For the inhabitants of Canaan, Sodom, and Gomorrah, God's act was one of judgment. For Christians, it is an act of grace; it warns us about the severe consequences of sin, allows us to see what our fate would have been apart from Christ, and helps us appreciate our forgiveness in Christ.

Noncombatants. It can be argued that the killing in Canaan focused on military personnel and people in the main cities, not the wholesale destruction of every person. In Deuteronomy 20:16–18, the Israelites were told to destroy the "cities" (עיר ['îr] in Hebrew). The Hebrew word is defined as a "permanent settlement without any reference to its size."[15] It was also used of tent encampments (Judg 10:4) and a fort within a city (2 Sam 12:26). From what we know from history and archaeology, most of the "cities" were nothing more than a walled fort where the ruler lived, along with his temple, treasury, and army. The "ruler" is usually called the "king" (*melek*), but he was more often than not a military commander who would answer to a greater *melek*, such as the *melek* of Jerusalem or the pharaoh in Egypt. For the most part, the people lived outside the city in small settlements, villages, or hamlets and would only retreat into the "city" for safety from invading armies. Joshua was instructed to totally destroy the centers of power that would continue to infect the Israelites with their pagan worship. It seems that the Israelites were not focused on destroying the noncombatants, and in fact there were many Canaanites who survived.[16]

Another interesting sidenote is the size of Jericho. Much is made in the text of Joshua's victory over Jericho, but Jericho was not a large city. Estimates are that it covered only a few acres, and the army protecting Jericho would have been about one hundred soldiers.[17] It was not a widespread slaughter, as might be imagined if Joshua had been marching against London or even Jerusalem.

This point may help a little, but at the end of the day God ordered the wholesale killing of men, women, children, and livestock. There is no question that Joshua's army slaughtered many people, but not all. It was a far cry from the genocide that many people imagine, and it was an act of judgment on unrepentant sin.

Conclusion

The picture of God in the Old Testament can be easily misunderstood. But once we realize that God is perfect love that moves to forgiveness, and perfect justice that moves to punishment, it is easier to accept by faith the loving and powerful nature of God and to believe that justice is what God does. What I cover in this chapter is what has guided me through the pains of my own life and helped me understand some of God's actions in the Old Testament. Before I start blaming God for not being a universal nanny, I have learned to look at my own life and what I have done and not done, directly or indirectly, to add to the pain and suffering in the world.

Notes

1. Richard Dawkins, *The God Delusion* (New York: Houghton Mifflin, 2008), 51.
2. When the Bible ceases to be the standard of truth, there can be no standard of truth; see David F. Wells, *No Place for Truth: Or Whatever Happened to Evangelical Theology?* (Grand Rapids: Eerdmans, 1993).
3. This point is made repeatedly by Clay Jones, *Why Does God Allow Evil? Compelling Answers for Life's Toughest Questions* (Eugene, OR: Harvest House, 2017).
4. Christopher J. H. Wright, *The God I Don't Understand: Reflections on Tough Questions of Faith* (Grand Rapids: Zondervan, 2008), 53.
5. Cited in Jones, *Why Does God Allow Evil?*, especially 50–56.
6. Jones, *Why Does God Allow Evil?*, 57.
7. See Jones, *Why Does God Allow Evil?*, 59, 68.

8. Wright, *The God I Don't Understand*, 32.

9. You can listen to my talk, "God and the Problem of Evil (Romans 8:28–30)," December 11, 2020, https://gk2.me/romans-8-28.

10. Shared in personal correspondence. Be sure to see Garrett's forthcoming commentary on Job in the Evangelical Exegetical Commentary series (Bellingham, WA: Lexham) and his full course on Job at www .biblicaltraining.org/book-of-job/duane-garrett.

11. See Wright, *The God I Don't Understand*, 109–57.

12. The best book I know of on the presence of pain in a believer's life is Jerry Sittser's *A Grace Disguised: How the Soul Grows through Loss*, 2nd ed. (1995; repr., Grand Rapids: Zondervan, 2004). Sittser tells the story of the tragic accident in which a drunk driver killed his wife, daughter, and mother.

13. See Richard Hess, *Joshua*, Tyndale Old Testament Commentaries (Downers Grove, IL: InterVarsity, 1996), 47.

14. Meredith G. Kline, "The Intrusion and the Decalogue," *Westminster Theological Journal* 16, no. 1 (November 1953): 1–22, www.meredith kline.com/files/articles/The-Intrusion-and-the-Decalogue-MGKline .pdf.

15. Ludwig Koehler and Walter Baumgartner, eds., *The Hebrew and Aramaic Lexicon of the Old Testament* (Leiden: Brill, 2001), 1:821.

16. See Hess, *Joshua*, 46–51. In *The Old Testament: A Historical, Theological, and Critical Introduction* ([Grand Rapids: Baker Academic, 2016], 191), Hess points out that Joshua was instructed to kill "everyone, 'men and women,' in Jericho (Josh. 6:21)." The Hebrew behind the phrase is *mēʾîš wěʿad ʾiššâ*, which literally means "from man and until woman" and "appears to be stereotypical for describing everyone." If women were present, they would have been killed. If only men were present, then all of them would have been killed. But the phrase doesn't mean that in every situation, both men and women died.

17. Cited in Hess, *Old Testament*, 190.

Chapter 13

THE HISTORICITY OF THE OLD TESTAMENT

In this chapter, we will look at how the Hebrew Bible was written and compiled, how the canon was established, and a few other issues, such as apparent contradictions and the use of large numbers, such as the ages of people before the flood.

Challenge

One of the big questions about the Hebrew Bible is whether or not it is historically reliable. How was it written? When was it written? Did the authors write accurate history? For many people, Genesis 1–11 reads more like a myth than history.

Many of these questions overlap with similar questions about the New Testament. In terms of authorship, many of the Old Testament books are anonymous, much like the Gospels. There are many accounts that sound so different from our own experiences that it's hard to believe they really happened. Was the universe created in six days (Gen 1:1–2:3)? Who were the "sons of God" who married human women and had children (6:2)? Could Methuselah really have lived 969 years (5:27)? Did the flood cover the entire earth (7:23)?

Jesus' Bible

Modern scholarship varies so widely on issues of date and authorship that it's hard to say there is a consensus on any issue. Some believe the Hebrew Bible is a postexilic creation, being written after the Israelites' return from the Babylonian exile (ca. 538 BC). What is called the "documentary hypothesis" in some form seems to dominate most Hebrew Bible scholarship; it postulates basically four different sources for the Pentateuch that were woven together—the different layers known as J, E, D, and P. Document J is the source that names God as "Jehovah," (*Yahweh*; a *y* sound in English is expressed with the letter *j* in German). Document E is the source that calls God "Elohim"; D is Deuteronomy; and P is priestly material. The permutations of this theory are almost endless.

I want to work backward in time, starting with Jesus. In one of his postresurrection appearances, Jesus said to his disciples, "This is what I told you while I was still with you: Everything must be fulfilled that is written about me in the Law of Moses, the Prophets and the Psalms" (Luke 24:44).

Jesus' Bible included three parts:

- "The Law of Moses," which is Genesis–Deuteronomy, also called the Pentateuch or the Torah.
- "The Prophets," which includes both the former prophets (Joshua, Judges, Samuel, Kings) and the latter prophets (Isaiah, Jeremiah, Ezekiel, the Twelve [Hosea–Malachi]).
- "The Psalms" is the first and largest book in the third collection of books generally called "the Writings." In Hebrew canonical order, this includes Psalms, Job, Proverbs, Ruth, Song of Songs, Ecclesiastes, Lamentations, Esther, Daniel, Ezra, Nehemiah, and Chronicles.

The Jewish name for their Bible is the "Tanak," an acronym standing for **T**orah (Pentateuch), **N**evi'im (Prophets), and **K**etuvim

(Writings), preserving the same threefold designation. Although the canonical order of the Hebrew Bible and the Christian Old Testament is different, they contain the same books (except for the Old Testament Apocrypha; see below). Jesus says that all these books ultimately point to him and are about him.

Elsewhere Jesus condemns the experts in the law when he says, "Therefore this generation will be held responsible for the blood of all the prophets that has been shed since the beginning of the world, from the blood of Abel to the blood of Zechariah, who was killed between the altar and the sanctuary. Yes, I tell you, this generation will be held responsible for it all" (Luke 11:50–51).

In Hebrew canonical order, Chronicles is the last book, so the last murder in the Bible is the killing of Zechariah (2 Chron 24:20–21). The first murder is that of Cain killing his brother Abel (Gen 4:8). Jesus' Bible extended from the beginning of Genesis to the end of Chronicles. In other places Jesus refers only to "the Law and the Prophets" (e.g., Luke 16:29, 31; 24:27). There is some debate as to whether the Writings had achieved full canonical status by Jesus' time, but most likely this twofold division is still to be understood as the entire Hebrew Bible.

Sirach (also called Ecclesiasticus) is a book of Wisdom Literature roughly paralleling Proverbs. It is part of the Old Testament Apocrypha and therefore found in the Catholic Bible but not in the Protestant Bible. Ben Sirach's grandson wrote a prologue to his grandfather's book and then translated the book into Greek in 138 BC. In the prologue, he refers to three parts of the Hebrew canon called "*the Law* and *the Prophets* and *the other ancestral books*"; the later collection he also calls "*the others that followed them*" and "*the rest of the books*."[1] Although Ben Sirach's grandson doesn't have a formal title for the third division of the Hebrew Bible, he does recognize the threefold division 138 years before Jesus.

In a real sense, what is important to Jesus is the final form of the Hebrew Bible and not so much how it was written and assembled. All of it — every piece of it — is "God breathed" (2 Tim 3.16), with the prophets speaking not what *they* wanted to say but what *God* wanted them to say "as they were carried along by the Holy Spirit" (2 Pet 1:21). Jesus affirmed his Bible to the point of every "jot" and "tittle" being fulfilled (Matt 5:18 KJV), "the smallest letter . . . the least stroke of a pen" (NIV).

Paul likewise affirmed the same Bible, down to the single word *seed*, emphasizing that the word is singular, thus pointing to Christ (Gal 3:16). This is why the New Testament authors reference so much of the Old Testament; they believed it had come from God. In other words, Jesus and the early church understood all of the Hebrew Bible to be from God, regardless of how it was historically constructed.

In most cases, the precise details concerning authorship and composition of the Hebrew Bible have been lost over the course of time. However, its authenticity and veracity are confirmed by Jesus, by the authors of the New Testament, and by the early church, regardless of how it was historically constructed. As Miles Van Pelt writes, "The New Testament provides the final, authoritative context from which God's people can rightly understand the message and design of the Old Testament."[2]

The Hebrew Canon

The history of the formation of the Hebrew canon is, admittedly, a bit of a mystery. We have substantially less information about it than we do about the New Testament canon. While this is not the place to go into this discussion in detail, I will summarize the basic understanding as background to this topic.[3]

When it comes to the formation of the canon, four decisive events took place in Israelite history: the destruction of the first temple by the Babylonians (586 BC), the widely held belief that God's prophetic voice ended with Malachi in the fourth century BC (Mal 4:6), the destruction of the temple by the Romans in AD 70, and the rise of Christianity and its writings.

As early as Deuteronomy, we read that there was a sensitivity to what writings were viewed as authoritative. Moses writes, "Do not add to what I command you and do not subtract from it, but keep the commands of the LORD your God that I give you" (4:2; cf. 12:32).

When the Babylonian exile came to an end, Ezra returned to Judah. He was "well versed in the Law of Moses" (Ezra 7:6), which means this collection of writings had been taken to Babylon at the beginning of the exile and was available for study during the exile. Ezra set out to teach "its decrees and laws" (7:10) to the Israelites. He even read the Book of the Law of Moses while the Israelites stood listening (Neh 7:73–8:8). There is little doubt that the Pentateuch was well-defined and accepted as authoritative by this time.

Because the Jewish people believed that the prophetic voice stopped with Malachi, there was no thought of accepting any new books into the canon (see the Old Testament Apocrypha section below). We believe that the Former and Latter Prophets were viewed as authoritative by the third century BC. Much like in the New Testament, the Pentateuch and the Prophets were the "core" of the Jewish canon, universally accepted as having come from God.

The process behind the acceptance of the Writings as canonical is less clear, and full acceptance of these books may not have occurred until the end of the first century AD. This section includes Psalms, Job, Proverbs, Ruth, Song of Songs, Ecclesiastes, Lamentations, Esther, Daniel, Ezra, Nehemiah, and Chronicles, listed in Hebrew canonical order.

The books that struggled to get into the canon were Ezekiel (appears at times to contradict the Law), Proverbs (some of them appear to contradict each other), Esther (doesn't include the name of "God," and some viewed it as secular history), Ecclesiastes (too pessimistic), and Song of Songs (too sexual). Nevertheless, there is a long-standing tradition of their full acceptance in Judaism.

With the growth of Christianity and its teaching that Jesus

fulfilled Old Testament prophecy, combined with the destruction of Jerusalem and its temple, which caused a redefining of the identity of the Jewish people, it was natural for the Jews to want to carefully define their canon. According to a later Jewish tradition in the Babylonian Talmud (*b. Gittin* 56a–b), a council was held at Jamnia after the destruction of Jerusalem but before the end of the century. It has been suggested that at this point, the Jewish canon was closed and further canonical discussion ended, although there is debate on this point.[4] Melito, the bishop of Sardis, claimed to have received a canon he found in Palestine in AD 170. There were other "Jewish" books we classify as the Old Testament Pseudepigrapha ("false writings"), but they were never accepted by mainstream Judaism.

The Old Testament Apocrypha

Up until the second or third century AD, the Hebrew books would have been written on scrolls and kept in the same location in a synagogue. Scrolls of other books also would have been kept in the same location. It wasn't until the invention of the codex that the accepted books would have been bound together and placed in a fixed order. This may explain historically why fifteen other books vied for inclusion in the canon, since they would have been stored with the canonical scrolls. These books became known as the Old Testament Apocrypha and are included in the Roman Catholic Bible.

The history of the development of the term *apocrypha* is difficult to determine. It means "hidden" or "concealed," and it was originally used of secret knowledge. In the fifth century AD, Jerome used the term to refer to the fifteen books not accepted by Judaism but accepted by some Christians; he differentiated the "canonical" from the "apocryphal" books, and this is how we tend to use the term today.

Following is a list of the books in question. In the Roman Catholic canon, they're interspersed throughout the Old Testament books.

	Protestant	Roman Catholic
1.	Tobit	Tobias
2.	Judith	Judith
3.	Wisdom of Solomon	Wisdom
4.	Ecclesiasticus (Sirach)	Ecclesiasticus
5.	1 Maccabees	1 Maccabees
6.	2 Maccabees	2 Maccabees
7.	Baruch	Baruch 1–5
8.	Epistle of Jeremiah	Baruch 6
9.	Additions to Esther	Esther 10:4–16:24
10.	Prayer of Azariah, and The Song of the Three Jews	Daniel 3:24–90
11.	Susanna	Daniel 13
12.	Bel and the Dragon	Daniel 14
13.	1 Esdras	3 Esdras (or 1 Esdras)
14.	2 Esdras	4 Esdras (or 2 Esdras)
15.	Prayer of Manasseh	Prayer of Manasseh

We do know that Judaism never accepted these books as authoritative, as seen in Josephus's comment in *Against Apion* 1.38.[5] Jesus never quotes from the apocryphal books.

The problem originated because at the time of Christ, some of these apocryphal books were interspersed throughout the canonical books. Our three most important Greek manuscripts of the Bible dating from the fourth and fifth century—Sinaiticus, Vaticanus, Alexandrinus—include some of these books. In other words, the Septuagint (the Greek translation of the Old Testament) did contain some of the Old Testament apocryphal books.

We also know that some of the early church fathers included some of the apocryphal books in their canonical lists and discussions, even if they felt the books were acceptable only for devotional reading (e.g., Augustine). Others argued they were clearly not part of the canon (e.g., Origen, Athanasius).

When Jerome translated the Bible into Latin (called the Vulgate), he included the fifteen books, although he stated his doubts of their authenticity. It appears that the general opinion was that these books were good to read for spiritual benefit but not authoritative in matters of faith and life.

The Reformers agreed that these books should not be part of the Bible, probably for several reasons:

1. Judaism never accepted them, and it is, after all, the Hebrew canon. This is the same rule of catholicity we see in the New Testament canonical process. The Apocrypha was not universally accepted by the Jewish people.
2. The apocryphal books were written after the cessation of the voice of God's Spirit in the fourth century BC (rule of authorship).
3. The Reformers found especially reprehensible certain doctrines supported by these books, such as making prayers for the dead[6] and the existence of purgatory (rule of orthodoxy).

In response to the Reformation, the Roman Catholic Church officially made the Apocrypha part of their Bible at the Council of Trent (1546) and pronounced an anathema on anyone not including them in the canon.

Martin Luther removed the apocryphal books from their historical position interspersed throughout the canonical books and placed them as a separate section between the Old and New Testaments. Eventually, they totally dropped out of Protestant Bibles.

Contradictions

Some people say they don't trust the Old Testament because of all the so-called contradictions. One of the apparent contradictions often pointed out is found in Proverbs 26:4–5. Should you, or should you not, answer a fool?

> Do not answer a fool according to his folly,
> > or you yourself will be just like him. (v. 4)

> Answer a fool according to his folly,
> > or he will be wise in his own eyes. (v. 5)

The placement in the book of these two verses and the similarity of grammar and content clearly suggest they are meant to be read together. Common sense suggests that thinking the verses are contradictory must be a misreading; no editor would put two contradictory statements side by side. The key is to understand the ambiguous Hebrew preposition כְּ (*ke*), translated below as "according to."[7] The Septuagint suggests the proper understanding:

> μὴ ἀποκρίνου ἄφρονι πρὸς τὴν ἐκείνου ἀφροσύνην, ἵνα μὴ ὅμοιος γένῃ αὐτῷ.
>
> Do not answer a fool *in accordance with* his folly, lest you become like him. (italics added)

> ἀλλὰ ἀποκρίνου ἄφρονι κατὰ τὴν ἀφροσύνην αὐτοῦ, ἵνα μὴ φαίνηται σοφὸς παρ' ἑαυτῷ.
>
> *But* answer a fool *according to* his folly, lest he appear to be wise to himself. (italics added)[8]

The inclusion of "but" (ἀλλά, *alla*) and the shift from "in accordance with" (πρός, *pros*) to "according to" (κατά, *kata*) show the correct meaning. Do not respond to a fool by speaking the same way he speaks; otherwise, you become like him. However, do respond to a fool so he will not think he is correct ("wise").

Another example of a supposed contradiction is seen in the second creation account (discussed below), where animals were created *before* Adam and Eve. However, in the third account, it can be surmised that animals were created *after* Adam: "Now the LORD God had formed out of the ground all the wild animals and all the birds in the sky. He brought them to the man to see what he would name them; and whatever the man called each living creature, that was its name" (Gen 2:19).

However, the "now" in Genesis 2:19 translates the simple Hebrew conjunction *waw* (the most basic Hebrew word for "and"), which doesn't require any sense of temporal sequence. This is why the CSB can leave the conjunction untranslated; the paragraph marker performs the same function. Also, the translation "had formed" makes the timing of the animal's creation indefinite (NIV, ESV). It's also possible that Adam and Eve together form "mankind," and therefore placing the creation of animals (1:20–25) before that of mankind (1:27) is theologically accurate.

These two passages serve to remind us of what we already saw in the New Testament: before pronouncing passages contradictory, be sure you have interpreted them correctly.

Multiple Accounts

Hebrew narrative is not always linear or chronological. It's often recursive. That is, it doesn't simply tell a story from beginning to end and then move on to the next story. It often starts the account, backs up and repeats itself from a different point of view, and then does so again until it gets to the end of the story. The three accounts of creation illustrate this technique.

The book of Genesis starts with these words: "In the beginning God created the heavens and the earth." This is the story of creation in its most basic form. It asserts that there is a beginning, that there is a God, that God created, and that he created everything. "Heaven and earth" is an expression that means "everything" (a "merism"), both the visible and invisible realms (Col 1:16).[9]

Genesis then repeats itself in 1:2–2:3. The account is, if nothing else, thematic. Light is created before the sun because God is so great that he doesn't need the sun to form light. (In other religions, the sun is the greatest God, but Yahweh doesn't even need the sun.) Only one verse is dedicated to the creation of human life (1:27).

Genesis repeats itself another time in 2:4–25, beginning with the introductory formula, "This is the account of the heavens and the earth when they were created, when the LORD God made the earth and the heavens." In this accounting, the writer focuses on the creation of Adam and Eve and their role in this new creation. These are not three different accounts of creation; this is one story told in a recursive manner.

Are these accounts contradictory and unreliable? No. Much like the Synoptics, they're retelling the same story to make different points.

Large Numbers

Some people have pointed to an issue with numbers that has led them not to trust the Bible. The main one is the age of the people in Genesis 1–11. Methuselah lived 969 years (5:27). Noah lived 950 years (9:29).

This is a difficult issue, and some people may not like my answer. In our modern culture, numbers tend to be precise, unless someone refers to even numbers. If someone says they're sixty-seven years old, it means sixty-seven, but if someone says they're sixty, it may be that they're precisely sixty years old or it may mean they're "in their sixties." If I say I'm six foot three inches tall and weigh two hundred pounds, we all understand that these figures are likely to be approximations. If I say that "thousands" of people turned out for a rally, we instinctively know I don't mean precisely "three thousand" people. In other words, sometimes numbers perform functions other than to count. They can be symbolic figures of speech. For example, a recurring phrase in the Bible is that something lasted for "forty days." It occurs with such frequency (twenty times) that it's possible it is a figure of speech indicating an indefinite, extended period of time, but not necessarily specifically forty days. This flexibility with numbers was especially common in ancient cultures.

One wonders if numbers in the Old Testament perform functions other than to count. Certainly, the primary significance of the age of the people before the flood is that life spans decrease after sin enters the world, and after the flood, the average life span becomes what we see as "normal." It could be that this is what the numbers are intending to tell us. The decreasing number of years in the biblical account is paralleled in the historical records of Mesopotamia.[10]

Of course, it could be that God intended people to live much longer than they do now and formed their bodies in a way that enabled centuries of life. In fact, perhaps God intended Adam and his descendants to live forever. One of the effects of sin was to reduce the number of years people live in their sin. I learned many years ago that it's unwise to dictate what God can and can't do.

We see other large numbers throughout the Hebrew Bible that similarly cause concern.[11] The solution is found in the academic term "numerical hyperbole," a nice-sounding phrase for exaggeration. In the literature from surrounding countries, we likewise see numbers that are too big to be believable. Since the numbers in the Hebrew Bible are bigger than the numbers in other literature, the thought is that these numbers were being exaggerated to make the theological statement that the God of Israel is greater than the gods of the neighboring countries.

In a sense, we do the same thing. Fishermen recount the size of the fish that got away. Pastors like to emphasize the size of their churches. In our culture, it's understandable that the fish was "really big" and that there are "lots" of people in the pews Sunday morning.

If this solution is acceptable, then it solves some of the problems caused by large numbers. The numbers are not meant to be understood precisely but are painting a picture. Different authors exaggerate different amounts to make different points.

Women

Many people reject the Bible because of its portrayal of women. One of the more common examples is the fate of Lot's daughters. When the men of the cities came to sexually abuse the two angels, Lot offers his daughters to them:

> Before they had gone to bed, all the men from every part of the city of Sodom—both young and old—surrounded the house. They called to Lot, "Where are the men who came to you tonight? Bring them out to us so that we can have sex with them."
>
> Lot went outside to meet them and shut the door behind him and said, "No, my friends. Don't do this wicked thing. Look, I have two daughters who have never slept with a man. Let me bring them out to you, and you can do what you like with them. But don't do anything to these men, for they have come under the protection of my roof."
>
> *Genesis 19:4–8*

The cultural issue was hospitality and the refusal of the men of Sodom to respect Lot's obligations to provide for the angels. In the New Testament, Peter says that Lot was "a righteous man, who was distressed by the depraved conduct of the lawless" (2 Pet 2:7), but that doesn't mean all his actions were righteous. In this case, they certainly were not. The Bible never says Lot was right to do this. The Bible never says it's right to treat your daughters as sexual objects who can be tossed aside. That philosophy may reflect the perspective of ancient culture, but that doesn't make it right.

Related is the story of Judah and Tamar in Genesis 38. Tamar's husband, Er, who was Judah's firstborn son, was wicked, and the Lord killed him. Er died without having children. The laws of levirate marriage required a brother to raise up children for Tamar, but the brother, Onan, refused, and the Lord killed him as well. Tamar eventually realized that the next brother, Shelah, also would not give her children, so she dressed up as a prostitute, seduced her father-in-law, Judah, and became pregnant. Judah was going to kill her until she proved that he was the father of the child. Judah says, "She is more righteous than I, since I wouldn't give her to my son Shelah" (v. 26).

No doubt this story strikes the modern reader as disgusting, although perhaps less so to a culture that practices levirate marriage. It does, after all, say that Tamar was "more righteous" than one of the patriarchs. The Bible certainly doesn't say Judah's behavior was right, nor that the misogyny of ancient culture is right. It does show the bravery of a woman who risked death to meet the cultural mandate of raising up children for her dead husband when the men in her family refused to meet their social obligations.

I should also mention that many women of faith are praised in the Hebrew Bible: Miriam, Deborah, Jael, Esther, Ruth, and the mothers of Samson and Samuel. There are more heroic women in the Hebrew Bible than in any other ancient Near Eastern literature I'm familiar with.

In the same way that some people wish the New Testament would clearly and unequivocally declare slavery to be sinful, so some wish that God had been more egalitarian in the Old Testament. But in the cases of both slavery and women, the biblical foundation was laid for the full emancipation of slaves and the viewing of women as created in God's image and of equal worth with men.

The doctrine of progressive revelation teaches that God reveals his will over a period of time. He doesn't teach Abraham, for example, everything we know to be true from the New Testament. He reveals himself slowly, probably at a rate people were able to grasp. So we don't learn about monogamy until the teachings of the New Testament, despite the reality of the clear implications of Genesis 2:24. We don't learn to love our enemies until Jesus' teachings in the New Testament

(Matt 5:43–45; 22:39), despite the reality of the teaching of Leviticus 19:18. We don't learn the full doctrine of the Trinity until after the time of the writing of the New Testament, although the seeds for the doctrine are clearly in Scripture. And so also the biblical view of women becomes clearer over time.[12]

Conclusion

It's credible to believe that the Hebrew Bible was fully assembled by the time of Jesus and accepted by him, Paul, and the early church. While there is some debate in Catholic and Protestant circles over fifteen other books, the core of the canon is accepted by both Catholics and Protestants and by Judaism. The Hebrew Bible is reliable and trustworthy as the revelation of the words and work of God from creation through the fourth century BC.

For Further Reading

Bruce, F. F. *The Books and the Parchments: How We Got Our English Bible.* 3rd ed. Old Tappan, NJ: Revell, 1984, 96–124.

Geisler, Norman L. *The Roots of Evil.* Eugene, OR: Wipf & Stock, 2002.

Gentry, Peter J. "The Text of the Old Testament." *JETS* 52, no. 1 (March 2009): 19–45.

Kaiser, Walter C. *The Old Testament Documents: Are They Reliable and Relevant?* Downers Grove, IL: IVP Academic, 2001.

Sailhamer, John H. *How We Got the Bible.* Grand Rapids: Zondervan, 1998.

Swinburne, Richard. *Providence and the Problem of Evil.* Oxford: Oxford University Press, 1998.

Wenham, John W. *The Goodness of God.* Downers Grove, IL: InterVarsity, 1974.

Advanced

Hess, Richard S. *The Old Testament: A Historical, Theological, and Critical Introduction.* Grand Rapids: Baker Academic, 2016.

Kitchens, K. A. *On the Reliability of the Old Testament.* Grand Rapids: Eerdmans, 2003.

Provan, Iain, V. Philips Long, and Tremper Longman III, *A Biblical History of Israel*. 2nd ed. Louisville, KY: Westminster John Knox Press, 2015.

Notes

1. "Sirach prologue" (italics added), in *A New English Translation of the Septuagint*, ed. Albert Pietersma and Benjamin G. Wright (Oxford: Oxford University Press, 2014), http://ccat.sas.upenn.edu/nets/edition /30-sirach-nets.pdf.

2. Miles Van Pelt, ed., *A Biblical-Theological Introduction to the Old Testament: The Gospel Promised* (Wheaton, IL: Crossway, 2016), 24.

3. For an excellent summary of the issues, see Craig L. Blomberg, *Can We Still Believe the Bible?* (Grand Rapids: Brazos, 2014), 45–55; see also Paul D. Wegner, *The Journey from Texts to Translations* (Grand Rapids: Baker, 1999), 101–18; Walter C. Kaiser, *The Old Testament Documents: Are They Reliable and Relevant?* (Downers Grove, IL: IVP Academic, 2001), 15–39. For a more academic discussion, see Lee M. McDonald and James A. Sanders, eds., *The Canon Debate* (Grand Rapids: Baker Academic, 2002), part 2, 21–263.

4. See Kaiser, *Old Testament Documents*, 31–32, who concludes that the canon was already accepted by AD 100 without the input from Jamnia.

5. "For we have not an innumerable multitude of books among us, disagreeing from, and contradicting one another [as the Greeks have:] but only twenty two books: which contain the records of all the past times: which are justly believed to be divine." Some attempt was undertaken to make the books in the Hebrew Bible number twenty-two, the number of letters in the Hebrew alphabet. This was done by combining books now divided in the Protestant canon.

6. "On the next day, as by that time it had become necessary, Judas and his men went to take up the bodies of the fallen and to bring them back to lie with their kinsmen in the sepulchres of their fathers. Then under the tunic of every one of the dead they found sacred tokens of the idols of Jamnia, which the law forbids the Jews to wear. And it became clear to all that this was why these men had fallen. So they all blessed the ways of the Lord, the righteous Judge, who reveals the things that are hidden; and they turned to prayer, beseeching that the sin which had been committed might be wholly blotted out. And the noble Judas exhorted the people to keep themselves free from sin, for they had seen with their own eyes what had happened because of the sin of those who had

fallen. He also took up a collection, man by man, to the amount of two thousand drachmas of silver, and sent it to Jerusalem to provide for a sin offering. In doing this he acted very well and honourably, taking account of the resurrection. For if he were not expecting that those who had fallen would rise again, it would have been superfluous and foolish to *pray for the dead*. But if he was looking to the splendid reward that is laid up for those who fall asleep in godliness, it was a holy and pious thought. Therefore he made atonement for the dead, that they might be delivered from their sin" (2 Maccabees 12:39–45 NRSV, italics added).

7. See Bruce K. Waltke, *The Book of Proverbs: Chapters 15–31*, New International Commentary on the Old Testament (Grand Rapids: Eerdmans, 2005), 349.

8. Albert Pietersma and Benjamin G. Wright, eds., *A New English Translation of the Septuagint* (Oxford: Oxford University Press, 2014).

9. Some people see Genesis 1:1 as the title of the first part of Genesis, in which case the writer only repeats himself once.

10. See Kaiser, *Old Testament Documents*, 72.

11. See especially David M. Fouts, "Numbers, Large Numbers," in *Dictionary of the Old Testament Historical Books*, ed. Bill T. Arnold and H. G. M. Williamson (Downers Grove, IL: IVP Academic, 2005), 750–54; see also J. W. Wenham, "Large Numbers in the Old Testament," *Tyndale Bulletin* 18 (1967): 19–53, www.godawa.com /Chronicles_of_the_nephilim/Articles_By_Others/Wenham%20%20 Large%20Numbers%20in%20the%20Old%20Testament.pdf.

12. For further discussion on topics related to the Old Testament, such as how the Old Testament was written and transmitted to us today, go to www.BillMounce.com/trust/14.

WHY I TRUST THE BIBLE

Mark was one of my students during his first semester in college. He took my New Testament Survey class as one of his required general education classes. I think he earned an A, but I never saw him again—until minutes after his graduation four years later.

We had just endured a horridly hot Southern California graduation ceremony. It went on far too long, considering the fact that we were clothed in our ridiculous long black gowns and funny black hats. I rushed back to my office, ripping off the gown as I ran, anxious to start my summer vacation. A knock on my door delayed my escape.

Mark's face was flushed red, and he was sweating. At first he was unable to speak in complete sentences. But he wasn't hot. He was terrified. "The Bible's true, isn't it? I think, maybe . . . Why do we think . . ." The sentence fragments piled up until I realized that he was asking why he should think the Bible was true. He was heading out of the cocoon of a Christian liberal arts university education, and now he was going to have to face the world. Thinking about that made him realize he didn't know what he believed, or why.

I thought to myself, *Why didn't Mark ask these questions earlier, when he had Christian professors and Christian friends to walk with him and help him process the answers?* And that's when I realized I had not sufficiently challenged him—or even told him why *I* think the Bible is reliable.

After he left, I sat down and got out my old college notes. I reflected a bit on why I believed the Bible and why I had failed to help Mark come to the same conclusion I had come to. I thought about my time with Craig Blomberg and Darrell Bock, and how it was all part of the Lord's plan to help me think through for myself why I accept the reliability of the Bible. My hope is that this book has helped you as well.

So why do I trust the Bible? I always start with the Bible's claims for itself. If the Bible never claimed to be from God, I would not say it was from God. Second, I trust the Bible because none of the challenges against it that we've considered are convincing. If there truly are contradictions, or clear evidence that the gospel writers were not interested in history, or if I knew we had the wrong books in the Bible, or if the copies of the copies of the manuscripts of the Bible were hopelessly corrupt, then I would certainly question the reliability of the Bible. But none of these arguments are convincing, and most are relatively easy to refute. At the end of the day, I believe that the Bible is accurate and deserves the benefit of the doubt. Yes, I still have a few questions, but for me, the burden of proof is on the person who says it can't be trusted.

I also trust the Bible because to do so is the most rational choice I can make. All of us have basic assumptions we hold about the world. These are *faith* assumptions, especially with regard to the possibility of the miraculous. For me, the Bible provides the best answers to the questions of life. The answers it gives make sense, though I recognize that it is God's Spirit who has helped me come to that decision. The Bible is consistent with itself and with reality, and this consistency provides a basis for believing it and trusting it.

So are you willing to take a leap of faith and believe that the Bible is true? That it is trustworthy? Even if I can't prove Christianity to be true, I am glad I don't have to put my brain on the shelf to believe. There is a lot of evidence that it is trustworthy, but evidence can't compel faith. We can't prove the Bible is historically reliable in everything it says. But since the Bible has been tested and found to be reliable in so many ways, it makes sense to give Scripture the benefit of the doubt and take that leap of faith, believing the Bible is trustworthy in all that it says. Yes, there will be mysteries, but you can trust it. That has been my journey.

A number of years ago, Lee Strobel interviewed renowned scholar and textual critic Bruce Metzger, asking him specifically about the topic of textual criticism (which we covered in chapters 7–9):

> Then I recall asking him how his many decades of intensely studying the New Testament's text had affected his personal faith. "Oh," he said, sounding happy to discuss the topic, "it has increased the basis of my personal faith to see the firmness with which these materials have come down to us, with a multiplicity of copies, some of which are very ancient."
>
> "So," I started to say, "scholarship has not diluted your faith—"
>
> He jumped in before I could finish the sentence. "On the contrary," he stressed, "it has built it. I've asked questions all my life, I've dug into the text, I've studied this thoroughly, and today I know with confidence that my trust in Jesus has been well placed . . . *Very* well placed."[1]

I trust that this book has helped you answer the questions you have about the Bible in the same way. Ask the hard questions. Don't be afraid to lean into the debate. Read other books. Watch online videos. The Bible is worthy of our trust, and it can stand up to scrutiny. I have staked my life and my future on it; I trust you will as well.

Notes

1. Lee Strobel, *The Case for the Real Jesus: A Journalist Investigates the Current Attacks on the Identity of Christ* (Grand Rapids: Zondervan, 2007), 99.